BOOK ONE IN THE LIGHTING HEAVEN'S WAY SERIES

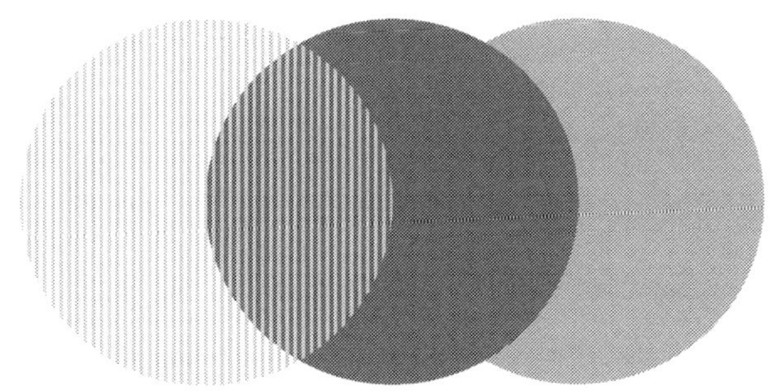

The KINGDOM of GOD is in OUR MIDST

THE PAROUSIA AS THE RELATIONAL UNVEILING OF CHRIST

JAMES CASO

The Kingdom of God Is in Our Midst

Published in the United States by Credo House Publishers,
a division of Credo Communications LLC, Grand Rapids, Michigan
credohousepublishers.com

ISBN: 978-1-62586-327-0

Cover and interior design by Frank Gutbrod
Editing by Donna Huisjen

Printed in the United States of America
First Edition

"The elements will burn and be dissolved."
(2 Peter 3:10)

CONTENTS

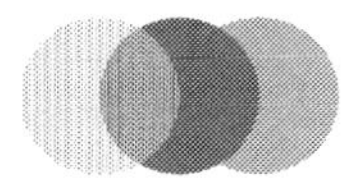

INTRODUCTION

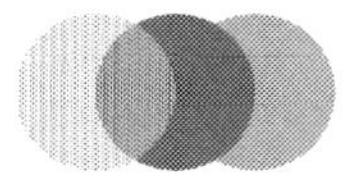

THE *PAROUSIA* AS TRANSFORMATIVE RELATIONAL REALITY

The concept of the *Parousia* holds a central position in Christian theology, particularly in the realm of eschatology. The Greek word *parousia* can be translated as "presence" or "coming." Traditionally, the emphasis has been on the latter meaning. The *Parousia* has been understood as the climactic moment of Christ's physical return, usually called the second coming, an event that concludes history and inaugurates the fulfillment of God's redemptive purposes. This anticipation has shaped theological frameworks, worship practices, and the Christian imagination, inspiring hope but also giving rise to speculative interpretations and debates over prophetic timelines. Too often this focus on external events has overshadowed the profound celestial realities at the heart of the *Parousia*, leading to divisions and fear-driven narratives.

The wholly anticipatory approach to the *Parousia* misses a big reality: the *Parousia* is not a distant event. It is not something that can be plotted on a timeline or calculated through a formula. Rather, its reality is already being unveiled in the lives of believers, often in ways that challenge our understanding of time, suffering, and transformation.

A striking example of this unveiling occurred in the life—and death—of Polycarp of Smyrna, a disciple of the apostle John and one of the most revered second-generation Church fathers.

In the year AD 155 Polycarp stood before the Roman authorities in Smyrna, accused of refusing to worship Caesar. The old man did not tremble as his sentence was pronounced: he was to be burned alive. His crime? His unyielding confession that Jesus Christ was Lord.

When the flames enveloped Polycarp, something extraordinary happened. Those who witnessed his faithfulness wrote,

> When he said "Amen" and finished his prayer, the men in charge kindled the fire. And as the flame blazed up in great fury, we, who were privileged to witness it saw a wonderous sight, and we have been spared in order to tell the others what happened. The fire took on the shape of a vault, like the sail of a ship filled with wind, and it surrounded the body of the martyr as with a wall. And he stood there in the midst, not as burning flesh but as bread that is being baked, or like gold and silver being refined in a furnace. And we perceived a fragrant smell, as of incense or some other precious spices (*The Martyrdom of Polycarp*, chapter 15).

Polycarp's martyrdom serves as a powerful example of the transformative relational nature of the *Parousia*—the revealing of Christ's presence. According to eyewitnesses the fire did not consume Polycarp, as would have been expected. Instead, the flames formed around him like a golden vault, encasing him as though he were being refined in a divine furnace. Instead of the stench of burning flesh, those present smelled a fragrance like incense. At that moment, from within his fiery vault, it wasn't his body but the world around him that burned. To Polycarp, the world—its threats, its power, its dominion—began to dissolve. The world and its filth were being purified by something more real than the fire that was trying to consume him. As the world burned around him, he was aware that Christ was present with him.

The fire that surrounded him did not merely signal death; it signified the unveiling of a greater reality.

Polycarp's final moments offer a profound vision of the *Parousia* as a transformative unveiling rather than an apocalyptic event. The world around him—its power structures, its threats, and even death itself—dissolved in the face of an eternal reality: Christ's reign is already present and active. This experience mirrors the apostle Peter's theological declaration that as the elements of the world dissolve, the eternal dwelling of righteousness—heaven—will appear.

Second Peter 3:10–13 reads,

> But the day of the Lord will come like a thief; on that day the heavens will pass away with a loud noise, the elements will burn and be dissolved, and the earth and the works on it will be disclosed. Since all these things are to be dissolved in this way, it is clear what sort of people you should be in holy conduct and godliness as you wait for the day of God and hasten its coming. Because of that day, the heavens will be dissolved with fire and the elements will melt with heat. But based on his promise, we wait for new heavens and a new earth, where righteousness dwells.

The dissolution about which Peter writes is not the annihilation of the world; rather, it is purification, much as the fire that refined Polycarp. It is the breaking away of what is temporary, corruptible, and fading. The "new heavens and . . . new earth" represent the unveiling of true reality—the eternal presence of Christ, not merely as a future hope but as an ever-present transformation within the believer.

The Kingdom of God Is in Our Midst explores the *Parousia* as a spiritual unveiling that is already at work. The *Parousia*, thus, is not simply a future event. Just as Polycarp's faith allowed him to step beyond the fear of death and into the presence of Christ, so too does the *Parousia* reveal a transformation in the believer's life. This unveiling is about not only the destruction of the old but also the emergence of the eternal—the presence of God manifesting in His people.

The theme of fire as transformation runs throughout Scripture. The refining of gold removes dross, revealing the purity that was always present beneath the impurities. Likewise, the *Parousia* is fundamentally about the purification of the world, revealing what has been hidden under corruption. Just as Polycarp was not destroyed by fire but transfigured within it, so the *Parousia* is not an end but a new beginning.

This book argues that the *Parousia* is a transformative, relational, and ongoing event. It is not about only what is to come but about what is already appearing in those who are in Christ. As the world fades—and with it the world's failed systems, its misguided self-reliance, and its perishable things—the presence and authority of Christ becomes clearer, like gold emerging from fire, like heaven breaking through the veil.

The question this book will explore is simple yet profound: What happens when the world dissolves and heaven appears? Importantly, this question is phrased in the present tense, because what happens is already happening now. In the following chapters we will examine how Scripture, theology, and Christian experience testify that the presence of Christ is the true unveiling of reality, already at work in the believer and moving toward God's ultimate fulfillment. Just as Polycarp stepped into that reality, so too are we called to live in the revelation of Christ's presence—a transformation that changes everything.

The central argument of this book is that the *Parousia* is not the future event that so many anticipate but an active transformation unfolding in the lives of believers.

At the heart of this reinterpretation is the theological framework of Nuncmillennialism, which views the *Parousia* as the transcendent unveiling of Christ's essence. Unlike traditional interpretations that confine the millennium to a future reign, Nuncmillennialism asserts that

Christ's reign is already active (*nunc* being Latin for "now"), manifesting through His Church and in the lives of believers (Ephesians 1:20–22). Nuncmillennialism (pronounced NOONK-millennialism) differs from amillennialism (no literal millennium), premillennialism (Christ will return before the millennium), or postmillennialism (Christ will return after the millennium of the Church). Understanding Christ's millennial reign as a present reality, Nuncmillennialism emphasizes Christ's present reign and His continual revelation in the lives of believers. By shifting the focus from awaiting external manifestations to engaging with Christ's transformative presence now, believers are invited to experience His reign as an active and dynamic reality.

In keeping with the Latin prefix, Nuncmillennialism could more colloquially be rendered "now-millennialism." The *Parousia*, as reinterpreted through Nuncmillennialism, represents not a singular, chronological event but an unfolding, transcendent relational reality. This perspective redefines the traditional understanding of Christ's coming, emphasizing His active reign and ongoing presence in the lives of His followers. In the nuncmillennialist view, The *Parousia* is not confined to a distant hope but is instead a present experience of Christ's transformative essence.

The *Parousia*, therefore, unfolds as a dynamic, ongoing reality, whereby Christ's presence transforms individuals and communities in alignment with His kingdom. This perspective invites us to shift our focus from awaiting external signs to engaging with the unveiled presence of Christ here and now. We can thus see the *Parousia* as an ongoing, transcendent unveiling of Christ's essence, present heavenly reign, and continual revelation in the lives of believers. Believers are invited to shift their focus from awaiting external manifestations to engaging with Christ's transformative presence now, experiencing His reign as an active and dynamic reality.

Through nuncmillennialism, this book illuminates the profound truth that the *Parousia* is both a present reality and a future hope, calling believers to live in the fullness of Christ's unveiled presence. This dual focus invites a life of active faith and enduring hope, empowering individual believers and the Church to reflect the glory of Christ's kingdom in a divided and longing world. As Jesus declared, "The kingdom of God is in your midst" (Luke 17:21).

A PARADIGM SHIFT: FROM EVENT TO PRESENCE

This book does not interpret the *Parousia* as a future global spectacle but rather as a present spiritual unveiling of Christ's essence to those who are "in Christ." While many traditions await a visible, physical return of Christ, this work explores how Scripture points to an ongoing relational appearing, one that transforms believers through revelation, not observation. As Christ is unveiled, His image is formed within us. This dynamic, ongoing manifestation of His presence is the heart of the *Parousia* we explore.

For centuries, eschatology has been centered on anticipated physical milestones—the rapture, tribulation, millennium, and the final judgment—most often framed as future events. However, the framework of *nuncmillennialism* offers a paradigm shift: these are not merely prophetic moments on a distant timeline but spiritual realities unfolding now in the lives of believers. The rapture is reimagined as the believer's present elevation into the heavenly realm through faith, seated with Christ by the indwelling of the Holy Spirit (Ephesians 2:6). The tribulation is understood not simply as a cataclysm to come but as the daily struggle to live out God's kingdom in a world bent toward rebellion (John 16:33).

The millennium is no longer a deferred reign but the active lordship of Christ exercised through His resurrected life and His Church (Revelation 20:4–6). Even the vision of a new heaven and a new earth is not postponed to the end of time but recognized in the ongoing renewal begun in Christ—a new creation that is already transforming those who are in Him (2 Corinthians 5:17). This reinterpretation calls believers to move beyond passive expectation and instead embrace the present power of Christ's *Parousia*—His unveiled presence—as the central force reshaping their lives and the world.

THE SYMBOLISM OF ESCHATOLOGICAL IMAGERY

Eschatological texts, especially those in Daniel and Revelation, are saturated with symbolic language—clouds, trumpets, and cosmic upheavals—designed to reveal profound spiritual realities rather than to forecast literal events. Within this symbolic framework, clouds consistently represent divine presence and authority, affirming Christ's ongoing reign and His transcendence over earthly powers (Daniel 7:13; Acts 1:9). Trumpets function as divine proclamations, awakening the faithful and calling them into greater spiritual awareness and readiness (1 Corinthians 15:52; Revelation 8:6).

Likewise, the dramatic cosmic imagery found throughout apocalyptic literature reflects not natural disasters but the breaking in of God's kingdom—a transformative unveiling that reshapes human history and perception. This symbolic language aligns with Christ's frequent use of parables, which conveyed eternal truths to those attuned to the Spirit's discernment (Matthew 13:10–17). Through this lens eschatology is not a roadmap of future catastrophes but a living revelation of Christ's presence—a continual *Parousia* that invites believers to see, hear, and respond to the spiritual reality already at work in the world.

PRACTICAL IMPLICATIONS FOR FAITH AND PRACTICE

This reinterpretation of the *Parousia* as a present, relational reality holds profound implications for faith and practice. Rather than centering Christian life on speculative timelines or apocalyptic anxieties, it redirects attention toward active discipleship and spiritual transformation. For individual believers the unveiled presence of Christ becomes the catalyst for ongoing renewal—a process captured in Paul's declaration that "we all, with unveiled faces, . . . are being transformed into the same image from glory to glory" (2 Corinthians 3:18). For the Church the *Parousia* offers a unifying framework for worship, mission, and service, as the community of faith lives out the reality of Christ's indwelling reign (Ephesians 1:22–23). Rooted in the heavenly certainty of Christ's rule rather than in earthly speculation, this perspective frees believers from fear-based narratives and empowers them to live with hope, resilience, and purpose. In doing so, the body of Christ becomes an active participant in the unfolding kingdom, embodying His essence and extending His light into every sphere of life.

Even the familiar apocalyptic imagery of judgment, the antichrist, and the mark of the beast take on renewed meaning when viewed through the lens of Christ's ascended reign. The resurrection, the cornerstone of Christian hope, is reinterpreted as both a future promise and a present reality. It embodies the victory of Christ's essence over sin, condemnation, and death, a victory that believers share through their union with Him (Romans 6:4–5). At its core the *Parousia* is the continuous revelation of Christ's glory, righteousness, and sovereignty.

This book is not a theological exercise; it is a call to relational transformation. It offers a robust, Christ-centered framework for eschatology that is both theologically sound and spiritually inspiring. It challenges traditional notions while empowering believers to live out their faith with clarity, purpose, and passion.

By embracing the *Parousia* as a present and actionable reality, Christians are invited into a new way of seeing and living. They are called to recognize the heavenly realities of Christ's reign and to allow those eternal truths to shape their daily choices, values, and identity. This perspective compels believers to actively participate in God's redemptive mission, becoming vessels through whom His essence is revealed to a world yearning for restoration. At the same time it cultivates a posture of hopeful anticipation—not for a distant event but for the ultimate renewal already set in motion by Christ's resurrection. Living within this unveiled reality, believers move forward with joy, purpose, and the assurance that the fullness of God's kingdom is both present and still unfolding.

THE *PAROUSIA* AS THE SPIRITUAL UNVEILING OF CHRIST

For centuries the *Parousia* has been widely regarded as the anticipated physical second coming of Christ, traditionally envisioned as a discrete event signaling the culmination of history and the fulfillment of God's redemptive plan. While this perspective has inspired hope and shaped eschatological thought within the Church, it has often been molded by assumptions that obscure the deeper biblical and theological significance of the *Parousia*. This book proposes a transformative reinterpretation: the *Parousia* is best understood as the transcendent unveiling of Christ's essence—His glory, authority, and divine power—manifesting within believers and creation itself.

Rooted firmly in Scripture and nuncmillennialism, which views Christ's millennial reign as having already begun, this view of the *Parousia* emphasizes His present reign and ongoing revelation in believers' lives. This unveiling is not theoretical but profoundly transformative as it becomes a lived experience within the lives of believers through the work of the Holy Spirit. The apostle Paul's declaration that "We all . . . are being transformed into the same image from glory to glory" (2 Corinthians 3:18) encapsulates this ongoing process of transformation and communion. The *Parousia*, therefore, emerges not as a distant theological concept but as a dynamic and present reality, inviting believers into deeper intimacy with Christ and active participation in His heavenly kingdom.

The Kingdom of God Is in Our Midst explores the *Parousia* across three critical dimensions to provide a robust and holistic understanding. First it looks at the linguistic and historical roots of the Greek term *parousia*, examining its cultural context, early Christian usage, and evolution within theological discourse. This analysis uncovers its original significance as denoting "presence" or "essence," reframing its implications for contemporary theology.

Second, the book considers the scriptural portrayal of the *Parousia*. Biblical texts often employ symbolic language for it that is rich with theological depth and divine insight. This book delves into these passages, revealing how they portray the essence of Christ as a continuous and transformative presence rather than a singular future event. Finally, by confronting and reassessing the historical preconceptions that have shaped Church doctrine, this book redefines the *Parousia* as the progressive revelation of Christ's essence—an ongoing unveiling of His glory, authority, and transformative work.

This reinterpretation challenges entrenched eschatological misconceptions, offering believers a renewed and vibrant understanding of Christ's transcendent presence. Rather than relegating the *Parousia* to the realm of speculative theology, this book presents an immediate invitation to live in communion with Christ now, allowing His unveiled essence to shape our worship, mission, and daily lives. Jesus's declaration that "the kingdom of God is in your midst" (Luke 17:21) resounds with the affirmation of His current heavenly reign and presence.

As a celestial unveiling, the *Parousia* transcends physical limitations, serving as a foundation for exploring its theological, practical, and eschatological dimensions. By beginning with its historical and linguistic context and progressing toward its transformative implications, *The Kingdom of God Is in Our Midst* challenges traditional boundaries while inspiring hope and purpose. It calls believers to a deeper experience of Christ's presence, urging them to live in the fullness of His essence and to reflect His glory in a world longing for renewal.

CHAPTER 1

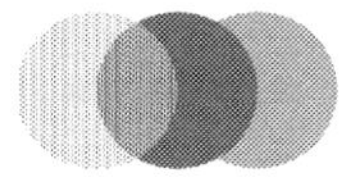

THE ETYMOLOGY OF *PAROUSIA* AND THE REVELATION OF CHRIST

The *Parousia* of Christ is not merely a religious concept but a cosmic reality that transcends theological speculation to reveal a profound spiritual truth. Yet this reality often remains obscured by layers of misunderstanding and misinterpretation. This is not the result of intentional misguidance but rather reflects how the unknown naturally gives rise to unasked and unimagined questions. To understand the *Parousia* is to embark on a journey of unveiling its purpose. "The purpose of a thing," as Aristotle taught (Metaphysics Book VII and Physics Book II), "defines its form."

This insight, which was adopted by the medieval theologian Thomas Aquinas, reminds us that knowing the purpose of something explains why it exists and how it functions. Simply put, design follows intent. The apostle Paul echoes this wisdom in Ephesians 2:10, declaring that believers are God's workmanship, created in Christ Jesus for good works that God prepared in advance for them to do. Our purpose "in Christ Jesus" shapes our identity and empowers our function as instruments of His will. Similarly, understanding the purpose of the *Parousia* is essential to interpreting God's intent for it. Knowing the intent of the *Parousia* helps us to determine its function, timing, and unveiling in the world.

A corollary of the above proverb is that purpose illuminates function. Just as believers discover their identity and mission through union with Christ, the *Parousia* unveils its transformative power when its divine purpose is fully grasped. This understanding forms the basis for our exploration of the ancient roots of the word *parousia*, shedding light on its significance and purpose in God's redemptive plan.

This chapter explores the etymological depth of the *Parousia*, its historical evolution, and its theological implications. Examining its Greek roots, its usage in ancient contexts, and its reinterpretation in early Christianity lays a foundation for understanding the *Parousia* as a dynamic, transformative, and heavenly relational reality and exploring how believers tangibly experience Christ's unveiled presence in their daily lives.

THE DEPTH OF THE TERM *PAROUSIA*

The term *parousia* carries with it a depth of meaning that extends beyond a mere arrival. Rooted in the Greek word, *parousia* conveys not only the coming of a person but also their presence and essence. It describes the act of one coming alongside another with intent and purpose. This dual meaning—presence and essence—provides a framework for understanding the *Parousia* as the simultaneous unveiling of Christ's nature and His active nearness to creation. This understanding of *Parousia* is integral to grasping the profound reality of Christ's coming—both His first advent and His ultimate return.

At its core, *parousia* encapsulates the tension between proximity and recognition. It is the simultaneous revelation of essence and the demand for a response. This is vividly portrayed in John 1:10–13: "He was in the world, and the world was created through him, and the world did not recognize him. He came to his own, and his own people did not receive him. But to all who did receive him, he gave them the right to be children of God, to those who believe in his name, who were born, not of natural descent, or of the will of the flesh, or of the will of man, but of God."

This passage serves as a touchstone, illustrating the dynamics of *Parousia*. Christ came alongside humanity, fully revealing His divine essence. Yet recognition was not universal. Those entrusted with the oracles of God—His chosen people—did not receive Him. Their rejection stemmed from a misalignment between their expectations and His revealed essence. However, those with faith, regardless of their physical lineage, recognized Him and were transformed by their reception of His life.

This dual response to Christ's first coming reflects the paradox inherent in the *Parousia*. It calls for both recognition and action, and this dynamic reverberates through Scripture. Just as Christ's first coming challenged preconceived notions and demanded faith, His eschatological *Parousia* will similarly unveil His essence, calling all of creation to respond.

BREAKDOWN OF THE GREEK COMPONENTS OF *PAROUSIA*

The Greek prefix *para* conveys an intrinsic sense of proximity, relational closeness, and nearness. It reflects a God who chooses to dwell with humanity, as seen in John 14:17, where Jesus promises the Holy Spirit's intimate presence with believers: "He remains with you and will be in you." The nearness is not just physical but relational, encapsulating Christ's ongoing engagement with His creation. Here the Spirit is described as dwelling with believers—a profound image of God's intimate nearness and relational presence.

When applied to *parousia*, *para* invites reflection on Christ's nearness to His creation. It reframes the *Parousia* not as a distant event waiting to unfold but as an ongoing and present reality. This is the God who walks alongside humanity, revealing His essence actively through His Spirit, His Word, and His people. Just as Christ walked alongside His disciples on the road to Emmaus, revealing Himself in the breaking of the bread (Luke 24:13–35), so His *Parousia* continues to reveal His presence in profound ways today.

The second component, *ousia*, carries much philosophical and theological weight. In classical Greek thought, *ousia* refers to the essence or substance of a thing—the fundamental reality underlying its appearance. The concept of *ousia* resonates with the declaration in John 1:14, "The Word became flesh and dwelt among us." Here the essence of God becomes tangibly revealed "in Christ," bridging the divine and the human. Aristotle, in his *Metaphysics*, expounds upon *ousia* as the core of existence, the essence that defines a being's true nature.

Aristotle's philosophical understanding finds a remarkable echo in Scripture. In Exodus 3:14 God declares to Moses, "I AM WHO I AM." This divine self-revelation speaks to God's unchanging and self-existent nature—a declaration of *ousia*. It is the essence of God's being made known to humanity.

In the person of Christ *ousia* takes on its fullest expression. The *Parousia* of Christ encompasses the continuous unveiling of His divine essence—His love, grace, truth, and authority. Whether through His incarnation, His presence through the Spirit, or His anticipated reign, Christ's *ousia* is not static but dynamically revealed. Hebrews 1:3 describes Him as "the radiance of God's glory and the exact expression of his nature." This radiance is the essence of Christ's being made visible and tangible to humanity, a presence that transforms and redeems.

When *para* and *ousia* are combined, the term product is a word with rich theological implications: "being alongside," or the manifestation of one's essence in presence or nearness. This understanding transcends a narrow focus on Christ's physical return and instead emphasizes His revealed essence made manifest among His people.

This interpretation challenges traditional eschatological frameworks that prioritize chronology and physicality. Instead it highlights the relational and spiritual dimensions of Christ's presence. His *Parousia* is not confined to a single moment in history; it is an ongoing, dynamic process through which His true nature is continually unveiled to the world. This understanding aligns with His promise in Matthew 28:20: "Remember, I am with you always, to the end of the age."

HISTORICAL USE IN GREEK LITERATURE

The historical uses of *parousia* in secular Greek literature offer valuable insights into its layered meaning and evolution. Initially a secular term, *parousia* described the presence or arrival of rulers, dignitaries, and other figures of authority. The word conveyed more than mere physical presence; it symbolized an event marked by authority, revelation, and transformation. Over time the term also found application in abstract and spiritual contexts, paving the way for its theological adoption by early Christians. This dual usage—both physical and metaphysical—provides a robust foundation for reexamining traditional interpretations of *Parousia* within Christian eschatology.

The secular roots of *parousia* emphasize the arrival of a powerful figure, often associated with the manifestation of their authority and glory. In contrast, its abstract applications highlight the revelation of essence or divine reality, suggesting that *parousia* transcends physical appearances. This historical flexibility challenges rigid eschatological interpretations and opens the door to understanding *Parousia* as a heavenly unveiling rather than merely a future physical event.

In classical Greek literature *parousia* frequently referred to the visit or presence of significant figures, particularly rulers or dignitaries. This usage is evident in the works of historians like Polybius and Plutarch. For example, Polybius, in his *Histories*, Book 29, chapter 27, section 7, describes the *parousia* of an emperor as an occasion marked by decrees, ceremonies, and the display of power that reinforced the ruler's authority. Plutarch, in his biography of *Demetrius I Poliorcetes*, section 23, speaks of the *parousia* of the ruler as an event that transformed the atmosphere of the city, not merely through physical arrival but by the demonstration of sovereignty and beneficence.

These accounts reveal that *parousia* was more than an appearance; it was a moment of profound impact, a manifestation of the ruler's essence and authority. For the public, the *parousia* of an emperor was transformative, signifying a tangible encounter with power and purpose. This secular understanding of *parousia* offers a compelling parallel to the theological concept of Christ's presence. Just as the *parousia* of a ruler revealed their sovereignty, so does Christ's *Parousia* unveil the essence of His divine authority and glory.

Parousia often denoted physical presence in secular contexts, and it also appeared in philosophical and metaphysical discussions. Plato's *Timaeus*, sections 37c–38a, describes the *parousia* of divine forms as the revelation of eternal truths within the temporal world. In this context *parousia* moves beyond physical presence to signify the manifestation of transcendent realities.

This abstract application of *parousia* introduces an essential dimension to its meaning: the presence of ultimate truth. For Plato the *parousia* of divine forms represented an encounter with eternal principles that shape and sustain the material world. This philosophical backdrop enriches the theological use of *parousia*, offering a precedent for interpreting it as more than a future physical event. In Christian theology *Parousia* signifies the ongoing revelation of Christ's essence and glory, experienced in the life of the believer, and the unfolding of divine truth in history.

The historical use of *parousia* in Greek literature demonstrates its capacity to bridge the physical and metaphysical, the temporal and the eternal. In secular contexts *parousia* emphasized the transformative presence of rulers and dignitaries and their effects on their constituents, while in philosophical writings it pointed to the manifestation of divine or abstract realities. This duality challenges traditional eschatological interpretations of *parousia* as a strictly physical future event.

By tracing its usage in Greek literature, we uncover the richness of *parousia* as a concept that transcends mere physical arrival. Instead, it embodies a dynamic unveiling of essence and authority. This understanding lays the foundation for reinterpreting *Parousia* as a multifaceted reality—a revelation of Christ's presence that offers profound theological vision and transformative possibilities for the Church and the world.

COMMON INTERPRETATIONS IN EARLY CHRISTIANITY

The term *parousia*, deeply rooted in Greek language and culture, underwent a remarkable transformation as it entered the lexicon of early Christian theology. In the shadow of Roman rule and influenced by Jewish eschatological hopes, early believers adopted *Parousia* to describe the anticipated return of Christ. However, the theological lens through which *Parousia* was understood varied significantly, reflecting a diversity of thought and expectation within the early Christian community.

Early Christians used the philosophical depth of *parousia* to expand the term's meaning. While retaining its connotations of authority and unveiling, *Parousia* also came to embody the spiritual and relational dimensions of Christ's presence. For some *Parousia* became synonymous with a dramatic and physical event: the triumphant return of Christ to judge the living and the dead and to establish His eternal kingdom. For others it represented an ongoing spiritual reality, emphasizing Christ's presence within the Church and in the lives of believers. These interpretations, shaped by cultural, theological, and scriptural influences, formed the foundation of Christian eschatology. Over time, however, certain perspectives were codified into rigid frameworks, limiting awareness of the term's richer, multifaceted meaning.

This section examines how the early Church interpreted *Parousia*, tracing its development from the apostolic age to the formation of established doctrine. By exploring these interpretations we uncover both the theological depth and the tensions surrounding *Parousia*, setting the stage for its reexamination.

The term *parousia*, originating in the Greco-Roman cultural lexicon, carried significant weight as it was adopted into early Christian theology. In secular Greek usage, as noted, *parousia* often referred to the ceremonial arrival or visit of a ruler or dignitary—an event marked by grandeur, authority, and the demonstration of power. Early Christian writers, recognizing the potency of this term, reappropriated it to describe the anticipated coming of Christ. This theological shift positioned Jesus as the ultimate sovereign, whose *Parousia* would surpass that of all earthly rulers in glory and authority.

The New Testament provides key examples of this conceptual adaptation. In 1 Thessalonians 4:15 Paul uses *Parousia* to describe the moment when Christ will descend from heaven, heralded by the voice of the archangel and the trumpet of God. Similarly, in Matthew 24:27 *Parousia* is likened to lightning illuminating the sky—an unmistakable and awe-inspiring event. These depictions align with the Greco-Roman understanding of a dignitary's arrival but elevate it to a cosmic and divine scale. In 2 Thessalonians 2:8 the *Parousia* of Christ is portrayed as a moment of decisive victory when Jesus destroys the lawless one with the mere breath of His mouth, underscoring the unparalleled authority of His coming.

Early church fathers such as Justin Martyr and Irenaeus reinforced this interpretation. Justin Martyr, in *Dialogue with Trypho*, chapter 110, describes the *Parousia* of Christ as the event during which the nations will see His glory and judgment will be rendered. Similarly, Irenaeus, in *Against Heresies*, book 5, chapter 30, emphasizes the *Parousia* as the culmination of God's promises when Christ will restore creation and vindicate the righteous. For these theologians the *Parousia* represented both the triumphant arrival of a divine king and the fulfillment of eschatological hope—a cornerstone of early Christian thought.

By adopting *parousia* as a term for the coming of Christ, early Christians connected their theological vision to a culturally familiar concept while imbuing it with profound spiritual significance. However, this reinterpretation also introduced tensions about whether the *Parousia* should be understood as a singular future event or an ongoing revelation of Christ's essence. This tension invites deeper exploration, particularly as it relates to the spiritual dimensions of *Parousia* in the lives of believers.

THE EVOLUTION OF THE *PAROUSIA*: FROM PRESENCE TO APOCALYPTIC EXPECTATION

The quiet wisdom of Polycarp, bishop of Smyrna, flowed from the same source as that of his mentor Ignatius and their teacher before them—John, the beloved disciple. Their theology was shaped by the apostle who had leaned against Christ's chest, the one who had seen the Word made flesh and recorded the great mysteries of Christ's abiding presence. For Polycarp and Ignatius, the *Parousia* was not a distant, cosmic event, nor was resurrection reserved for some final apocalyptic unveiling. Instead, these early disciples understood the mystery of Christ's presence already at work in those who belonged to Him.

Ignatius, journeying to his martyrdom in Rome, wrote of Christ's indwelling power, urging believers to remain united in His presence (Letter to the Ephesians 15:1–2, Letter to the Magnesians 1:2). His letters reflect an understanding that the kingdom of God was not only coming but was already breaking forth in the suffering, unity, and faith of the Church. Ignatius saw his own impending death not as an end but as a final unveiling of Christ's presence—a personal *epiphaneia* (manifestation or unveiling—the root of the English word *epiphany*) wherein his union with Christ would be fully realized (Letter to the Romans 6:1; cf. Galatians 2:20).

Polycarp shared this conviction. He wrote not of waiting for Christ's return but of being raised with Him now, living out the resurrected life even in the present age (Epistle to the Philippians 2:1–2) He saw resurrection through the lens of Paul, who declared, "If we have been united with him in the likeness of his death, we will certainly also be in the likeness of his resurrection" (Romans 6:5). For Polycarp the resurrection was not only future but present—it was the ongoing transformation of the believer into the image of Christ (Epistle to the Philippians 5:2; cf. Romans 6:4–5; 2 Corinthians 3:18). And when the time of his own death came, he did not wait for a distant judgment or a far-off resurrection. Instead he proclaimed, "May I be received among the martyrs in the presence of Christ today" (Martyrdom of Polycarp 14:2). His *Parousia* was happening at that moment in time.

But as the Church grew and the generations that had known the apostles faded, the focus of the *Parousia* began to shift. By the late second century the Church was expanding, facing philosophical opposition from Greek thinkers and theological challenges from Gnostics. In this environment, Irenaeus of Lyons and Justin Martyr sought to defend the physicality of Christ's work, ensuring that Christianity would not be reduced to a spiritualized, mystical faith that abandoned the world.

Irenaeus, deeply influenced by Polycarp, still upheld the present reality of Christ's presence in the believer's life. He affirmed that resurrection was already being experienced by those transformed into Christ's image. The faithful, he taught, had already begun to "rise" with Christ and participate in His reign. But he also emphasized a future restoration—a time when Christ would physically return to bring about the full redemption of creation (Against Heresies 5.36.3).

Justin Martyr took a similar stance. Writing against the philosophers of Rome, he argued that Christ's first coming had already inaugurated the transformation of those who followed Him but that a future return would bring final judgment and the renewal of all things (First Apology 45). Unlike Polycarp and Ignatius, who saw the *Parousia* as an ongoing relational unveiling, Justin increased the emphasis on a future event. He never fully abandoned the present transformative reality of Christ's reign, but the seeds of a shifting eschatology had been planted.

As the second century gave way to the third, the theological focus of the Church underwent a profound change. The once-balanced tension—between the immediate presence of Christ and His future fulfillment—began to tip. A new dominant perspective emerged: the *Parousia* was no longer primarily an unveiling of Christ's presence in that time but had become, above all else, a cataclysmic event in the future.

Two major Church leaders cemented this transition: Tertullian and Origen. Tertullian, a fiery theologian and apologist from Carthage, developed one of the earliest clear systems of apocalyptic eschatology. In reaction to heresies that denied Christ's bodily nature, he heavily emphasized the physical return of Christ as a future event. His theology reflected a growing fear of Roman persecution and the Church's desire for vindication. He saw history moving toward an ultimate moment when Christ would return visibly, in power, to judge the wicked. By this time the relational unveiling of Christ's presence—so central to first- and second-century believers—had been overshadowed by a coming eschatological battle. The early martyrs had seen death as their personal unveiling, but by Tertullian's time many Christians looked forward to an external triumph.

Origen, writing in the early third century, took a different approach from that of Tertullian. He spiritualized much of Christian doctrine, seeing Christ's coming as an inward reality, transforming believers on a mystical level. However, while he preserved an element of the ongoing *Parousia*, he also framed Christ's return as a future culmination of all things, by which believers would be fully absorbed into God's divine life. For Origen the real *Parousia* was the soul's progressive ascent into God, yet he still maintained that there would be a final event whereby this reality would be universally fulfilled.

Thus, by the third century the Church's view of the *Parousia* was fundamentally changed. What had begun as a deeply relational theology—where Christ's *Parousia* was an ongoing unveiling in the life of the believer—morphed by the third century into a primarily apocalyptic event. Yet the traces of the transformative relational *Parousia* never disappeared. Even in later centuries, theologians like Augustine and writers within the Eastern Orthodox tradition would reclaim elements of the present unveiling of Christ's presence alongside the future hope of His return.

The transformation of *Parousia* theology from a present unveiling of Christ's presence to a future apocalyptic expectation is critical to understanding how the early Church perceived Christ's reign and resurrection life. While the earliest disciples of John—Ignatius and Polycarp—saw Christ's *Parousia* as an ongoing reality, progressively revealed through faith, martyrdom, and transformation, later theologians such as Irenaeus and Justin Martyr attempted to hold both the present experience of Christ's presence and the expectation of a future fulfillment in tension. However, by the third century under Tertullian and Origen, the emphasis had largely moved toward an eschatological framework wherein the physical return of Christ became the dominant understanding of the *Parousia*. But despite this shift, the threads of the transformative relational *Parousia* never disappeared. They remained embedded in theological thought, resurfacing in later traditions that recognized the *Parousia* as both a present and a future reality.

TRANSITION TO THEOLOGICAL USE AS THE SECOND COMING OF CHRIST

As Christian theology evolved, the term *parousia* underwent a significant transition. Initially a concept encompassing presence and manifestation, it became increasingly associated with a narrowly defined eschatological event: the second coming of Christ. This shift reflects the growing emphasis within early Christian thought on the ultimate fulfillment of God's redemptive plan through a future, visible and climactic return of Jesus.

In the New Testament this eschatological focus is evident in passages such as Revelation 1:7: "Look, he is coming with the clouds, and every eye will see him, even those who pierced him. And all the tribes of the earth will mourn over him. So it is to be. Amen." Here the *Parousia* is depicted as a global and unmistakable event, marked by divine glory and universal recognition. This imagery resonates with Old Testament motifs, such as Daniel 7:13, where the Son of Man is described as coming with the clouds of heaven—a scene that early Christians saw as prefiguring Christ's return.

Over time apocalyptic expectations like these coalesced into a dominant theological framework in which the *parousia* symbolized not only the culmination of history but also the fulfillment of divine judgment and restoration. However, as the *Parousia* became increasingly associated with Christ's physical return, its spiritual and metaphorical dimensions were often overshadowed. Initially, the term carried the connotation of presence, emphasizing Christ's nearness and active participation in the lives of believers. Yet in the face of external pressures—such as persecution and the apparent delay of Christ's return—Christian communities increasingly focused on the future and visible aspects of the *Parousia*. This expectation provided hope and encouragement for suffering believers, assuring them that vindication and deliverance were imminent.

The historical and cultural context of the early Church thus played a critical role in this theological shift. Living under Roman oppression and facing marginalization, early Christians found profound hope in the promise of Christ's return. The anticipation of a physical *Parousia* served as both a theological anchor and a rallying cry, reinforcing the belief that Christ would triumph over all enemies. Yet as this expectation took precedence, it left little room for exploring the broader implications of *Parousia* as a continuous revelation of Christ's essence.

At the same time, the narrowing of its meaning raises important questions that lay the groundwork for reexamining the *Parousia* within the framework of this book: Have traditional interpretations of the *Parousia* overlooked its spiritual dimensions? Can the *parousia* be reclaimed as not merely a future event but a transformative reality that permeates the believer's present experience?

CONCLUSION

Chapter 1 has laid the groundwork by revisiting the linguistic and theological foundations of *parousia*, challenging long-held assumptions of a physical second coming and proposing instead a biblically consistent alternative—the spiritual unveiling of Christ's essence. Through an examination of etymology, historical usage, and theological evolution, we have uncovered how Christ's presence is an ongoing transformative reality rather than a distant apocalyptic event.

This understanding sets the stage to explore the scriptural roots of the term itself. As we turn to Scripture's unfolding revelation, we will see how God's desire to dwell among His people—first in the Garden of Eden and then in the tabernacle and the temple—forms the basis for the New Testament revelation of the *Parousia*. In doing so we will discover how Christ's presence, unveiled through His kingdom, transforms believers into His image, revealing the fullness of God's eternal purpose.

CHAPTER 2

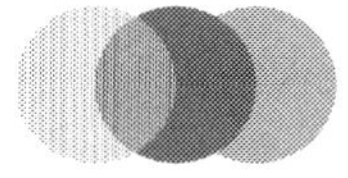

OLD TESTAMENT NEAR-SYNONYMS FOR *PAROUSIA*

To fully grasp the theological depth of the New Testament concept of *Parousia*, we must first examine its roots in the Old Testament. This chapter explores the concept of *parousia* through two key lenses: the Hebrew terms that embody aspects of divine presence and the Greek translations in the Septuagint that bridge the Old and New Testament contexts. By examining these elements we uncover the theological continuity and progression that culminates in Christ.

While the Greek word *parousia* does not appear explicitly in the Hebrew scriptures, its equivalents and themes are unmistakably present there. The Old Testament frequently describes divine manifestations, or theophanies, where God's presence is revealed to His people in profound and transformative ways. These moments, ranging from visible signs and angelic messengers to God's voice speaking directly, serve as precursors to the New Testament understanding of Christ's unveiling. They highlight the continuity of God's relationship with humanity and His ongoing effort to reveal His essence.

This chapter explores how Old Testament accounts of God's presence illuminate the broader context of *Parousia* as a transformative relational unveiling. Key examples include the cloud and fire guiding Israel through the wilderness (Exodus 13:21–22), the glory of God filling the tabernacle and temple (Exodus 40:34–35; 1 Kings 8:10–11), and encounters with God experienced by patriarchs, prophets, and national leaders (e.g., Genesis 28:12–17; Isaiah 6:1–5). These were not merely physical manifestations but profound spiritual revelations of God's character, authority, and mission. Through these narratives the Old Testament establishes a framework for understanding how God's presence transforms His people and prepares them for the fuller revelation to come in Christ.

One pivotal aspect of these theophanies is their role as both moments of divine nearness and invitations to faith. For example, when God spoke to Moses at the burning bush (Exodus 3:1–12), He not only revealed His name and essence as "I AM" but also called Moses into a covenantal mission. Similarly, the divine glory that filled the temple symbolized God's willingness to dwell among His people while simultaneously demanding their holiness and devotion. These moments underscore the duality of God's presence as both awe inspiring and deeply relational—a reality that finds its fullest expression in Christ's *Parousia*.

By examining these equivalents to *parousia*, this chapter demonstrates that the unveiling of God's essence has always been central to His relationship with humanity. The Old Testament accounts challenge us to see *parousia* not as a novel New Testament concept but as the culmination of a consistent biblical theme: God's desire to make His presence known, to dwell among His people, and to invite them into deeper relational fellowship with Him. This perspective bridges the Old and New Testaments, showing how the heavenly unveiling of God's presence finds its ultimate fulfillment in Christ. Yet it remains rooted in the rich theological soil of the Hebrew scriptures, offering a lens through which to understand the eternal consistency of God's expression of self-revelation.

HEBREW WORDS RELATED TO THE CONCEPT OF *PAROUSIA*

The Old Testament employs various Hebrew terms that reflect dimensions of God's presence, appearance, or coming. While none wholly equates to the Greek term *parousia*, these words reveal key theological and spiritual themes that later influenced the New Testament's usage. Each term underscores aspects of God's interaction with His people, laying the foundation for the fuller revelation of His essence in Christ.

The Hebrew term pānîm (פָּנִים), often translated as "face" or "presence," carries profound theological significance in the Old Testament. It encapsulates the idea of relational closeness and an intimate awareness of God's nearness to His people. Far more than a mere acknowledgment of God's existence, pānîm conveys the reality of experiencing His presence as if one were standing "before His face." This term serves as a powerful expression of God's unwavering commitment to dwell among His people and guide them in their journey.

A pivotal example of pānîm is found in Exodus 33:14, where God reassures Moses, saying, "My presence [pānîm] will go with you, and I will give you rest." Here God's presence is not depicted as a distant or occasional visitation but as an enduring companionship that brings peace and assurance. The Israelites understood this as a defining aspect of their covenant relationship with God, a presence that signified divine favor, protection, and guidance.

The theological depth of pānîm finds its fulfillment in the New Testament concept of Parousia, which similarly conveys the abiding presence of Christ. Just as pānîm in the Old Testament denotes God's continuous nearness to His people, Christ's promise in Matthew 28:20 ("Remember, I am with you always, to the end of the age.") reflects the enduring nature of His relational presence in the lives of believers. This connection reveals that the *Parousia* of Christ is not merely an anticipated future event but an ongoing relational reality, where Christ's essence is continually unveiled to those who abide in Him.

Through pānîm, the Old Testament lays the foundation for understanding the *Parousia* as more than a moment of arrival; it is a sustained and transformative relational presence that shapes the lives of God's people. It invites believers to live in the reality of divine nearness, walking in communion with Christ and experiencing His presence in their daily lives. The concept of pānîm presents a profound understanding of God's presence as an ongoing, intimate reality—one that is not merely observed but deeply experienced in relationship.

This sustained nearness is complemented by another crucial aspect of divine interaction found in the Hebrew Scriptures: the concept of bôʾ (אוֹבּ), meaning "to come" or "to arrive." This term speaks to the dynamic movement of God in history. While pānîm assures believers of God's abiding presence, bôʾ conveys the anticipation and fulfillment of His coming, revealing the moments when His presence manifests in decisive acts of intervention, redemption, and covenant fulfillment.

Together these terms offer a comprehensive picture of God's engagement with His people—one that is both enduring and expectant, constant and climactic. As we move from the relational closeness of pānîm to the anticipatory nature of bôʾ, we gain a fuller appreciation of how the *Parousia* integrates both the ever-present reality of Christ's essence and the unfolding fulfillment of God's redemptive purposes.

Bôʾ carries a rich theological significance throughout the Old Testament. It is often associated with divine visitation, intervention, and fulfillment of covenantal promises. A profound example of bôʾ is found in Malachi 3:1, where the Lord declares, "'See, I am going to send my messenger, and he will clear the way before me. Then the Lord you seek will suddenly come to his temple, the Messenger of the covenant you delight in—see, he is coming [bô],' says the Lord of Armies."

This passage not only highlights the imminent arrival of God's intervention but also points to a deeper reality: the coming of the long-awaited Messiah, who embodies the fulfillment of God's promises and brings restoration to His people. The suddenness of this coming underscores the sovereign timing of God, whose arrival often defies human expectation and yet fulfills divine purposes with precision.

The theological implications of bôʾ resonate deeply with the New Testament concept of parousia. Just as bôʾ in the Old Testament describes God's arrival in response to His covenant, the *Parousia* of Christ signifies His coming to fulfill the ultimate redemptive work of God. Christ's first coming fulfilled the covenant by bringing salvation, while His ongoing presence through the Holy Spirit continues to usher believers into the reality of His kingdom. The mysterious promise of Christ's future coming remains as a culmination of this divine narrative, when all things will be fully restored under His reign.

Thus, bôʾ serves as a bridge between anticipation and realization, showing that God's redemptive acts are not isolated events but part of an unfolding divine plan. The arrival of Christ in history and His continuous unveiling in the lives of believers through the *Parousia* reflect the essence of bôʾ—a fulfillment of God's promises and an assurance that He remains active and present in the unfolding story of redemption.

In this way bôʾ enriches our understanding of the *Parousia* by emphasizing both the expectancy and fulfillment inherent in God's plan. It calls believers to live with readiness and hope, recognizing that Christ's essence is continually revealed in their lives while they anticipate the final consummation of His kingdom. The concept of bôʾ captures the dynamic anticipation of God's coming, emphasizing divine intervention and fulfillment of covenantal promises. This movement of God into the lives of His people reflects the forward-looking nature of redemption, highlighting both the certainty and the hope of His appearing.

However, the experience of God's coming is not limited to moments of divine intervention; it also encompasses intentional encounters wherein His presence is acknowledged and celebrated by His people. This brings us to the Hebrew term yirʿarâh, which expands our understanding of divine presence by emphasizing the visible and ceremonial aspects of appearing before God. Usually translated "to appear," the term yirʿarâh conveys the idea of manifestation—moments when God's presence is not only experienced but also acknowledged through sacred interaction. It often appears in contexts where individuals or the community come before God in worship and covenant renewal, recognizing His authority and seeking communion with Him.

In Exodus 34:24 God commands His people to appear before Him three times a year, assuring them of His protection and provision when they fulfill their covenantal obligations: "I will drive out nations before you and enlarge your territory. No one will covet your land when you go up three times a year to appear [*yirʿarâh*] before the Lord your God." This appearance before God is not merely a physical act; it represents a deeper spiritual reality—an acknowledgment of dependence, devotion, and alignment with His divine purposes.

Theologically, yirʿarâh underscores the significance of engaging with God through sacred encounters, foreshadowing the New Testament's emphasis on beholding Christ's unveiled glory. The apostle Paul in 2 Corinthians 3:18 describes the transformative power of encountering Christ's presence: "We all, with unveiled faces, are looking as in a mirror at the glory of the Lord and are being transformed into the same image from glory to glory." Just as Israel's festivals and sacred assemblies were opportunities to reaffirm the Israelites' covenant relationship with God, so too the *Parousia* invites believers to continually behold and reflect the unveiled essence of Christ in their daily lives.

Together with pānîm and bôʾ, the concept of yirʿarâh enriches our cultural understanding of the *Parousia* by highlighting the intentional response of believers to God's presence. It reveals that the unveiling of Christ's essence is not only an act of divine initiative but also an invitation for believers to relationally draw near to, worship, and be transformed by His revealed glory.

Building upon the idea of appearing before God conveyed by yirʿarâh, another Hebrew term, gālâ (הָלָג), deepens our understanding of the *Parousia* by emphasizing the act of divine unveiling and revelation.

While yir'ârâh highlights the intentional response of humanity in approaching God, gālâ, meaning "to reveal" or "to uncover," shifts the focus to God's initiative in making Himself known. This term conveys the act of uncovering or revealing, portraying divine self-disclosure as an essential aspect of the believer's experience of His presence.

Gālâ signifies the removal of a covering, exposing what was previously hidden. It frequently appears in the Hebrew Scriptures in contexts where God reveals His will, character, and redemptive purposes to His people. In Isaiah 40:5 the prophet declares, "The glory of the LORD will appear [be revealed, gālâ], and all humanity together will see it, for the mouth of the LORD has spoken." This unveiling is not merely an abstract concept but a tangible encounter with the essence of God, drawing His people into a deeper understanding of His nature and plans.

Theologically, gālâ captures the heart of the *Parousia* as the unveiling of Christ's essence. "In Christ" the hidden mysteries of God are revealed, bringing the fullness of divine truth and presence into the lives of believers. The apostle Paul echoes this sentiment in Colossians 1:26–27 when he speaks of "the mystery hidden for ages and generations but now revealed to his saints. God wanted to make known among the Gentiles the glorious wealth of this mystery, which is Christ in you, the hope of glory." Just as gālâ in the Old Testament signifies God lifting the veil to reveal His purposes to Israel, so too the *Parousia* unveils Christ's presence and essence, transforming believers from within.

This unveiling is not passive; it calls for an active response of faith and surrender. As the Church experiences the *Parousia* through the Holy Spirit, the Word, and sacramental life, the hidden realities of Christ's kingdom are made known in greater measure. The ongoing unveiling invites believers to live with an awareness that they are part of a divine narrative in which Christ's presence is progressively being revealed in and through them.

By examining these Hebrew terms we see a rich tapestry of themes that converge in the New Testament's portrayal of *parousia*. Each term reflects a facet of God's presence, from His intimate relational nearness to His majestic and transformative unveiling. The Hebrew terms pānîm, bô', yirʿarâh, and gālâ establish a rich theological foundation, emphasizing relational nearness, divine intervention, and the unveiling of God's glory. These concepts provide a theological bridge between the Old and New Testaments, highlighting the consistency of God's self-revelation throughout Scripture. These terms collectively anticipate the ultimate *Parousia* of Christ, in which God's presence is fully realized and unveiled in the lives of believers.

THE SEPTUAGINT

As the Scriptures were translated into Greek, new linguistic frameworks were employed to capture these profound theological realities, bridging the Old Testament's covenantal self-revelation to the New Testament's eschatological and heavenly unveiling of Christ. Transitioning from the Hebrew Scriptures to the Septuagint—the Greek translation of the Hebrew Bible—allows us to glimpse how the concept of divine presence evolves and deepens across the biblical narrative. The Septuagint demonstrates significant linguistic and theological connections between the Old and New Testaments, particularly regarding the concept of divine manifestation.

While the specific term parousia does not appear in the Septuagint, its thematic foundations are evident in other Greek terms that convey God's presence, revelation, and intervention. Words such as epiphaneia (ἔπιφάνεια, "appearance") and erchomai (ἔρχομαι, "to come") express the profound reality of divine self-disclosure, anticipating the New Testament's full articulation of Parousia as the unveiling of Christ's essence. These terms, respectively, reflect the Hebrew Scriptures' consistent portrayal of God's nearness, His active engagement with creation, and His desire to reveal Himself to His people.

One of the most compelling terms used in the Septuagint is epiphaneia, which signifies the visible manifestation of divine glory and authority. This word appears in passages such as Isaiah 40:5, which declares, "The glory of the Lord will appear [epiphanei], and all humanity together will see it." The term communicates an expectation of divine intervention—of God revealing Himself in ways that transform history and humanity. The New Testament later adopted epiphaneia to describe Christ's appearing, particularly in passages such as 2 Timothy 4:8, which speaks of His coming as the moment when justice is rendered and faith is rewarded. The transition from Old Testament theophanies to the New Testament use of epiphaneia highlights a central truth: God's self-revelation is not only a future hope but a present reality, progressively unveiled in the lives of those who have eyes to see.

This concept of appearance, revelation, and recognition leads naturally to the idea of epiphany—a moment of spiritual awakening in which the truth of God is suddenly and deeply perceived. Within the framework of parousia, epiphany represents the transformative moment when a believer truly "sees" Christ for who He is—not merely as Savior in a doctrinal sense but as the living essence of divine power, authority, and presence. This realization is not an abstract theological concept; it is the pivotal turning point in a person's spiritual journey. The disciples themselves experienced this progression, moving from intellectual belief to transformative epiphany, particularly at moments like Peter's confession of Jesus as the Christ (Matthew 16:16–17) or Thomas's exclamation, "My Lord and my God!" (John 20:28) after encountering the resurrected Christ.

Another Greek term in the Septuagint closely associated with divine coming is erchomai (ἔρχομαι), meaning "to come" or "to arrive." This term frequently translates the Hebrew bôʾ (אוֹב), which conveys the active and imminent nature of God's movements in history. A significant example appears in Malachi 3:1, which proclaims, "The Lord you seek will suddenly come to his temple." Here the prophecy speaks of God's arrival as both judgment and fulfillment, marking a decisive moment in redemptive history. This expectation of God's imminent arrival carries over into the New Testament, where erchomai describes Christ's coming—not only in His incarnation but also in His ongoing presence through the Spirit. The continuity between God's covenantal movements in the Old Testament and Christ's revealed presence in the New Testament affirms that His redemptive work is never static; it is always unfolding, always revealing itself, always calling humanity more deeply into communion with Him.

The absence of parousia in the Septuagint is noteworthy, as it underscores its subsequent development as a distinctively Christian concept, not one simply borrowed from Judaism. While epiphaneia and erchomai laid the groundwork for the concept of divine revelation and coming, the New Testament writers adopted parousia to express something even greater—the unveiling of Christ's essence. Rather than limiting Christ's coming to a single future event, they presented parousia as a dynamic and ongoing reality, experienced through faith, discerned through spiritual awakening, and revealed through the Holy Spirit's work. The introduction of this term in Christian theology does not replace the Old Testament's themes of divine manifestation but rather fulfills and expands them.

The theological harmony between the Hebrew and Greek Scriptures is evident in the transition from *pānîm* (מ׳נָפ), "face" or "presence," in Hebrew thought to epiphaneia in the Greek tradition. Likewise, the movement from bôʾ (God's coming) to erchomai (Christ's arrival and continued presence) reflects a consistent divine pattern of self-disclosure. The Septuagint acts as a bridge, preserving the Old Testament's emphasis on God's tangible presence while expanding its application in light of Christ's mission. This connection reinforces the central dynamic of the *Parousia*: God's presence is not an eschatological event to be awaited but an unveiling reality to be experienced.

Ultimately, the Septuagint provides the linguistic and theological foundation for the New Testament's use of parousia. The consistent themes of divine presence, revelation, and fulfillment woven throughout the Septuagint affirm God's unchanging desire to dwell with His people. Yet this reality is not merely an abstract theological construct but a present and transformative experience for those who surrender to His unveiling. This experience of seeing Christ with spiritual clarity—the moment of epiphaneia—is what defines true participation in the *Parousia*. It is in this surrender and recognition that believers move beyond mere belief to true transformation, experiencing the full weight of Christ's revealed essence in their lives.

CONCLUSION

In subsequent chapters we will explore how the sacred spaces of the Old Testament—the Garden of Eden, the tabernacle, and the temple—prefigure the *Parousia* as the ultimate fulfillment of God's eternal plan for communion with His people. These physical manifestations of divine presence were never meant to be endpoints but serve as signposts pointing toward the greater revelation to come. "In Christ," these sacred dwellings find their fulfillment, for He is the true tabernacle, the very dwelling place of God among humanity (John 1:14). This exploration will further illuminate the continuity between the divine presence in sacred spaces and the *Parousia* as the indwelling of Christ in the lives of believers.

Throughout the Old Testament and the Septuagint God's unveiling presence follows a consistent and intentional pattern—one that finds its culmination in the revealed essence of Christ. The linguistic and conceptual insights explored in this chapter serve not merely as historical observations but as keys to understanding the transformative nature of the *Parousia*. From the prophetic declarations of God's coming to the sacred spaces of divine habitation to the linguistic shifts from Hebrew to Greek, all point toward a singular and profound truth: the essence of Christ is unveiled not merely in history but in the very heart of the believer.

Yet divine self-disclosure was never limited to language alone. It was intricately expressed through physical spaces; covenantal relationships; and, ultimately, the incarnation itself. As we move forward we will see how the marriage covenant—one of the most intimate and sacred human relationships—serves as another profound analogy for the *Parousia*. Just as betrothal in the ancient world signified a binding union even before its consummation, the Church, as the bride of Christ, exists in the tension of already being united with Him while awaiting the full revelation of that reality. The next chapter will examine this profound analogy, exploring how the marriage covenant deepens our understanding of the *Parousia* as the unveiling of Christ's essence in the life of the believer.

CHAPTER 3

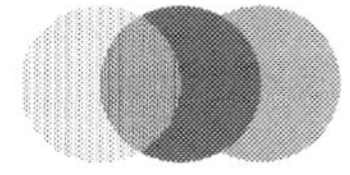

THE MARRIAGE ANALOGY AND THE *PAROUSIA*

The *Parousia*—the unveiling of Christ's essence—is not merely a theological concept; it is a deeply relational reality woven into the fabric of God's redemptive plan. Scripture presents this reality through the profound metaphor of marriage, portraying Christ as the bridegroom and the Church as His bride. This sacred analogy conveys both the present and the future dimensions of the *Parousia*, revealing a union that is already established yet awaits its ultimate consummation. In ancient Israelite culture betrothal was not a mere engagement but a binding covenant with the full legal weight of marriage, affirming the couple's relationship long before the wedding ceremony. Similarly, the Church, as the bride of Christ, lives in the present reality of her union with Him, even as she anticipates the final fulfillment of that relationship.

This marriage analogy transforms the *Parousia* from a distant hope into a present experience, inviting believers to embrace Christ's unveiled presence in their daily lives. The betrothal period, with its covenantal commitments and preparations, provides a rich context for understanding the believer's relationship with Christ and the anticipation of His full revelation. This chapter explores the intricate details of ancient Israelite betrothal customs, their scriptural significance, and the transformative implications of seeing the *Parousia* as the divine marriage of Christ and His Church. It calls believers to embrace their identity as the bride of Christ, living in the joy and anticipation of their union while reflecting His presence in the world.

THE BETROTHAL STAGE IN ISRAELITE CULTURE

The betrothal period in ancient Israel carried profound significance, far surpassing the modern concept of engagement. It was not merely a promise of future marriage but an established covenant that carried both legal and relational weight. This understanding of betrothal provides a powerful framework for interpreting the Church's relationship with Christ in the present age.

In the eyes of Israelite law, a betrothed woman was already considered legally married to her groom. Deuteronomy 22:23–24 affirms this by treating unfaithfulness during betrothal with the same gravity as adultery after marriage. The binding nature of this covenant meant that breaking a betrothal required a formal process of divorce, underscoring the seriousness of the commitment. In the same way the Church is not awaiting a future relationship with Christ but is already in a binding covenant with Him, secured by His redemptive work.

During this time of betrothal the groom's responsibility was to prepare a place for his bride, often an additional room in his father's house. This custom serves as a powerful parallel to Christ's promise in John 14:2–3: "I am going to prepare a place for you." Just as the bride lived in the assurance of her future dwelling, believers live in the confident hope of their eternal union with Christ, knowing that He is actively preparing a place for them in the Father's house.

The groom bore the primary responsibility for ensuring the readiness of their future home and life together. This period of preparation involved both physical and financial commitment, demonstrating his devotion and ability to provide for his bride. One of the most significant aspects of this preparation was the payment of the bride price—an expression of the groom's love and commitment as well as of the value he placed upon his bride (Genesis 24:53). This act finds its ultimate fulfillment in Christ, who paid the highest price for His Church—not with silver or gold but with His own precious blood (1 Corinthians 6:20; 1 Peter 1:18–19). In giving Himself fully, Christ demonstrated His unwavering love and commitment to His bride, securing her place in His eternal kingdom.

Christ, as the bridegroom, continues to fulfill His role by preparing His Church, guiding and sanctifying her through the Holy Spirit. His provision is not passive but active, working in the hearts and lives of believers to transform them into a bride ready for His appearing. The Church is thus called to live in a posture of preparedness, fully assured that her groom is actively engaged in readying her for their eternal union.

While the groom prepared the home, the bride devoted herself to preparation as well. Her role during the betrothal period was characterized by purity, anticipation, and readiness. Revelation 19:7 captures this beautifully: "His bride has prepared herself." In ancient Israel this preparation often included crafting wedding garments, symbolizing the bride's dedication to presenting herself in beauty and righteousness. This imagery speaks profoundly to the Church's call to holiness and sanctification through the Spirit, as believers prepare their hearts and lives for the fullness of Christ's presence.

The Church, like the betrothed bride, is called to live with unwavering faithfulness, keeping her heart fixed on the promise of Christ's appearing. This season of waiting is not passive but active, marked by spiritual growth, devotion, and mission. The anticipation of the final consummation fuels a life of worship and service, reflecting the bride's longing for the moment when she will be fully united with her bridegroom.

LIVING IN THE REALITY OF THE BETROTHAL

The betrothal framework reveals a profound theological truth: believers are not waiting to enter into a relationship with Christ;

they are already bound to Him through the new covenant. Just as the bride lived in the reality of her marriage during betrothal, the Church exists in the present reality of her union with Christ, experiencing His unveiled essence through the Spirit. This understanding transforms how believers live, worship, and engage with the world, anchoring them in the present reality of their transformative relationship with Christ while looking forward to its ultimate fulfillment.

In embracing this identity as the bride of Christ, believers are called to live in the confidence of their union with Him, allowing His presence to shape every aspect of their lives. The *Parousia*, therefore, is not just a future hope but an ongoing relational experience that empowers the Church to embody the love, faithfulness, and mission of Christ until the day of ultimate consummation.

The metaphor of marriage as a covenant between God and His people is deeply woven throughout Scripture, reflecting the profound nature of God's love and His desire for an intimate relationship with His people. This imagery finds its roots in the Old Testament, where God frequently portrays Himself as the faithful husband and Israel as the oft wayward bride. Despite Israel's repeated failures and infidelities, God's steadfast love remains unwavering, pointing to the ultimate fulfillment of this divine relationship in Christ. Hosea 2:19–20 captures this covenantal love, as God declares, "I will take you to be my wife forever. I will take you to be my wife in righteousness, justice, love, and compassion." Similarly, in Jeremiah 31:31–32 God reaffirms His commitment, promising a new covenant with His people—one that would be fulfilled through the redemptive work of Christ, the true Bridegroom.

The joy and intimacy of this divine union are vividly expressed in Isaiah 62:5, where the prophet writes, "As a groom rejoices over his bride, so your God will rejoice over you." This passage anticipates the delight and fulfillment Christ finds in His Church, underscoring the depth of His love and the celebratory nature of their union. Throughout

Scripture marriage serves as a consistent theme that points forward to the *Parousia*—the full unveiling of Christ's presence within His people.

THE WEDDING BANQUET IN MESSIANIC PROPHECY

The theme of marriage reaches its climactic expression in the prophetic imagery of a wedding banquet, representing the culmination of God's redemptive plan and His ultimate union with His people. Isaiah 25:6–8 presents a vision of a grand banquet, where the Lord prepares a feast for all nations, removing sorrow and death and ushering in an era of joy and communion. Similarly, Psalm 45:6–9 celebrates the splendor and majesty of the King's marriage to His bride, portraying a scene of divine fulfillment and rejoicing that echoes through the New Testament vision of the marriage supper of the Lamb.

Jesus Himself embraced and expanded upon this analogy, explicitly referring to Himself as the Bridegroom. In Matthew 9:15 He asks, "Can the wedding guests be sad while the groom is with them?" signaling the fulfillment of Old Testament prophecies concerning God's union with His people. The parables of the wedding feast (Matthew 22:1–14) and the ten virgins (Matthew 25:1–13) emphasize essential aspects of the kingdom: preparation, participation, and joyful anticipation. These teachings invite believers to embrace their role in the unfolding reality of the *Parousia*, living in readiness for the full consummation of their union with Christ.

John the Baptist, recognizing Christ's role as the Bridegroom, declared, "He who has the bride is the groom" (John 3:29), affirming Jesus as the One who calls, loves, and redeems His bride. This statement reflects the relational essence of the *Parousia*, whereby the Church is not only waiting for Christ's return but is already experiencing His presence and love in the present age.

The apostle Paul further develops this rich analogy, portraying the Church as the bride of Christ, sanctified and cleansed by His sacrificial love. In Ephesians 5:25–27 Paul writes that Christ "loved the church and gave himself for her to make her holy, cleansing her with the washing of water by the word." This imagery reveals Christ's ongoing work in His Church, unveiling His essence within His people and preparing them for the day when they will appear with Him in glory (Colossians 3:4). The *Parousia*, therefore, is not solely a future event but a present reality in which believers are continually being transformed into the likeness of Christ.

LIVING IN THE REALITY OF THE *PAROUSIA*

The marriage of Christ and the Church is a present reality, experienced through the ongoing unveiling of His presence. Just as the betrothal period in ancient Israel required preparation, the Church is called to a life of sanctification, worship, and mission, all empowered by the Holy Spirit. Revelation 19:7–8 declares, "His bride has prepared herself. She was given fine linen to wear, bright and pure." The fine linen represents the righteous acts of the saints, demonstrating that the preparation of the bride is an active and continual process of transformation.

Communion and fellowship with Christ serve as a foretaste of the ultimate wedding feast, which will be fully realized at the consummation of the *Parousia*. Jesus's parables of the kingdom as a wedding banquet (Matthew 22:2–4) underscore that this participation is not reserved for the future alone but is extended to believers now.

The marriage analogy of the *Parousia* carries profound implications for believers, calling them to a life of preparation, reflection, and anticipation. First, believers are to prepare for the Bridegroom. Believers are called to actively engage in the sanctification process, aligning their lives with Christ's essence through prayer, worship, and obedience. This ongoing preparation mirrors the bride's anticipation and readiness in the betrothal period, cultivating a heart of faithfulness and devotion.

Second, believers must seek to reflect Christ's essence: living in the reality of the *Parousia* requires believers to embody the love, purity, and mission of Christ in their daily lives. The world sees Christ unveiled through the Church's holiness and service as she participates in acts of worship and proclamation. Revelation 19:7–8 portrays this preparation as an ongoing process, while Christ's prayer in John 17:22–23 affirms the present reality of their union: "that they may be one as we are one . . . that they may be made completely one."

Finally, believers anticipate consummation with Christ. Faith anchors the believer's present experience in the promise of future fulfillment. Paul writes in 2 Corinthians 5:7, "For we walk by faith, not by sight," underscoring the Church's confidence in the unseen yet present reality of her union with Christ. The anticipation of the final marriage feast fuels a life of hope and purpose, shaping the believer's actions and aspirations.

THE MYSTERY OF THE UNION ALREADY REVEALED

The apostle Paul presents the union between Christ and the Church as a profound mystery—one that was hidden for ages but is now revealed to the saints. Drawing from Genesis 2:24, Paul writes, "For this reason a man will leave his father and mother and be joined to his wife, and the two will become one flesh. This mystery is profound, but I am talking about Christ and the church" (Ephesians 5:31–32). This covenantal language reflects not only the intimacy of the relationship but also its spiritual reality: the Church is already the bride of Christ. This is not a future role to be assumed; it is a present identity, established by grace and secured in the indwelling presence of Christ.

This union is the foundation of the *Parousia*. As Paul affirms, "Christ in you, the hope of glory" (Colossians 1:27). The *Parousia* is not merely an event on the horizon of time but a transformative unveiling already occurring within the life of the Church. In this ongoing revelation the bride is being renewed and sanctified day by day (2 Corinthians 4:16), called to live in active faithfulness as she reflects the character of her bridegroom.

The imagery of Revelation 19:7–8—"His bride has prepared herself. She was given fine linen to wear, bright and pure"—reminds believers that the *Parousia* invites not passive waiting but wholehearted preparation. Through prayer, worship, holiness, and service, the Church embodies the beauty of the bride adorned for her groom. This is both a personal and a communal calling, as the Church together becomes a living testimony of Christ's love, purity, and mission in the world.

Yet even as the bride walks in the unveiled presence of Christ through the Spirit, the consummation is still to come: the marriage supper of the Lamb. The Church lives in this "already-but-not-yet" tension, where faith holds the unseen promises of glory while participating in the present unveiling of Christ's reign. As Paul declares, "We walk by faith, not by sight" (2 Corinthians 5:7), and this journey by faith is how the bride matures into the fullness of her calling.

The marriage analogy is not a symbolic flourish; it is central to God's eternal longing to dwell with His people. From the garden to the tabernacle, from the Incarnation to the indwelling Spirit, God has relentlessly pursued intimate communion with humanity. The *Parousia* is the culmination of this divine romance—where the mystery once hidden is now being revealed in Christ and through His bride. As we turn to the next chapter we will trace this relational thread through Scripture and see how the presence of God, once confined to sacred places, now fills the hearts of those who believe.

CHAPTER 4

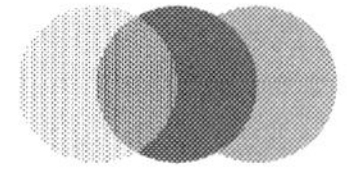

THE GARDEN TO THE TEMPLE: A RELATIONAL JOURNEY FULFILLED

The longing of God to dwell with humanity serves as the golden thread that weaves through the tapestry of Scripture, beginning in the sacred Garden of Eden and culminating in the radiant glory of the New Jerusalem. This desire is not merely a theological concept but the very heartbeat of God's redemptive plan—a relentless pursuit of unbroken communion with those created in His image. Throughout the biblical narrative, sacred spaces such as Eden, the tabernacle, and the temple stand as tangible expressions of this divine longing. These spaces are not only historical landmarks; they foreshadow the ultimate fulfillment found in Christ, who embodies God's presence among His people.

In the Garden of Eden, God's presence was immediate and intimate, fostering perfect communion with Adam and Eve. However, the intrusion of sin shattered this harmony, and humanity's exile from Eden became a poignant symbol of their broader estrangement from their Creator. Yet even in the aftermath of the fall, God's redemptive plan unfolded, carving out pathways for restored fellowship through covenants, sacrifices, and divine laws. The establishment of the tabernacle and the temple offered both provisional meeting places and powerful reminders of the separation caused by sin, emphasizing the holiness of God and humanity's need for redemption.

The fullness of God's desire to dwell with humanity is ultimately realized in Christ—*Immanuel*, "God with us" (Matthew 1:23). Through His incarnation, atoning death, resurrection, and ascension Christ bridges the chasm between heaven and earth, inaugurating a new era of divine presence. The *Parousia*—the spiritual unveiling of Christ's essence—continues to manifest this divine purpose, making God's indwelling presence a lived reality for believers. Through the Holy Spirit the Church becomes a living temple (1 Corinthians 3:16), a visible manifestation of God's presence and an active participant in His redemptive mission.

This chapter explores the profound implications of God's desire to dwell with humanity, tracing the relational journey from Eden to the temple and ultimately to the New Jerusalem. It seeks to uncover how these sacred spaces, deeply ingrained in the Jewish consciousness, prepared the way for the ultimate unveiling of God's presence in Christ. Approaching this journey through the lens of the *Parousia* allows believers to grasp how God's dwelling presence transforms individuals, communities, and all of creation.

A rich exploration of the continuity and fulfillment of divine dwelling across the ages provides practical insights into how the *Parousia* shapes the believer's personal identity, worship, and mission today. Through the *Parousia* God's dwelling is no longer merely a future hope but a present reality—a transformative relational gift that draws believers into intimate communion with their Creator.

THE GARDEN OF EDEN: GOD'S FIRST DWELLING PLACE WITH HUMANITY

The Garden of Eden stands as the primordial symbol of God's desire to dwell with humanity. More than just a physical paradise, Eden was a sacred space where divine and human realities intersected in perfect harmony. God's presence was immediate and unhindered, reflecting

His deep longing for relational communion with His creation. Here humanity was invited into a life of intimate fellowship with their Creator, mirroring His image and fulfilling His divine purpose.

Eden was uniquely designed as a shared space, a meeting place where heaven and earth coexisted in perfect unity. In Genesis 3:8 we see a glimpse of this intimate relationship as God is described as walking in the garden in the cool of the day. This imagery reveals a profound truth: God's intention was always to be near His creation, dwelling with them in a relationship of love, trust, and purpose. Humanity, made in His image (Genesis 1:26–27), was given the extraordinary role of reflecting His glory and stewarding the earth within the sacred communion of His presence.

The garden served as more than a dwelling; it was the blueprint of God's relational purpose. The sacredness of Eden was defined not merely by geography but by the divine presence that filled it. In this space God's glory was fully unveiled, accessible, and transformational. Humanity lived in perfect obedience and harmony, its identity and function wholly aligned with God's original design. This sacred communion highlights the core truth that humanity was never meant to exist apart from God's dwelling presence.

THE DISRUPTION OF COMMUNION: THE FALL

However, the beauty of Eden was soon overshadowed by the tragic disruption of sin. In seeking autonomy apart from God, Adam and Eve fractured the sacred space, introducing separation, shame, and death into the human experience. This rupture was not simply a physical departure from Eden but a profound spiritual severance, one that barred direct access to God's presence. Genesis 3:23–24 records humanity's expulsion from the garden, where cherubim and a flaming sword guarded the entrance, emphasizing the weight of separation from divine holiness.

The fall introduced several theological consequences that would shape the biblical narrative moving forward. For starters, there was a loss of intimacy: humanity's exile symbolized the loss of direct communion with God, necessitating a mediated approach to His presence. Accompanying the loss of intimacy was the invasion of death and corruption: with separation came mortality, corruption, and alienation from God, casting a shadow over humanity's purpose (Romans 5:12). Still there was the promise of redemption: even in the midst of judgment, God's redemptive plan was already in motion. The protoevangelium of Genesis 3:15 introduced the promise of a coming Redeemer who would crush the serpent's head and restore what had been lost.

THE NECESSITY OF SHARED SPACE FOR RESTORATION

Our exile from the Garden of Eden underscores the vital truth that humanity cannot fulfill its God-given purpose apart from His presence. The longing for Eden's restoration permeates Scripture, as God continually provides ways to reestablish shared space with His people. This desire is fulfilled progressively through covenants and sacred institutions and ultimately in Christ, who brings humanity back into divine communion.

The necessity of shared space is rooted in core truths. First, humanity flourishes only in the presence of God, where His holiness, wisdom, and love provide true meaning and purpose. Thus, apart from God, attempts at self-sufficiency lead to fragmentation and brokenness, as illustrated in the post-Edenic narrative of Genesis. Finally, true restoration requires not just proximity to God but a reestablished relationship of trust and obedience.

Despite humanity's exile from Eden, God's desire to dwell among His people has never wavered. His presence continued to manifest in tangible ways in the Old Testament, first through the tabernacle and later in the temple—each pointing forward to the ultimate fulfillment in Christ.

Through Christ the lost paradise of Eden is ultimately restored. In Him believers experience the unveiling of God's presence once again. The *Parousia*, as the spiritual unveiling of Christ's essence, restores the shared space between God and humanity, renewing the sacred relationship first established in Eden. "In Christ," the sacred space is no longer limited to a garden but is found within the hearts of believers. Paul writes in 2 Corinthians 5:17, "If anyone is in Christ, he is a new creation." The indwelling of the Holy Spirit transforms each believer into a living temple, wherein God's presence resides and restores what was lost.

This restoration, however, is not only personal but cosmic. The grand vision of Revelation 21:3 proclaims, "Look, God's dwelling is with humanity, and he will live with them. They will be his peoples." The final fulfillment of the *Parousia* ushers in the ultimate restoration of Eden, where God's presence permeates all of creation, just as He had originally intended.

THE TABERNACLE: A MOBILE DWELLING OF GOD'S GLORY

Following humanity's expulsion from Eden, God's longing to dwell among His people did not wane. Instead it found new expression in the wilderness as the children of Israel journeyed toward the promised land. The tabernacle, a sacred and mobile dwelling, became the tangible representation of God's abiding presence with His covenant people. Far more than a physical structure, the tabernacle was a theological declaration of divine nearness, a profound expression of God's holiness, love, and desire for communion with a fallen and wandering people. It provided Israel with a visible assurance that their God journeyed with them, leading, guiding, and dwelling in their midst.

The establishment of the tabernacle was not an arbitrary decision but a divine initiative, reflecting God's unwavering commitment to restore the shared space lost in Eden. It stood as a microcosm of that original communion, pointing both backward to the lost paradise and forward to the future restoration that would be fully realized "in Christ." In this sacred space God's presence was made manifest, offering His people a foretaste of the ultimate *Parousia*—the full unveiling of Christ's essence and the permanent dwelling of God with humanity.

The construction of the tabernacle was not left to human ingenuity but was carefully orchestrated by divine command. God's instructions were precise, emphasizing the necessity of holiness, obedience, and reverence in hosting His presence. Exodus 25:8 records God's intention: "They are to make a sanctuary for me so that I may dwell among them." These words capture the essence of the tabernacle's purpose. It was a visible declaration of God's desire to live among His people despite their sinfulness.

The design of the tabernacle reflected a profound theological reality with its threefold structure—the outer court, the Holy Place, and the Most Holy Place—serving as a representation of the varying degrees of access to God's presence. The Most Holy Place, where the Ark of the Covenant resided, symbolized God's throne on earth, containing the tablets of the covenant, the manna, and Aaron's rod. Every intricate detail of the tabernacle, from its materials to its colors and furnishings, pointed to divine perfection, foreshadowing Christ's glory and the ultimate redemption He would bring.

Beyond its physical design, the tabernacle was a daily reminder of God's holiness and Israel's dependence on Him. The sacred rituals performed within its courts underscored the tension between God's immanence—His nearness—and His transcendence, highlighting the need for mediation, atonement, and holiness to sustain the covenant relationship.

The true significance of the tabernacle was revealed when God's glory—His *Shekinah*—descended upon it, visibly marking it as His chosen dwelling. Exodus 40:34–35 describes this awe-inspiring moment: "The cloud covered the tent of meeting, and the glory of the LORD filled the tabernacle." So overwhelming was this manifestation that not even Moses could enter the tent. The pillar of cloud by day and fire by night that accompanied Israel's journey became a constant assurance of God's presence, guiding them in the wilderness and providing divine direction (Exodus 13:21–22).

The tabernacle thus became more than a structure; it was a sacred meeting place where divine and human interaction took place. In Exodus 33:9–11 we see a remarkable depiction of God speaking to Moses "face to face, just as a man speaks with his friend." This moment underscores the tabernacle's role as an intermediary space—one that allowed for personal communion with God, albeit through a divinely appointed mediator. This reality foreshadowed the ultimate Mediator, Christ, who would grant believers direct access to God without barriers.

THE TABERNACLE AND THE COVENANT RELATIONSHIP

The tabernacle was not merely a dwelling place but a physical embodiment of the covenant relationship between God and Israel. Following the giving of the Law at Mount Sinai, its construction signified God's tangible commitment to His people. The sacrificial system instituted within its courts underscored the necessity of atonement and holiness in maintaining this relationship. Each sacrifice and ritual pointed to the gravity of sin and the need for redemption—a theme that would find its ultimate expression in the atoning work of Christ.

Moreover, the portability of the tabernacle reflected God's faithfulness throughout Israel's journey. As the Israelites wandered through the wilderness, the tabernacle moved with them, demonstrating that God's presence was not confined to a fixed location but was dynamically involved in their daily lives. Numbers 9:15–23 describes how the cloud covering the tabernacle directed Israel's movements, ensuring that they followed God's will in every step of their journey.

This mobile expression of God's faithfulness revealed His desire to be known and worshiped even in the uncertainty of the wilderness. It assured the people of Israel that, despite their failings and fears, God's presence remained steadfast, guiding them toward the fulfillment of His promises.

The tabernacle's ultimate significance lies in its foreshadowing of the *Parousia*—the unveiling of Christ's essence and God's permanent dwelling with humanity. In John 1:14 the apostle declares, "The Word became flesh and dwelt [tabernacled] among us. We observed his glory." Christ's incarnation serves as the full expression of God's longing to dwell with humanity. He is the true tabernacle—the living intersection of heaven and earth where divine glory is fully revealed and accessible.

The sacrificial system of the tabernacle pointed to Christ, whose atoning death and resurrection established a new covenant, granting believers unrestricted access to God (Hebrews 9:11–15). No longer bound by physical structures, believers themselves become the living tabernacle, indwelt by the Holy Spirit (1 Corinthians 6:19). Through the *Parousia* the Church now embodies God's presence in the world, continuing His mission of revealing divine glory and extending His kingdom.

This fulfillment does not end with Christ's first coming but looks forward to the ultimate restoration of all things. Revelation 21:3 offers the climactic promise of God's dwelling: "Look, God's dwelling is with humanity, and he will live with them. They will be his peoples." The temporary nature of the tabernacle gives way to the permanence of the New Jerusalem, where God and humanity will dwell together eternally, unhindered by sin or separation.

THE TEMPLE: A PERMANENT STRUCTURE OF GOD'S PRESENCE

The construction of the temple in Jerusalem marked a significant milestone in the biblical narrative, signifying a profound progression in God's desire to dwell among His people. Unlike the mobile tabernacle that had accompanied Israel through the wilderness, the temple stood as a permanent and centralized dwelling place—a visible declaration of God's enduring presence among His covenant nation. More than an architectural wonder, the temple embodied the depth of God's covenantal faithfulness, holiness, and commitment to humanity. Its grandeur was not merely for the admiration of the Israelites but was meant to serve as a constant reminder of the sacred relationship between God and His people.

The temple's significance extends beyond its physical structure; it represented the intersection of heaven and earth, a place where God's presence was made known and accessible through the prescribed system of worship and sacrifice. Yet even in its splendor the temple foreshadowed a greater reality to come—the ultimate fulfillment in Christ and the ongoing unveiling of His presence through the *Parousia*. This section explores the theological importance of the temple, its role in the spiritual life of Israel, and how it serves as a foreshadowing of the ultimate dwelling of God with humanity.

The temple's construction was not simply a human endeavor; it was rooted in divine initiative, reflecting God's desire for a dwelling among His people. The covenant made with King David provided the foundation for this sacred edifice, with God's promise to establish His presence in the temple contingent upon Israel's faithfulness. In 1 Kings 6:12–13 God declared to Solomon: "As for this temple you are building—if you walk in my statutes, observe my ordinances, and keep all my commands by walking in them, I will fulfill my promise to you, which I made to your father David. I will dwell among the Israelites and not abandon my people Israel."

This covenantal promise emphasized both divine commitment and human responsibility, reinforcing the truth that God's presence required a response of obedience and faithfulness from His people. The temple became a visible sign of God's nearness and a tangible reminder of the conditions necessary for continued fellowship with Him.

At the temple's inauguration God's glory descended in a dramatic display of His acceptance. As recorded in 1 Kings 8:10–11, "When the priests came out of the holy place, a cloud filled the Lord's temple, and because of the cloud, the priests were not able to continue ministering, for the glory of the Lord filled the temple." This event mirrored the filling of the tabernacle in the wilderness (Exodus 40:34–35), affirming the temple as God's chosen dwelling and a sacred intersection between heaven and earth.

The temple was the spiritual heart of Israel, serving as the focal point for worship, sacrifice, and covenantal relationship with God. It provided a sacred space where God's holiness was upheld, His presence revered, and His redemptive purposes enacted through the sacrificial system.

Central to the temple's function was the sacrificial system, which allowed for atonement and reconciliation between God and His people. Leviticus 17:11 highlights its significance: "For the life of a creature is in the blood, and I have appointed it to you to make atonement on the altar for your lives, since it is the lifeblood that makes atonement." These offerings not only addressed individual and communal sins but also foreshadowed the ultimate sacrifice of Christ, whose atonement would surpass the limitations of the Levitical system (Hebrews 10:11–14).

While the temple primarily served Israel, God's vision for it extended beyond national boundaries. Isaiah 56:7 declares, "For my house will be called a house of prayer for all nations." This inclusivity reflected God's desire to draw the nations to Himself, a reality fulfilled in Christ as the gospel extended beyond Israel to the entire world. The temple festivals—Passover, Pentecost, and Tabernacles—further reinforced its centrality in Israel's worship, celebrating God's past faithfulness while pointing forward to His ultimate redemptive work.

THE TEMPLE AS A SYMBOL OF SEPARATION AND ACCESS

Despite its grandeur and purpose, the temple also symbolized the tension between God's holiness and humanity's sinfulness. Its structure, with the distinct areas of the outer court, the Holy Place, and the Most Holy Place, illustrated the degrees of proximity to God's presence. The veil that separated the Holy Place from the Most Holy Place underscored the barrier created by sin, granting access only to the high priest once a year on the Day of Atonement (Leviticus 16:2).

However, Christ's crucifixion marked a pivotal turning point. Matthew 27:51 records that "the curtain of the sanctuary was torn in two from top to bottom." This dramatic event symbolized the removal of the separation between God and humanity, granting direct access to His presence through Christ's atoning work. No longer would God's presence be confined to a physical structure; it would now dwell within believers through the Holy Spirit.

While the physical temple stood as a monumental expression of God's presence, its ultimate fulfillment was realized in Christ, who declared Himself to be the true temple. John 1:14 proclaims, "The Word became flesh and dwelt [tabernacled] among us." Christ embodied the presence of God in human form, and through His resurrection He established a new and living temple—His body.

Jesus foreshadowed this reality in John 2:19, stating, "Destroy this temple, and I will raise it up in three days," referring to His resurrection. This marked the transition from a physical building to a spiritual dwelling, where God's presence would be experienced directly through faith in Christ.

Through the *Parousia* believers themselves become the living temple of God, indwelt by the Holy Spirit (1 Corinthians 3:16). The Church now serves as the visible expression of God's presence on earth, revealing His glory and extending His kingdom.

THE DESTRUCTION OF THE PHYSICAL TEMPLE

The destruction of the Jerusalem temple in AD 70 underscored the transition from reliance on physical structures to recognition of spiritual realities. Stephen, in his final address, declared, "The Most

High does not dwell in sanctuaries made with hands" (Acts 7:48–50), emphasizing that God's presence is no longer confined to a building but found in the hearts of His people. This transition fulfilled Christ's prophecy and reaffirmed that the *Parousia*—the spiritual unveiling of Christ's essence—had established a new reality.

The destruction of the temple marked a decisive shift in salvation history, affirming that through the *Parousia* God's presence is now universally accessible, no longer bound by walls of stone but dwelling within His people worldwide. The tearing of the temple veil at Christ's crucifixion had already signified this reality, making way for the indwelling of God's presence in a new and transformative way.

THE NEW JERUSALEM: THE ULTIMATE TEMPLE

The vision of the New Jerusalem in Revelation 21 represents the culmination of God's redemptive plan and His eternal longing to dwell with humanity. Unlike the tabernacle and the temple, which were confined to specific locations and limited access, the New Jerusalem embodies a reality in which God's presence permeates all of creation without restriction. It is the ultimate fulfillment of the *Parousia*—the complete unveiling of Christ's essence—and signifies the transformative power of dwelling perpetually in the presence of God. In this heavenly city the barriers that once separated humanity from divine communion are forever removed, ushering in an era of unbroken fellowship and radiant glory.

The New Jerusalem represents a world in which the presence of God saturates every aspect of existence, erasing all separation between Creator and creation. It transcends the limitations of former sacred spaces, offering an unmediated, eternal communion that humanity has long yearned for. In Revelation 21:22 John describes the absence of a physical temple in the New Jerusalem, proclaiming, "I did not see a temple in it, because the Lord God the Almighty and the Lamb are its temple." This profound declaration reveals that God Himself, in perfect unity with Christ, becomes the dwelling place of His people. The physical structures that once mediated access to God's presence are no longer needed, as His glory now fully inhabits and sustains all things. This fulfillment echoes the prophetic vision of Isaiah 6:3, "His glory fills the whole earth" now realized in its fullest expression.

The city itself radiates with divine light, dispelling all darkness and illuminating the hearts of those who dwell within. Revelation 21:23 affirms this reality: "The city does not need the sun or the moon to shine on it, because the glory of God illuminates it, and its lamp is the Lamb." The unveiled essence of Christ provides not only physical light but also spiritual illumination, truth, and eternal life. This radiant glory is not just a future hope but a present reality that believers begin to experience through the *Parousia*, as they walk in the light of Christ's revealed presence.

The New Jerusalem is not only the restoration of creation; it is the fulfillment of God's promise of intimate communion with His people. While the *Parousia* is now experienced through the indwelling of the Holy Spirit—Christ's presence unveiled within His bride—it also points forward to a glorious consummation. The New Jerusalem represents this future fullness: the unveiled and eternal dwelling of God with His people, face-to-face. In this way believers live in a foretaste of what is to come, walking in the presence of Christ now, even as they long for the day when all things will be made new.

The apostle John captures this promise in Revelation 21:3, declaring, "Look, God's dwelling is with humanity, and he will live with them." This eternal fellowship restores the intimacy first experienced in Eden, where humanity walked with God in perfect harmony. What was once lost through sin is now fully restored through the *Parousia*, offering believers a foretaste of this reality even in the present.

The pinnacle of this transformation is seen in Revelation 22:4–5: "They will see his face, and his name will be on their foreheads. Night will be no more." The unveiling of Christ's face symbolizes the deepest level of communion possible—the full revelation of His glory and the complete transformation of those who belong to Him. As 1 John 3:2 proclaims, "When he appears, we will be like him, because we will see him as he is." This eternal vision of Christ fulfills the believer's ultimate longing, transforming them into His likeness as they dwell in His unveiled presence.

Moreover, the New Jerusalem stands as the fulfillment of God's covenantal promises to Abraham, David, and Israel, now extended to all who are in Christ. Paul affirms this in Galatians 3:29: "If you belong to Christ, then you are Abraham's seed, heirs according to the promise." The *Parousia*, therefore, is not merely a distant hope but an active, living reality, offering believers a present relational, transformative participation in the inheritance of God's eternal kingdom.

ANTICIPATING THE NEW JERUSALEM THROUGH WORSHIP AND MISSION

Although the New Jerusalem is a future reality, its implications are transformative in the present, shaping how believers live, worship, and engage with the world. As the bride of Christ, the Church is called to embody the values and mission of the New Jerusalem, serving as a foretaste of God's eternal dwelling among humanity.

In Revelation 22:17 the invitation resounds: "The Spirit and the bride say, 'Come!' Let the one who hears, say, 'Come!'" This dual role of invitation and anticipation defines the Church's mission in the present age—calling the world to Christ while living in expectation of His ultimate appearing. Worship becomes an act of faith and prophetic hope, reflecting the glory of the coming kingdom, while mission serves as the Church's active participation in extending God's presence to the world.

Philippians 3:20 reminds believers of their true citizenship, stating, "Our citizenship is in heaven, and we eagerly wait for a Savior from there, the Lord Jesus Christ." This heavenly citizenship is not a passive waiting but an active calling, shaping every aspect of life in anticipation of the New Jerusalem. Living as citizens of this coming reality means embracing holiness, justice, and love, reflecting Christ's essence in a world longing for redemption.

THE RENEWAL OF ALL CREATION THROUGH THE *PAROUSIA*

The impact of the New Jerusalem extends beyond humanity to encompass the renewal of all creation. Paul describes this cosmic restoration in Romans 8:21: "The creation itself will also be set free from the bondage to decay into the glorious freedom of God's children." The *Parousia* unveils God's redemptive work not only in the lives of believers but in the very fabric of creation itself.

Revelation 21:4 paints a picture of this transformation: "He will wipe away every tear from their eyes. Death will be no more; grief, crying, and pain will be no more, because the previous things have passed away." The ultimate unveiling of God's presence will bring an end to suffering, brokenness, and separation, ushering in an eternal reality where the former things are replaced with unending joy and communion with God.

Through the *Parousia* believers experience a foretaste of this renewal, allowing the hope of the New Jerusalem to sustain them amid the struggles of life. This assurance provides not only comfort but also motivation to live faithfully, knowing that God's redemptive work is both present and future.

In the New Jerusalem the longing of humanity to dwell with God finds its ultimate fulfillment. However, the reality of the *Parousia* reminds us that this sacred dwelling is not just a distant hope but an ongoing invitation to abide "in Christ" today. As the Church anticipates the final unveiling of Christ's essence, it is called to live in the light of His presence now—worshiping, serving, and proclaiming the transformative relational reality of His indwelling glory.

CONCLUSION: THE JOURNEY FROM THE GARDEN TO THE NEW JERUSALEM

The unfolding story of God's dwelling with humanity begins in the sacred intimacy of the Garden of Eden and reaches its climactic fulfillment in the radiant glory of the New Jerusalem. This grand narrative, woven throughout Scripture, reveals the unchanging desire of God to dwell among His people and the transformative power of His presence. From the earliest moments of creation to the promise of eternal communion, each stage of this journey—the Garden, the tabernacle, the temple, and finally the New Jerusalem—illuminates the profound truth that God's presence is both the source and the fulfillment of human existence.

In the Garden of Eden humanity experienced unbroken fellowship with God, reflecting creation's ultimate purpose: to dwell in perfect harmony with the Creator. However, sin shattered this sacred communion, introducing separation, exile, and longing. The loss of Eden was not merely a physical displacement but a spiritual rupture that necessitated God's redemptive intervention. Yet even in humanity's failure, God's desire to restore His dwelling remained steadfast, initiating a divine pursuit that would unfold through the tabernacle and the temple.

The tabernacle, a mobile dwelling, signified God's willingness to journey with His people, a reminder of His covenantal faithfulness and intimate nearness despite their wilderness wanderings. As Israel matured, the temple in Jerusalem became a more permanent representation of God's dwelling, standing as the sacred meeting place between heaven and earth. However, these physical structures, with their sacrifices and rituals, pointed beyond themselves to a greater fulfillment—a fulfillment found "in Christ."

In the incarnation Christ became the ultimate meeting place between God and humanity. His life, death, and resurrection transcended the limitations of the physical temple, inaugurating a new and living way into God's presence. Through the *Parousia*—the ongoing unveiling of Christ's essence—this sacred relationship is no longer confined to a geographical location but is made accessible to all who are "in Christ." The indwelling Holy Spirit transforms believers into living temples, embodying God's presence in their daily lives and within the collective body of the Church.

The journey reaches its final fulfillment in the New Jerusalem, where God's redemptive plan finds its ultimate expression. In this heavenly city the barriers of sin and death are forever removed, and God's glory saturates all of creation. Revelation 21:22 declares, "I did not see a temple in [the city], because the Lord God the Almighty and the Lamb are its temple." This signifies that the presence of God, once mediated through sacred spaces, now fully permeates every aspect of existence. The unveiled essence of Christ illuminates the New Jerusalem, making all things new and restoring the communion humanity once experienced in Eden.

Understanding the trajectory from the Garden to the temple and ultimately to the New Jerusalem invites believers to see their own lives as part of this divine narrative. Through the *Parousia* Christ's essence is continually unveiled, drawing humanity closer to the eternal reality of dwelling with God—a reality that transforms individuals, communities, and the entire creation.

This journey, however, did not emerge in isolation; it was deeply shaped by the theological and cultural framework of ancient Israel. The sacred spaces and covenantal structures of the Old Testament were intricately interwoven with the spiritual life of God's people. In the next chapter we will explore how Jewish theology and cultural traditions provided the foundation for understanding the *Parousia* as the ongoing unveiling of Christ's essence. By examining the historical and cultural context in which these ideas developed, we gain a richer understanding of how the relational and transformative nature of the *Parousia* continues to fulfill God's eternal purpose.

CHAPTER 5

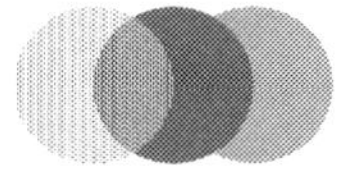

FORGED IN THE FIRE: ISRAEL'S COVENANT IDENTITY IN HISTORY

The journey of the Jewish people is a powerful testament to resilience, identity, and divine purpose—a narrative woven together through generations of trials, exile, and enduring covenantal hope. From the nomadic wanderings of the patriarchs to the golden era of the united monarchy, and from the sorrow of Babylonian captivity to the challenges of Roman occupation, every chapter of their history had been instrumental in shaping their understanding of God's presence and purpose. This story is not one of a people chosen for their strength or virtue but rather of a nation whose relationship with God was tested, refined, and sanctified through the fires of hardship and divine intervention.

Throughout Scripture the dwelling of God with humanity is depicted in sacred spaces such as the Garden of Eden, the tabernacle, and the temple, each representing His unchanging desire to commune with His creation. Yet these were never meant to be static symbols confined to time and space; rather, they served as dynamic representations of a relational God who actively engaged with His covenant people in the midst of their evolving circumstances. As external forces of war, exile, and foreign dominion pressed upon them, and as internal theological traditions developed through covenantal obligations and prophetic insight, the Jewish people grew in their understanding of Yahweh's justice, mercy, and redemptive purpose.

This chapter explores the interplay between these external pressures and internal theological reflections that have shaped Jewish thought. The tension between divine holiness and covenantal faithfulness finds expression in the lived experiences of God's people through wars and exiles, through idolatry and repentance, and through the wisdom and prophetic literature that provided guidance and hope. This intricate tapestry of theology and culture was not merely a record of the past but a profound anticipation of God's ultimate fulfillment in the person of the Messiah, Jesus Christ.

The sacred spaces that once defined Israel's understanding of God's dwelling presence find their ultimate realization in the *Parousia.* "In Christ" the limitations of physical structures are transcended, and the promise of divine presence is fully realized. Through this lens we gain a deeper appreciation for the richness of God's revelation and His continuing work through Christ and His Church. In tracing this journey we uncover not only the story of a people forged in the fire but also the enduring faithfulness of a God who desires to dwell among His people and transform their lives for His redemptive purpose.

Throughout their history the Jewish people encountered relentless external pressures that profoundly shaped their identity and theological understanding. Their journey was one of survival, perseverance, and unwavering faith in the midst of constant warfare, exile, and the seductive pull of idolatry. These challenges were not merely historical incidents but served as divine instruments of refinement, shaping their perception of God's presence and purpose. The struggles of Israel reinforced their awareness of Yahweh as both a warrior and a covenantal protector, deepening their understanding of their unique relationship with Him and strengthening the theological fabric of Scripture.

WAR AS A TEST OF FAITHFULNESS

The persistent cycles of war played a defining role in shaping Israel's theology, particularly their recognition of Yahweh as their warrior-king and ultimate protector. Exodus 15:3 declares, "The LORD is a warrior; the LORD is His name," affirming that God's power and sovereignty were central to Israel's existence and success. Each battle they faced was a test of their faith and reliance on divine intervention rather than human strength.

Early conflicts with formidable enemies such as the Amalekites, the Philistines, and Canaanite tribes revealed the depth of Israel's dependence on God for deliverance. These military encounters were not merely political in nature; they were deeply theological, demonstrating Yahweh's covenant faithfulness and power to save. The Ark of the Covenant, carried into battle, was more than a sacred object; it represented the tangible presence of God among His people. The miraculous conquest of Jericho, as recorded in Joshua 6:6–15, stands as a testament to God's intervention and the importance of absolute obedience. Israel's victories, such as Gideon's triumph with just three hundred men (Judges 7), underscored the truth that success was never determined by military might but by faith in the Lord's promises.

Israel's victories and defeats served as spiritual barometers, revealing the connection between covenant faithfulness and divine favor. When the Israelites walked in obedience to God's commands they experienced triumphs like the victory at Jericho, where their unwavering trust in Yahweh led to miraculous conquest. However, when they failed to uphold the covenant they faced devastating losses, such as their defeat at Ai (Joshua 7), which was attributed to disobedience and sin within the camp.

The book of Judges captures the cyclical pattern of Israel's sin, judgment, repentance, and deliverance, emphasizing that their survival depended not on strategic alliances or military prowess but on adherence to God's covenant. These historical accounts provided enduring theological lessons, illustrating the interplay between divine justice and mercy and the critical importance of human responsibility in maintaining the covenant relationship.

Through these experiences Israel's understanding of Yahweh evolved. He was not a distant, passive observer but an active participant in their history, fighting for them, calling them to obedience, and deepening their trust and dependence on Him. These lessons laid the foundation for the Messianic hope, as the Jewish people longed for a deliverer who would rescue them, not just from earthly adversaries but from the spiritual bondage of sin and death.

COVENANT PURPOSE IN WAR

Israel's military struggles were not arbitrary; they were imbued with deep theological significance and covenantal purpose. Each conflict was a divine test, a call to reaffirm faith in Yahweh and commitment to His plan. God's assurance of victory was clear in passages such as Deuteronomy 20:1–4, where He commanded them not to fear their enemies, for He would fight on their behalf. This promise reinforced Israel's identity as God's chosen people and highlighted the necessity of trust and obedience over human strength.

Symbolically, the presence of the Ark of the Covenant in battle served as a visible reminder of God's power and the necessity of faith. The victories achieved when they relied on God, such as the destruction of Jericho, underscored the supremacy of faith and obedience. Conversely, defeats—like the failure at Ai—exposed the dire consequences of disobedience and the theological reality that divine favor was contingent upon covenantal fidelity.

The wars Israel fought were not merely for territorial expansion or survival; they were spiritual testing grounds where their identity as a set-apart people was constantly reaffirmed. These conflicts underscored Yahweh's role as both protector and judge, teaching Israel to trust in His guidance and promises. The narratives of war in the Old Testament served to deepen their understanding of God's nature and pointed to the ultimate fulfillment of God's redemptive plan in the Messiah, who would bring victory not through military conquest but through the defeat of sin and death.

THE EGYPTIAN BONDAGE AND DELIVERANCE: A FOUNDATIONAL NARRATIVE OF REDEMPTION

Two specific experiences, slavery and exile, were defining crucibles that refined their understanding of identity, purpose, and the unwavering faithfulness of Yahweh. These periods of profound suffering and displacement challenged Israel's covenant relationship with God, forcing them to grapple with questions of divine justice, purpose, and ultimate redemption. Yet within these trials they discovered deeper insights into God's redemptive purposes and His enduring commitment to their restoration.

The story of Israel's enslavement in Egypt and subsequent deliverance stands at the heart of its national and theological identity. This formative experience became a defining paradigm, shaping their self-understanding as a people chosen by God and redeemed for His purposes. The oppression endured under Pharaoh's harsh rule served as a backdrop against which God's mighty acts of salvation were revealed.

The deliverance from Egypt was not merely an act of liberation; it was a profound demonstration of Yahweh's covenantal faithfulness and unrelenting compassion. In Exodus 6:6–7 God declared His intent with unmistakable clarity: "I will rescue you . . . from slavery to them. . . . I will take you as my people, and I will be your God." These words not only affirmed Israel's special status as God's covenant people but also underscored the foundational truth that its identity was rooted in divine grace rather than human achievement.

Central to Israel's deliverance was the institution of the Passover (Exodus 12:24–27), which became an enduring symbol of God's power and faithfulness. Each year as the Israelites observed this sacred feast, they were reminded of their miraculous redemption and their ongoing covenant relationship with Yahweh. Through the blood of the lamb, they were spared from judgment, a reality that foreshadowed the ultimate redemption through Christ—the true Passover Lamb.

Beyond its immediate impact the Exodus provided a theological framework for understanding future redemptive acts. This pattern of bondage, deliverance, covenant, and worship became a lens through which Israel interpreted their history, guiding their expectations of God's continued intervention. It established the expectation that Yahweh would remain faithful even in the darkest moments of exile and suffering.

THE BABYLONIAN EXILE: A SEASON OF LAMENT AND THEOLOGICAL TRANSFORMATION

Centuries later the Babylonian exile plunged the Israelites into another season of profound suffering, which tested their faith and forced a reexamination of their relationship with God. The destruction of the temple and the loss of their homeland were not just political tragedies; they were theological crises that shook the very foundations of their identity. The question arose: Could they still be God's chosen people without the land and the temple?

The anguish of exile is poignantly captured in Psalm 137:4: "How can we sing the Lord's song on foreign soil?" This lament expresses the deep sorrow of a people separated from their sacred space of worship and struggling to maintain their spiritual identity in a foreign culture. Stripped of their physical symbols of faith, they were compelled to rediscover God's presence in new and unexpected ways.

During this time prophetic voices such as those of Jeremiah and Ezekiel offered messages of hope and reassurance, reminding the exiles that Yahweh's presence was not confined to the temple in Jerusalem. In Jeremiah 29:11–14 God's words brought a promise of future restoration: "For I know the plans I have for you . . . plans for your well-being, not for disaster." Similarly, Ezekiel 11:16 provided a groundbreaking theological shift, declaring that God Himself would be a sanctuary for His people, even in foreign lands.

These prophetic reinterpretations expanded Israel's understanding of God, emphasizing His relational presence rather than a localized dwelling place. The exile became a time of theological innovation during which the focus shifted from physical structures to the internalized experience of God's nearness, preparing the way for the ultimate indwelling of God's presence through Christ.

Despite their displacement, the exile also became a period of covenant renewal and spiritual reflection. Leaders like Ezra and Nehemiah emphasized a renewed commitment to the Law and the centrality of worship in defining national identity. In the absence of the temple the Torah took on an even greater role, reinforcing the idea that faithfulness to God was dependent not on location but on obedience and devotion.

The exile also sharpened Israel's messianic hope, as the longing for a deliverer grew more fervent. The prophetic voices of Isaiah and Daniel painted a vision of a future ruler who would establish an everlasting kingdom. Isaiah 9:6–7 foretold the coming of a divine King: "For a child will be born for us. . . . He will reign on the throne of David." Similarly, Daniel 7:13–14 provided a vision of the "Son of Man" coming in glory, pointing to the ultimate fulfillment of God's redemptive plan in Christ.

DENUNCIATION, REPENTANCE, AND RENEWAL

The periods of bondage and exile were not without purpose. They served as refining fires, stripping away superficial elements of Israel's faith and revealing the core of their relationship with God. Through their suffering they came to understand Yahweh as both just and merciful, a God who disciplines His people yet remains steadfast in His covenant love.

These experiences reinforced the reality that God's presence is not confined to sacred geography but is dynamically present wherever His people seek Him. The lessons learned in exile would shape the future of Jewish faith, fostering a resilient hope that would ultimately find its fulfillment in the coming of the Messiah. Through Him the exile of humanity from God's presence would be reversed and the long-anticipated restoration of communion would be fully realized.

Throughout their history the people of Israel were constantly surrounded by nations that practiced idolatry, presenting an ongoing challenge to their covenantal fidelity to Yahweh. The allure of foreign gods and cultural assimilation tested Israel's commitment to the one true God and played a significant role in shaping their theological understanding of holiness and devotion. These external influences served as both a temptation and a catalyst, forcing Israel to confront their unique identity as a people set apart for God's purposes.

The presence of polytheistic cultures surrounding Israel created a constant tension between their call to the exclusive worship of Yahweh and the temptation to conform to the prevailing religious practices of their neighbors. The challenge of maintaining their distinct identity in the face of cultural influence became a recurring theme throughout their history.

One of the most poignant examples of this struggle is found in the golden calf incident (Exodus 32). Even as God was establishing His covenant with Israel at Mount Sinai, the people, influenced by their past experiences in Egypt and the cultural pressures around them, succumbed to idolatry. They crafted a golden image and proclaimed it as the god who had delivered them from Egypt, highlighting their vulnerability to external influences and their struggle to remain faithful to Yahweh alone.

Similarly, during the period of the monarchy the infiltration of Canaanite religious practices, particularly the worship of Baal, became a pervasive issue. The Israelite kings, in their desire for political alliances and cultural acceptance, often tolerated or even promoted the worship of foreign gods, leading the nation into spiritual compromise. The tension between devotion to Yahweh and assimilation into surrounding cultures was a persistent theme, illustrating the difficulty of living as a holy nation in an idolatrous world.

In response to Israel's recurring idolatry, the prophets of Yahweh arose as voices of warning and correction, calling the nation back to their covenantal relationship. Prophets such as Elijah, Hosea, and Jeremiah passionately condemned idolatry, likening it to spiritual adultery—a betrayal of their covenant with God.

Hosea's prophetic imagery presents Yahweh as a faithful husband seeking to restore His wayward bride. In Hosea 2:16–20 God declares His enduring love for Israel despite their unfaithfulness, emphasizing His relentless pursuit of their hearts. This powerful metaphor underscores the depth of Israel's covenant relationship with Yahweh and the pain caused by their idolatry.

One of the most dramatic prophetic confrontations occurs in 1 Kings 18:20–40, where Elijah challenges the prophets of Baal on Mount Carmel. In this encounter Elijah calls on Yahweh to demonstrate His supremacy over Baal, and through a miraculous display of fire from heaven God reaffirms His power and exclusivity. Elijah's challenge—"If the Lord is God, follow him. But if Baal, follow him" (1 Kings 18:21)—captures the essence of Israel's struggle and the need for unwavering devotion.

Jeremiah, often referred to as the "weeping prophet," issued stern warnings against the consequences of idolatry, reminding the people that their spiritual unfaithfulness would lead to judgment and exile. His messages were a plea for repentance, urging Israel to forsake their false gods and return to the covenant with Yahweh.

Despite their recurring failures Israel's theology ultimately returned to the foundational truth of monotheism: the belief in one true God, Yahweh. This conviction found its most profound expression in the Shema, the central declaration of Jewish faith: "Listen, Israel: The Lord our God, the Lord is one" (Deuteronomy 6:4–5). This declaration served as a theological and cultural anchor, reinforcing their unique identity and calling as God's chosen people. The Shema was more than a statement of belief; it was a call to wholehearted devotion. It instructed Israel to love the Lord with all their heart, soul, and strength, emphasizing that true worship was not just about rituals but about an all-encompassing relationship with God.

The repeated affirmation of God's oneness set Israel apart from their polytheistic neighbors and solidified their distinct identity as a holy nation (Leviticus 20:26). This unwavering commitment to monotheism helped Israel navigate the pressures of cultural assimilation and reaffirmed their understanding of Yahweh's exclusivity. Through cycles of repentance and renewal they came to realize that their true strength and purpose lay in their fidelity to God alone.

THE THEOLOGICAL IMPACT OF IDOLATRY ON ISRAEL'S COVENANT IDENTITY

The persistent struggle with idolatry ultimately deepened Israel's understanding of God's holiness, justice, and mercy. The Israelites learned that faithfulness to Yahweh required more than external observance; it demanded internal devotion and a constant renewal of their covenant relationship.

The trials of idolatry served to refine Israel's theology, making them acutely aware of their need for a Redeemer who could transform their hearts and establish an unbreakable covenant. This expectation set the stage for the coming of the Messiah, who would ultimately fulfill and embody the covenant relationship between God and His people.

The external pressures of wars, exile, and idolatrous influences acted as refining fires, shaping Israel's theology and strengthening their covenantal identity. These experiences taught them to rely fully on Yahweh, clarified their understanding of His justice and mercy, and nurtured a resilient hope in His promises.

The lessons learned through Israel's struggles provide a rich foundation for understanding His transformative work. The trials faced by Israel reveal the unchanging character of God and His redemptive plan, culminating in the ultimate revelation of His presence through Christ. The *Parousia* fulfills God's ultimate desire to dwell with His people.

The experiences of the past were not in vain; they were instrumental in preparing God's people for the fulfillment of His covenant in Jesus. Israel's battles, exiles, and struggles with idolatry all point to a deeper reality: God's unwavering faithfulness and His desire to dwell among His people. These historical trials forged Israel's covenant identity, refining their understanding of holiness, justice, and mercy. As the *Parousia* unveils the fullness of God's indwelling presence, the story of Israel's formation becomes a vital lens through which we comprehend His redemptive work. The God who walked with Abraham, spoke through Moses, and preserved a remnant through exile is the same God who now walks with His people in Christ. In this way Israel's history becomes sacred preparation for the unfolding glory of the *Parousia*.

CHAPTER 6

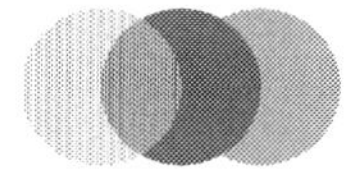

WOVEN BY THE SPIRIT: THE THEOLOGICAL TAPESTRY OF ISRAEL'S SCRIPTURES

Ultimately, the Old Testament's theological diversity anticipates the fulfillment of God's promises in Jesus Christ. The varied voices of literary traditions within Israel's Old Testament Scriptures are not competing viewpoints but complementary threads woven into a unified tapestry of divine revelation. Together they prepare the way for the *Parousia*—God's full unveiling in Christ—and invite us to see continuity between the covenantal faithfulness of Yahweh and the incarnate presence of the Messiah.

While Israel's external history shaped her covenantal identity, her internal theological framework was equally formative. The sacred writings of the Old Testament are not only historical records; they are the inspired expressions of a people reflecting deeply on God's nature, human responsibility, and the unfolding of divine purpose. These writings emerged from within Israel's covenant life and contain layers of prophetic, priestly, and relational insight that continue to shape the faith of God's people today.

The development of Jewish theology was not static but dynamic—an ever-growing revelation rooted in the covenant and enriched through prophetic vision, wisdom tradition, and liturgical practice. This theological tapestry wove together diverse voices and traditions to express the mystery of divine presence. As we explore these traditions—the Yahwist, Priestly, and Covenantal—we will see how they anticipated the fullness of the *Parousia*, now unveiled in Christ and echoed in the New Testament's use of the Hebrew Scriptures.

THE YAHWIST, PRIESTLY, AND COVENANTAL TRADITIONS

Within the fabric of Israel's theological identity three significant traditions emerged—often referred to by scholars as the Yahwist, Priestly, and Covenantal traditions. While some associate these terms with source-critical theories about composition of the Old Testament, this work engages them more theologically than historically: as interpretive lenses that highlight distinct but complementary dimensions of Israel's relationship with God. Each tradition offers a unique emphasis—whether on divine intimacy, sacred order, or covenantal responsibility—and together they form a unified theological tapestry. Rather than being in tension, these perspectives enrich one another and contribute to a fuller understanding of Yahweh's presence, character, and purpose in the life of His people.

The Yahwist tradition presents Yahweh as a deeply personal and relational God who walks among His people and desires close fellowship with them. Using vivid anthropomorphic language, this tradition emphasizes God's nearness and His covenantal commitment. In Genesis 2 and 3 Yahweh is depicted as walking in the Garden of Eden, engaging directly with Adam and Eve. This imagery of divine companionship highlights His original intent to dwell in harmony with humanity, reflecting a profound relational dynamic that underpins all subsequent theological developments. The Yahwist tradition reinforces the idea that God's presence is not distant or abstract but immediate and personal.

Additionally, this tradition underscores God's covenantal promises, particularly through His relationship with Abraham. The divine pledge in Genesis 12:1–3, where God promises to make Abraham's descendants a blessing to all nations, establishes the foundation for Israel's identity and mission. These covenantal assurances reveal God's unchanging purpose to restore humanity's relationship with Him, despite their failures.

In contrast to the Yahwist's intimate portrayal of God, the Priestly tradition emphasizes Yahweh's holiness and the structured means by which His people can approach Him in reverence. This tradition is concerned with order, sacred rituals, and maintaining purity within the covenant relationship. The central tenet of the Priestly tradition is captured in Leviticus 19:2, where God commands, "Be holy because I, the LORD your God, am holy." This call to holiness reflects Yahweh's transcendence and the necessity for His people to mirror His character through obedient living and worship.

The tabernacle and, later, the temple were central to the Priestly worldview, serving as the physical loci of God's presence. The elaborate instructions for their construction and use, detailed in Exodus 25 to 31, demonstrate the importance of sacred space and ritual purity in maintaining communion with God. Sacrifices, festivals, and priestly duties were not merely religious customs but essential elements of Israel's identity and theological framework, ensuring that their worship reflected divine order and facilitated atonement.

The Covenantal tradition provides the ethical and moral framework for Israel's relationship with Yahweh, highlighting the reciprocal nature of their covenant. It frames Israel's history as an ongoing narrative of divine faithfulness and human responsibility, where obedience results in blessing and disobedience leads to consequences. The covenant established at Sinai, detailed in Exodus 19–24, laid out the terms of this relationship, with Deuteronomy 28 outlining blessings for obedience and curses for rebellion. The covenant shaped Israel's self-understanding, reinforcing their identity as a holy nation set apart for God's purposes.

During times of suffering and exile covenantal theology provided Israel with a lens through which to interpret their hardships. Their struggles were understood not merely as political or military failures but as divine discipline—a call back to covenantal faithfulness. Yet embedded within this theology was also a message of profound hope: a promise that repentance would bring restoration.

Deuteronomy 30:1–10 speaks of a day when God would gather His people, circumcise their hearts, and dwell with them once more. This promise does not merely point backward to Israel's return from exile but also forward to the ultimate renewal fulfilled in the *Parousia*. In Christ the covenant is both restored and transformed, as the indwelling presence of God becomes the very means by which the hearts of His people are made new. The *Parousia*, then, is the covenant's consummation—the realization of God's promise to dwell intimately with His people, not only after exile but forever.

PROPHETIC CONTRIBUTIONS: SHAPING ISRAEL'S THEOLOGICAL VISION

The prophets of Israel played a crucial role in shaping and refining the nation's theology. They served as God's messengers, calling the people to righteousness, warning of judgment, and offering hope for future restoration.

The prophets consistently emphasized that genuine worship must be accompanied by justice and ethical living. Ritual observance without moral integrity was condemned, as seen in Isaiah 1:17, which calls the people to "learn to do what is good. Pursue justice. Correct the oppressor. Defend the rights of the fatherless. Plead the widow's cause." Similarly, Amos decries hollow religious rituals, declaring in Amos 5:21–24 that God desires justice to "flow like water." These prophetic calls reinforced the idea that faithfulness to God extended beyond temple sacrifices to how the people treated one another, particularly the vulnerable and marginalized.

Amid warnings of judgment the prophets also spoke of a future hope when God's kingdom would be fully realized. The prophetic writings contain glimpses of the coming Messiah, the restoration of Israel, and the establishment of an eternal kingdom. Isaiah 9:6–7 prophesies the birth of a ruler who would bring justice and peace, while Ezekiel envisions a restored temple symbolizing renewed communion with God. Daniel's visions of an eternal kingdom ruled by the "Son of Man" (Daniel 7:13–14) lay the foundation for New Testament expectations of Christ's appearing and reign.

The prophetic voices introduced greater complexity into Israel's theological understanding. Jeremiah speaks of a "new covenant" written on the hearts of believers (Jeremiah 31:31–34), moving beyond external observance to an internal transformation. This laid the groundwork for New Testament teachings on spiritual renewal and the indwelling of the Holy Spirit.

WISDOM AND POETRY TRADITIONS: CONTEMPLATING DIVINE ORDER

Beyond covenant and prophecy, Israel's theological reflections extended into wisdom and poetry literature, addressing universal questions about suffering, divine sovereignty, and human purpose. Wisdom literature, such as Proverbs, presents a vision of life governed by divine order and wisdom. Trusting in God's guidance is seen as the key to a flourishing life, as expressed in Proverbs 3:5–6, which urges reliance on God's wisdom rather than on human understanding.

While Proverbs offers practical instruction, books like Ecclesiastes and Job wrestle with deeper existential questions, reflecting on the nature of suffering and the limits of human knowledge. These texts provide theological depth by acknowledging the complexities of life and encouraging a trust in God's ultimate justice and wisdom.

The internal theological dynamics of Israel reveal a rich and evolving tapestry of traditions and insights that shaped their understanding of God and their role in His redemptive plan. The Yahwist, Priestly, and Covenantal traditions illuminate distinct aspects of their relationship with Yahweh, while the prophetic voices challenge and expand their theology, pointing to a future fulfillment in the Messiah. Wisdom literature, in turn, provides a broader perspective, addressing the complexities of faith and human experience.

Together these theological developments anticipate the *Parousia*, where the fullness of God's presence is revealed and realized in the lives of believers. The development of Jewish theology was not a linear progression but a dynamic interplay of diverse perspectives, each contributing to a comprehensive understanding of God's revelation and Israel's covenantal experience. The Yahwist, Priestly, Covenantal, Prophetic, and Wisdom traditions—though distinct in their emphases—did not exist in isolation. Instead they engaged in an ongoing theological dialogue, shaping a richly woven tapestry of divine truth. This complex interplay is essential for interpreting the Old Testament as a unified narrative that ultimately finds its fulfillment in the person and work of Jesus Christ.

MUTUAL INFLUENCES AND THEOLOGICAL CROSS-POLLINATION

The diverse theological traditions of ancient Israel interacted in profound ways, each complementing and refining the others to provide a multifaceted portrayal of God's nature and His relationship with His people. Throughout Israel's theological history the tension between God's immanence and transcendence remained a central theme. The Yahwist tradition emphasized Yahweh's relational closeness, depicting Him as intimately involved in human affairs. In Genesis 3:8 God is portrayed as walking in the Garden of Eden, highlighting His nearness and desire for fellowship with humanity. This perspective reassured Israel of God's personal concern and accessibility.

Conversely, the Priestly tradition underscored God's holiness and transcendence, emphasizing the sacred boundaries that governed divine-human interaction. The grandeur of God's glory filling the tabernacle, as recorded in Exodus 40:34–35, illustrated His majestic presence, which required reverence and meticulous observance of purity laws. Together these traditions balanced the understanding of God as both intimately present and gloriously exalted, creating a theological framework that fostered both trust and awe.

The Covenantal tradition served as a unifying thread that wove together the diverse theological perspectives of Israel's history. The Yahwist's focus on God's promises to the patriarchs, such as the covenant with Abraham in Genesis 12:1–3, was complemented by the Priestly tradition's emphasis on covenantal rituals that safeguarded Israel's relationship with Yahweh, exemplified in the observance of the Day of Atonement (Leviticus 16).

The prophets reinforced this covenantal framework by calling the people back to faithfulness, often critiquing empty religious observance in favor of genuine devotion. In Hosea 6:6 God declares, "For I desire faithful love and not sacrifice, the knowledge of God rather than burnt offerings." This prophetic voice served to deepen Israel's understanding of covenant, highlighting both divine mercy and the call to ethical living.

The Wisdom tradition provided a reflective and universal dimension to Israel's theology, addressing fundamental questions of human existence, suffering, and divine justice. Wisdom writings such as Proverbs offered practical guidance for aligning one's life with God's order, as seen in Proverbs 3:5–6, which urges trust in Yahweh's guidance.

At the same time Wisdom literature grappled with profound theological dilemmas, challenging simplistic notions of divine justice. The book of Job, for instance, presents a nuanced exploration of suffering and divine sovereignty, resonating with prophetic themes of restoration and redemption. The prophetic depiction of the suffering servant in Isaiah 53 echoes Job's reflections, deepening the theological narrative with a foreshadowing of Christ's redemptive work.

THE ROLE OF HISTORICAL CONTEXT IN THEOLOGICAL DEVELOPMENT

Historical events served as pivotal moments that catalyzed theological reflection and the synthesis of diverse traditions. As we have seen, Israel's history was marked by crises that necessitated reevaluation and adaptation of their theological frameworks.

The Babylonian exile stands as a prime example of how theological thought evolved in response to national catastrophe. The destruction of the temple forced a rethinking of God's presence, leading to an increased focus on internalized faith and covenantal renewal. The Priestly tradition sought to preserve Israel's identity through ritual and law, while the Prophetic tradition offered visions of hope and restoration.

Ezekiel 37:1–14 presents the vision of the Valley of Dry Bones, symbolizing national renewal and divine restoration, while Jeremiah 31:31–34 introduces the concept of a "new covenant" written on the hearts of the people, pointing toward a more profound spiritual transformation.

The crisis of exile also led to the emergence of eschatological hope, with the prophets envisioning a future when God's promises would be fully realized. Ezekiel 40–48 draws on Priestly imagery to describe a restored temple, while Isaiah 7:14 presents the promise of "Immanuel," a prophetic foreshadowing of Christ's incarnation.

Wisdom literature, such as Ecclesiastes, provided a complementary perspective by affirming God's sovereignty in the midst of uncertainty, encouraging trust in His ultimate justice and purpose (Ecclesiastes 12:13–14).

Israel's interactions with surrounding nations often tested their theological distinctiveness, leading to both confrontation and adaptation. The Priestly tradition responded by emphasizing ritual purity and separation, codifying laws to guard against assimilation, as seen in the dietary and purity regulations of Leviticus 11–15.

Simultaneously, Wisdom literature engaged with broader philosophical questions, reflecting influences from surrounding cultures while maintaining a distinctly Yahwistic perspective. Parallels between Proverbs and other ancient Near Eastern wisdom texts demonstrate a willingness to engage with external ideas while reaffirming Israel's theological identity.

The interplay of diverse theological perspectives within ancient Israel reflects a community actively wrestling with the complexities of divine revelation and human experience. Rather than existing as isolated streams, the Yahwist, Priestly, Covenantal, Prophetic, and Wisdom traditions informed and enriched one another, contributing to a holistic and multifaceted understanding of God's purposes.

THEOLOGICAL DIVERSITY WITHOUT CONTRADICTION

This diversity, rather than being a source of contradiction, is a testimony to the unity of God's redemptive plan. Each tradition brought its own emphasis—intimacy and holiness, justice and mercy, suffering and hope—yet together they formed a cohesive witness to God's covenantal faithfulness and His call to holiness.

The unity within these traditions finds its ultimate expression "in Christ," where intimate presence and holiness, justice and mercy, and suffering and restoration are perfectly embodied. Through the *Parousia* the theological threads of the Old Testament converge in the New, revealing God's redemptive plan in its fullest and most transformative expression.

The Old Testament stands as a remarkable tapestry of theological perspectives, historical contexts, and cultural influences, woven together to reveal the multifaceted nature of God's relationship with humanity. Rather than its being a collection of conflicting viewpoints, the diversity within its pages enriches our understanding of God's covenantal faithfulness, His call to holiness, and His redemptive purpose. This amalgamation of perspectives presents a unified message that finds its ultimate fulfillment in Christ, demonstrating the continuity and depth of divine revelation.

The richness of the Old Testament lies in its ability to present distinct theological voices that, rather than contradicting one another, converge to offer a fuller picture of God's character and His interaction with His people. Each theological tradition within the Old Testament contributes a unique dimension to the understanding of God's nature and His covenant with Israel. The Yahwist tradition emphasizes God's relational intimacy, highlighting His covenant with Abraham as a cornerstone of Israel's identity (Genesis 12:1–3). In contrast, the Priestly tradition underscores God's holiness and the necessity of maintaining ritual purity, as outlined in the meticulous laws of Leviticus. The Prophetic tradition, exemplified in the writings of Isaiah and Amos, calls Israel to justice and repentance while offering hope for restoration (Isaiah 11:1–9; Amos 5:24).

Far from being disjointed, these perspectives intertwine to reflect a God who is both near and transcendent, just and merciful, holy and compassionate. Together they reveal the depth and breadth of divine revelation, allowing readers to encounter the fullness of God's character across the diverse contexts of Israel's history.

Despite the variety of voices and historical settings, the Old Testament maintains a coherent theological message, anchored in three central themes. The first theme is God's covenantal faithfulness: whether in times of blessing or judgment, God's steadfast love remains unshaken, as declared in Exodus 34:6–7 and reaffirmed through the prophet Hosea's depiction of God's enduring commitment (Hosea 2:19–20). The second theme is the call to holiness; this theme permeates every aspect of Israel's life, from the priestly regulations concerning purity (Leviticus) to the ethical exhortations of the prophets (Micah 6:8) and the Wisdom tradition's pursuit of righteousness (Proverbs 9:10). And the third theme is the hope of restoration; from the covenant with Abraham to the prophetic visions of a restored Zion, the Old Testament consistently points forward to God's redemptive plan, culminating in the Messiah who will establish a kingdom of justice and peace.

The final arrangement of the Old Testament reflects a deliberate theological design that integrates these diverse perspectives into a cohesive whole. The Pentateuch lays the foundation for Israel's covenantal relationship with God, providing the legal and moral framework. The Historical Books illustrate Israel's successes and failures in living out this covenant, while the Prophetic Books serve as divine commentary, offering correction and hope. The Wisdom Literature, with its reflective and philosophical insights, brings depth to the understanding of God's justice and human responsibility, addressing universal themes that resonate across generations.

A UNIFIED PURPOSE IN CHRIST

When viewed through the lens of Christ, the theological diversity of the Old Testament converges into a single redemptive narrative. Jesus stands as the fulfillment of its promises, laws, and prophetic hopes, uniting the Old Testament's themes into a cohesive testimony of God's saving work—a work that continues to unfold through the *Parousia* as Christ's presence is unveiled in the lives of His people and throughout history.

Jesus embodies the covenantal promises made to Abraham, fulfilling the divine intention to bless all nations through his lineage (Matthew 1:1; Galatians 3:16). He upholds the holiness demanded by the Law and surpasses it by offering Himself as the final and perfect sacrifice, as described in Hebrews 9:11–12. The prophetic visions of a coming Redeemer, such as those found in Isaiah 9:6–7, find their realization in Christ, whose kingdom of justice and righteousness is inaugurated through His ministry.

Jesus Himself affirmed this unity when He declared in Luke 24:44, "These are my words that I spoke to you while I was still with you—that everything written about me in the Law of Moses, the Prophets, and the Psalms must be fulfilled." In Him the diverse elements of the Old Testament—covenant, law, prophecy, and wisdom—together reach their intended culmination.

Understanding the Old Testament through the lens of Christ allows believers to appreciate its theological unity and ongoing relevance. The Yahwist tradition, with its emphasis on covenantal intimacy, finds its highest expression in Christ, who fulfills God's promises to Abraham and his descendants (Galatians 3:16). The Priestly tradition reaches its pinnacle in Jesus, the ultimate High Priest who provides eternal redemption (Hebrews 9:11–14). The Prophetic tradition's call for justice and restoration comes to fruition in Christ's mission to establish the kingdom of God on earth (Isaiah 9:6–7; Matthew 5:17–20).

Even the Wisdom Literature, which offers practical insights into righteous living, finds its fulfillment in Christ, who is described as the embodiment of all wisdom and knowledge (Colossians 2:3). His life and teachings bring harmony to the philosophical and ethical concerns raised throughout the Old Testament.

THE OLD TESTAMENT UNVEILED IN THE NEW TESTAMENT

Recognizing the Old Testament as an amalgamation of perspectives encourages believers to engage with it deeply and reverently, drawing insights that are both historical and eternally relevant, revealing God's unchanging character. The Old Testament consistently portrays God as both holy and compassionate, offering a balanced view of His justice and mercy. It also speaks to the human condition; the narratives, laws, and prophecies highlight humanity's recurring struggles with sin and the need for divine intervention and redemption. Finally, it points to the hope of restoration: the prophetic promise of a coming Messiah is realized in Christ, offering believers a firm foundation for their faith and an assurance of God's ultimate plan for redemption.

The fulfillment of Jewish theology reaches its pinnacle in the person and work of Jesus Christ. As the embodiment of the Old Testament's covenantal promises, prophetic visions, and theological reflections, Christ unites the Law, the Prophets, and the Writings into a singular redemptive narrative. Through His life, death, and resurrection and the ongoing *Parousia*, Christ reveals the fullness of God's presence and plan, extending the blessings of the covenant to all humanity and offering a renewed understanding of divine purpose.

Jesus serves as the interpretive key to unlocking the Old Testament's depth and meaning. Through His teachings and actions He affirmed the authority of Scripture, while bringing its ultimate fulfillment into view. Christ consistently upheld the Old Testament as divinely inspired, demonstrating its continued relevance in light of His mission. He illuminated the Scriptures, revealing that they pointed to Him as their ultimate fulfillment. In Luke 24:27 Jesus, speaking to His disciples, "beginning with Moses and all the Prophets . . . interpreted for them the things concerning himself in all the Scriptures." Similarly, in Matthew 5:17 He declared, "Don't think that I came to abolish the Law or the Prophets. I did not come to abolish but to fulfill."

Through His teachings Jesus demonstrated that the Old Testament was not a relic of the past but an unfolding of God's covenantal faithfulness and redemptive plan, brought to completion in Him. Jesus not only upheld the Law but fulfilled its deepest intent, elevating it beyond external adherence to an inward transformation of the heart. His teachings, particularly in the Sermon on the Mount (Matthew 5–7), emphasized the moral and spiritual essence of the Law, calling believers to a righteousness that flows from love and devotion to God.

The sacrificial system of the Old Testament, which served as a foreshadowing of atonement, found its culmination in Christ's ultimate sacrifice. Hebrews 10:1 reflects this fulfillment: "Since the law has only a shadow of the good things to come, and not the reality itself of those things, it can never perfect the worshipers." Through His death and resurrection Jesus completed the requirements of the Law, providing eternal redemption and access to God (Hebrews 9:11–14).

The prophetic hopes of justice, peace, and restoration anticipated in the Old Testament are fully realized "in Christ." As the long-awaited Messiah Jesus inaugurated the kingdom of God, embodying the visions of Isaiah, Jeremiah, and Ezekiel. Isaiah 9:6–7 proclaimed, "For a child will be born for us, a son will be given to us. . . . The dominion will be vast, and its prosperity will never end." Jesus confirmed this fulfillment in Luke 4:18–21, declaring Himself to be the anointed One sent to proclaim good news to the poor and liberty to the captives.

Beyond His earthly ministry Christ's work continues through the *Parousia*, where the ultimate unveiling of His essence will bring the full restoration of creation and the fulfillment of prophetic expectations. This progressive unveiling is evident throughout Jesus's ministry, but it reaches a pivotal moment when He turns to His disciples and asks, *"Who do you say that I am?"* (Matthew 16:15). This question is not just about information—it is an invitation to revelation. It is the moment when human perception is tested against divine illumination.

Among all the voices it is Peter who responds, declaring, "You are the Messiah, the Son of the living God" (Matthew 16:16). This is no ordinary realization—it is an *epiphaneia*, a moment of divine revelation granted by the Father. Yet even this unveiling is incomplete, as Peter soon struggles to reconcile his understanding of Messiahship with the suffering and death that Jesus begins to foretell.

But six days later Peter would experience another unveiling—one that would shake his understanding even further. Jesus took Peter, James, and John up a high mountain, away from the crowds, away from the familiar, away from everything they thought they knew. And there, before them, He was transfigured: "His face shone like the sun; his clothes became as white as the light" (Matthew 17:2).

For a brief moment the veil of His humanity was lifted, and His divine essence radiated before their eyes. This was not a new reality—this was the eternal reality of Christ breaking through into the present. The *Parousia* was before them—not in some distant future but in the now, revealing Jesus as He always had been and always will be.

As if to confirm this moment as the ultimate *epiphaneia*, two figures appeared beside Jesus—Moses and Elijah. Here stood the very embodiments of the Law and the Prophets, testifying that everything in Israel's history culminated in Christ.

Yet even as Peter beheld this vision, his instinct was to contain it, to control it, to hold onto the moment: "Lord, it's good for us to be here. If you want, I will set up three shelters here: one for you, one for Moses, and one for Elijah" (Matthew 17:4). But *epiphaneia* cannot be contained. It is not meant to be preserved in structures or confined to a place—it is meant to transform the beholder. Before Peter could act on his impulse a voice from heaven interrupted: "This is my beloved Son, with whom I am well-pleased. Listen to him!" (Matthew 17:5).

At Jesus's BAPTISM the Father's voice had spoken to affirm Him; now, at the Transfiguration, the Father's voice spoke to instruct the disciples. They were no longer to look to Moses for the Law or to Elijah for the prophetic word—they were to look to Christ alone. The full unveiling of the *Parousia* would come not through visions but through hearing His voice.

Terrified, Peter, James, and John fell to the ground. But Jesus in His mercy touched them and spoke words that have echoed through every *epiphaneia* moment since: "Get up; don't be afraid" (Matthew 17:7). And when they lifted their eyes Moses and Elijah were gone. Only Jesus remained. This was the message of the Transfiguration: all that had come before had served its purpose, and now Christ alone stood as the fulfillment of all things.

Yet the Transfiguration was only a glimpse, a foretaste of the full *Parousia* yet to come. The disciples still did not fully comprehend that the path to glory led through suffering. But the trajectory was set—they had seen the glory. And soon, through the cross, the resurrection, and the outpouring of the Spirit, they would come to know it in its fullness: "For God who said, 'Let light shine out of darkness,' has shone in our hearts to give the light of the knowledge of God's glory in the face of Jesus Christ" (2 Corinthians 4:6).

Christ not only fulfills the Law and the Prophets but also embodies divine wisdom, guiding humanity in the ways of righteousness and truth. Colossians 2:3 affirms, "In him are hidden all the treasures of wisdom and knowledge." His parables reflect the thoughtful and practical nature of Wisdom literature, offering insights into God's kingdom and human responsibility.

Additionally, the messianic Psalms, such as Psalm 22 and Psalm 110, find their ultimate expression in Jesus's suffering, exaltation, and eternal reign. Through Him the longing for divine justice, guidance, and deliverance expressed in the Psalms becomes a present reality for believers.

"In Christ" the diverse theological strands of the Old Testament converge, demonstrating God's unbroken faithfulness and the completion of His promises.

Jesus fulfills the covenants made with Abraham and David, bringing them to their intended fulfillment in the New Covenant. Galatians 3:16 declares, "Now the promises were spoken to Abraham and to his seed, . . . who is Christ," affirming that Jesus is the promised descendant through whom all nations are blessed.

Likewise, the Davidic covenant reaches its culmination in Christ's eternal kingship. As the angel proclaimed to Mary in Luke 1:32–33, "The Lord God will give him the throne of his father David. . . . His kingdom will have no end." Through His reign Christ establishes an unbreakable relationship between God and humanity, sealed by His blood in the New Covenant (Jeremiah 31:31–34; Luke 22:20).

Jesus reinterpreted and fulfilled key symbols and practices of the Old Testament, revealing their deeper spiritual significance. He declared in John 2:19–21, "Destroy this temple, and I will raise it up in three days," signifying the shift from the physical temple to Himself as the true dwelling place of God.

Similarly, in John 6:35–58 Jesus identified Himself as the Bread of Life, fulfilling the provision of manna in the wilderness and offering eternal sustenance for the soul. In these and other instances Christ reframed Israel's religious practices in light of His mission to bring ultimate redemption and transformation.

CONCLUSION

The *Parousia* brings the Old Testament's diverse theological threads into their unified fulfillment. "In Christ" the covenantal promises, priestly holiness, prophetic visions, and wisdom traditions converge, revealing the fullness of God's redemptive plan. As Ephesians 1:10 declares, God's purpose is "to bring everything together in Christ, both things in heaven and things on earth in him."

This grand culmination fulfills Israel's eschatological hope and humanity's longing for restored communion with God. As Revelation 21:3 affirms, "Look, God's dwelling is with humanity. . . . [He] will be their God." Through the *Parousia* this indwelling becomes a present reality, not merely a future hope.

The theological richness of Israel's journey—shaped by intimacy, holiness, justice, and wisdom—prepared the way for Christ, who embodies and fulfills it all. His ongoing unveiling calls believers to live as participants in this redemptive mission, reflecting His glory, embodying His holiness, and anticipating the day when all things are made new in Him.

CHAPTER 7

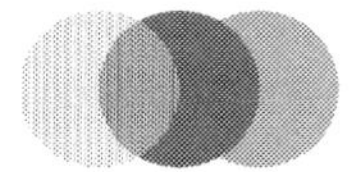

FULFILLMENT AND TRANSFORMATION OF EXPECTATION: DISCIPLES' USE OF *PAROUSIA*

The story of Jewish theology and culture is a profound testament to divine revelation, resilience, and preparation, culminating in the person of Jesus Christ, the promised Messiah. Throughout their history the Jewish people were shaped by the trials of war, exile, and idolatry, experiences that not only tested their covenantal faithfulness but also deepened their understanding of God's holiness, justice, and unwavering mercy. These trials refined Israel into a people uniquely prepared to receive and proclaim God's redemptive purpose to the world.

The journey of Israel reflects God's sovereign hand guiding His people through adversity, shaping a covenantal identity through the Law, the Prophets, and the Writings. The theological richness of the Old Testament, whether in the intimacy of Yahwism, the structure of priestly law, the passion of prophetic justice, or the meditations of Wisdom literature reveals diverse glimpses of God's nature and His dealings with humanity. Yet each stream, despite their differences, was aimed toward one ultimate fulfillment.

"In Christ" these traditions converge. He is the embodiment of God's promises to Abraham, the holiness demanded by the Law, and the vision foretold by the prophets. In Him the scattered revelations of the Old Testament come into sharp, unified focus. Jesus does not stand apart from Israel's history—He stands as its fulfillment.

His life and ministry fulfilled the Law not only by perfect obedience but by revealing its deepest intention: to form a people who love God and neighbor with holy devotion. His death and resurrection did not abolish the covenant; they completed it, enabling all people, Jew and Gentile, to enter into God's eternal rest through faith. The longings of the prophets for peace, justice, and a new heart find their answer in His kingdom. And the Wisdom literature finds its voice in His teachings and His paradoxical triumph through suffering.

The *Parousia* of Christ does not sever the Church from its Jewish roots; rather, it reveals the purpose for which Israel was chosen: to be a vessel through whom the nations would be blessed. Through Christ that purpose is realized. He extends the blessings of the covenant to all who believe, creating one new humanity reconciled to God.

This chapter will explore how Jewish theological traditions prepared the world for the Messiah, how Jesus fulfills and transforms those traditions, and how His *Parousia* reveals the unity of God's redemptive plan. Understanding this continuity is essential for seeing the Scriptures as one story, culminating in the reign of Christ and the present participation of believers in His kingdom. From covenant to Christ, from shadow to substance, the unfolding glory of God finds its center in Jesus, the fulfillment of all things.

The theological richness of Jewish history and culture provides a vital foundation for understanding the continuity of God's redemptive work across time. The varied traditions, shaped by historical and spiritual trials, ultimately find their fulfillment and unity in Jesus Christ. This is especially evident when we consider the expectations of Jesus's first disciples, who—steeped in Jewish eschatological hopes—anticipated a visible, political restoration of Israel's kingdom. Yet Christ's *Parousia* unveils something far more profound: it ushers believers into the eternal reality of God dwelling with His people.

This profound truth challenges believers to engage with Scripture in a more meaningful way, to see its unified message through the lens of Christ, and to live out the transformative power of His presence. As partakers in God's redemptive mission they are called to embody His kingdom values and to anticipate the ultimate fulfillment of His promises when all things are made new in Him.

TRANSITION FROM OLD TESTAMENT MESSIANIC EXPECTATIONS

The disciples' expectations of the Messiah and their understanding of *Parousia* were profoundly influenced by the Jewish apocalyptic worldview. This perspective, deeply rooted in sacred texts such as Isaiah, Ezekiel, Daniel, and 1 Enoch, provided a theological framework that anticipated divine intervention in human history. Central to this worldview were grand themes of cosmic upheaval, divine judgment, ultimate restoration, and the vindication of God's people. In the face of suffering, exile, and oppression these texts conveyed an unwavering hope in God's sovereign plan—one that envisioned a climactic "Day of the Lord" when He would establish His eternal rule, vanquish evil, and restore righteousness throughout creation.

Jewish apocalyptic literature frequently pointed to the arrival of a divinely appointed figure who would act as God's agent in establishing His kingdom. The vision in Daniel 7:13–14, which depicts "one like a Son of Man" coming with the clouds of heaven and receiving dominion from the "Ancient of Days," became a cornerstone for messianic expectation. This portrayal of the Messiah as a powerful, triumphant ruler deeply influenced Jewish hopes for national deliverance and divine intervention.

Early Christians, shaped by these expectations, came to recognize Jesus as the fulfillment of these long-cherished hopes. However, they reinterpreted His mission in a way that emphasized spiritual transformation rather than political or military conquest. While many envisioned the Messiah as a liberator who would free Israel from earthly oppressors, Jesus's teachings revealed a deeper mission, one that aimed to rescue humanity from the bondage of sin and death. In doing so He redefined the apocalyptic vision, shifting the focus from national restoration to the redemption of all creation through His life, death, and resurrection.

The Jewish apocalyptic imagination often used vivid cosmic imagery to describe divine intervention, depicting events such as the shaking of the heavens, darkened suns, and celestial signs (Isaiah 13:10; Joel 2:31). These dramatic portrayals symbolized God's sovereign action within human history, signaling the transition from one era to another. The New Testament writers adopted this language to convey the profound significance of Christ's *Parousia*. In Matthew 24:30 Jesus describes the coming of the Son of Man with power and great glory, mirroring the apocalyptic imagery of the Old Testament and emphasizing the cosmic scope of His reign.

However, rather than viewing these descriptions as literal predictions of physical events, the New Testament interprets them as symbolic representations of spiritual realities. The *Parousia* reveals Christ's supreme authority, permeating creation with His truth and light, dispelling darkness, and asserting His reign over all things.

A defining feature of Jewish eschatology was its division of history into two distinct ages: "this age," characterized by sin, suffering, and rebellion against God, and "the age to come," marked by divine justice, peace, and universal restoration. This dual framework profoundly influenced the early Christians' thought, shaping their understanding of *Parousia*. The New Testament presents *Parousia* within the framework of the "already-but-not-yet" tension, acknowledging that Christ's first appearing inaugurated the kingdom of God, while its full realization remains in the future.

In this light *Parousia* is both a present experience and a future hope. Believers are called to live in the transformative power of Christ's presence now (Colossians 1:27), while eagerly anticipating the ultimate renewal of creation (Revelation 21:1–5). This perspective empowers Christians to actively participate in God's unfolding redemptive work, embodying the values of the coming kingdom while awaiting its final consummation.

A recurring theme in Jewish apocalyptic thought is the eventual vindication of God's people amid suffering and injustice. Scriptures such as Isaiah 25:8 and Daniel 12:2–3 offer powerful visions of resurrection, divine justice, and eternal reward for those who remain faithful to Yahweh. The New Testament echoes this hope, portraying the *Parousia* as the moment when Christ will fully vindicate the faithful and establish His eternal reign. In 1 Thessalonians 4:16–17 Paul reassures believers that Christ will return to gather His people and bring them into His glorious presence.

For the early church, facing persecution and hardship, the promise of *Parousia* provided immense encouragement. It affirmed that their trials were not in vain and that God's justice would ultimately prevail. The anticipation of Christ's appearing inspired perseverance, urging believers to remain steadfast in faith and commitment to their calling.

While the New Testament understanding of *Parousia* is deeply rooted in Jewish apocalyptic tradition, it also reinterprets and expands these themes through the lens of Christ's life, death, resurrection, and ascension. "In Christ" the role of the Messiah extends beyond national deliverance to encompass the redemption and restoration of all creation. *Parousia* thus emerges as a profound expression of God's ongoing presence with His people, offering both immediate spiritual renewal and the promise of ultimate transformation.

The eschatological hope that once looked forward to a distant intervention now finds fulfillment in the person of Jesus, whose presence permeates every aspect of life. Through Him the ancient expectations of divine intervention and cosmic renewal are realized, and believers are invited to participate in the unfolding reality of God's kingdom.

THE MESSIAH'S REINTERPRETATION OF GOD'S EXPECTATIONS

In His earthly ministry Jesus redefined and expanded the long-held Jewish expectations concerning God's kingdom and the fulfillment of divine promises. Rather than conforming to the prevailing anticipation of a political or military deliverer, Jesus presented the kingdom of God as a reality that was both present and yet to be fully realized. Through His teachings and parables He unveiled a kingdom characterized by spiritual transformation, faithfulness, and active participation, calling His followers to live in a state of readiness and alignment with God's purposes.

Jesus proclaimed that the kingdom of God was not solely a distant event to be anticipated but a present reality that had already begun to take shape in His presence and work. In Luke 17:21 He declared, "The kingdom of God is in your midst," emphasizing that His appearing inaugurated God's reign in a way that was already accessible to those who embraced Him. At the same time He spoke of a future culmination, teaching that the kingdom would reach its full expression at a time known only to the Father and urging His followers to remain vigilant and faithful.

Through His parables Jesus communicated the necessity of spiritual preparedness and perseverance in light of the kingdom's unfolding reality. The parable of the ten virgins (Matthew 25:1–13) vividly illustrates the importance of readiness, as it portrays a group awaiting the bridegroom's arrival—some wisely prepared with oil, while others were caught unprepared when the moment arrived. This story reinforces the call to live in expectation, being spiritually equipped for the revelation of God's purposes. Similarly, the parable of the talents

(Matthew 25:14–30) underscores the responsibility of believers to faithfully steward what has been entrusted to them, emphasizing that their faithfulness will be evaluated when the master returns.

Through these teachings Jesus introduced a profound reinterpretation of apocalyptic expectations. While Jewish thought often focused on an abrupt, cataclysmic intervention of God to restore Israel, Jesus revealed a more comprehensive and transformative vision. His use of *Parousia* did not point to a singular dramatic event but to an ongoing, unfolding reality in which His presence was actively shaping the world. This redefinition emphasized both the "already" (His presence among His people) and the "not yet" (the ultimate fulfillment when He would return in glory).

Jesus's reframing of apocalyptic themes had a lasting impact on the New Testament writers, shaping their understanding of *Parousia* as more than just the future return of Christ. They came to see it as the continuing manifestation of Christ's essence and reign in the life of the believer and the church. In passages like Matthew 24:44–46 Jesus urged His followers to remain faithful and expectant, underscoring the reality that His appearing would not only mark the consummation of all things but was a present reality to be lived out in daily faith and obedience.

Ultimately, Jesus's reinterpretation of God's expectations called for a shift in focus—from longing for an external political salvation to embracing an internal, transformative relationship with God. His teachings reoriented the concept of *Parousia*, presenting it as an ongoing spiritual unveiling that empowers believers to live in the reality of His presence while remaining watchful for the day when the fullness of His kingdom will be revealed.

As Jesus redefined the meaning of God's kingdom and reshaped the expectations of His disciples, the early Church was left with a profound reality: the Messiah had come not to fulfill national hopes but to inaugurate a new creation through His presence. What remained was to understand how His ongoing presence—His *Parousia*—would shape theology, worship, and daily life. That was the task of the New Testament writers and is the focus of the next chapter.

ANALYSIS OF KEY SCRIPTURAL PASSAGES ON THE *PAROUSIA*

The New Testament presents the *Parousia* as more than a future event; it is an ongoing, transformative reality that shapes the lives of believers. Through key passages we see *Parousia* as an unveiling of Christ's presence that offers comfort, hope, and victory amid life's uncertainties. These passages provide a theological and relational framework, guiding believers to live with trust, readiness, and purpose in the light of Christ's revealed essence.

In Matthew 24:3–27 the disciples approach Jesus with questions about the signs of His coming and the end of the age, reflecting their longing for certainty in an uncertain world. Jesus responds with vivid imagery, likening His *Parousia* to lightning flashing across the sky—sudden, unmistakable, and all encompassing. However, rather than indulging speculative concerns about the future, Jesus shifts their focus to trust, vigilance, and faithfulness in the present.

His words reassure the disciples that His appearing will be undeniable, emphasizing His sovereign authority over all things: "For as the lightning flashes from horizon to horizon and lights up the sky, so the Son of Man will be in his day" (Luke 17:24). This striking imagery of lightning reveals both the universality and the sudden, inescapable nature of His presence—transformative and uncontainable. In the midst of world chaos and instability, such language offers hope: the *Parousia* will not be hidden or obscure but revealed with unmistakable clarity and power to all who have eyes to see.

Christ's *Parousia* serves as a beacon of clarity and hope, providing assurance that His presence will bring order and fulfillment to life's uncertainties. Beyond a future event, Christ's *Parousia* invites believers into a relationship of trust and dependence on His care and authority in the present moment. For believers today this passage offers encouragement to navigate uncertainty with confidence in Christ's enduring presence. It calls them to live expectantly, embracing hope and readiness while trusting in God's sovereignty.

In 1 Thessalonians 4:15–17 Paul addresses the fears and grief of the Thessalonian believers over loved ones who had passed away. Concerned that the departed might miss out on the blessings of Christ's return, they sought reassurance. Paul comforted them by declaring, "We who are still alive at the Lord's coming will certainly not precede those who have fallen asleep," affirming that "the dead in Christ will rise first" and that then all believers, both living and deceased, "will be caught up together with them . . . to meet the Lord in the air." In this way Paul assured them that all who belong to Christ will be united with Him forever in His appearing.

This passage paints *Parousia* as a profound moment of reunion in which separation and sorrow will be replaced by eternal communion with Christ and fellow believers. The hope it offers transcends the fear of death, grounding believers in the certainty of God's redemptive plan. *Parousia* signifies more than an event; it embodies the ultimate restoration of relationships, offering hope that transcends physical death. Christ's appearing fulfills the longing for unity, reaffirming His promise of eternal fellowship with His people. This passage speaks to the hearts of those experiencing loss, encouraging them to live in the anticipation of eternal reunion. It calls believers to embrace a perspective of hope and endurance, trusting in the certainty of Christ's promises.

This hopeful vision of union with Christ is not only future oriented; it is rooted in the present spiritual reality of being "in Christ." Paul's own words in Philippians 1:21–23, written well before the destruction of the temple in AD 70, confirm this perspective. He openly longed to "depart and be with Christ," which he describes as "far better," demonstrating his belief that death ushers the believer immediately into the unveiled presence of the Lord, not into unconscious waiting but into a fuller life. This affirms that the "catching up" Paul describes in 1 Thessalonians 4:17 is not about physical removal, or rapture, but about being spiritually gathered into Christ's glory. After the *Parousia* those who die "in Christ" do not "sleep" but enter directly into eternal communion with Him. Paul's confident expectation reveals that the *Parousia* inaugurates a new reality in which the faithful are never separated from the presence of Christ—either in life or in death or in the world to come.

After Paul addresses the Thessalonians about rising evil and deception, he presents Christ's *Parousia* as the moment when the lawless one" will be revealed and defeated by the sheer brilliance of Christ's appearing (2 Thessalonians 2:8–9). This passage underscores the triumph of Christ's authority over the forces of darkness and deception, highlighting the transformative and victorious nature of His presence.

Paul's message reassures believers that no force of evil can withstand the radiance of Christ's unveiled essence. The brightness of His coming symbolizes not only His cosmic victory but also the power of His presence to bring personal renewal and liberation from sin. The key insight of his passage is that the *Parousia* reveals Christ's ultimate victory, dispelling darkness and establishing His righteous reign. It understands the presence of Christ as not only a future hope but also a present reality that empowers believers to overcome sin and live in the light of His truth. This passage calls believers to confidence and courage, reminding them that Christ's power is already at work within them. It challenges them to reflect His light in a world overshadowed by confusion and fear.

As Jesus prepared His disciples for His departure, He spoke of a coming transition—from His physical presence to a deeper, spiritual indwelling through the Holy Spirit. In John 16:16–33 He assured them that, although they would experience sorrow at His absence, their grief would turn to joy as they came to understand the enduring nature of His presence.

Jesus redefines the concept of His presence, emphasizing that His essence will remain with them in a transformative way. The sorrow of separation gives way to the joy of spiritual communion as believers come to know Him in an even deeper, more intimate way through the Spirit. The *Parousia* thus is not confined to physical manifestation but represents an ongoing unveiling of Christ's essence, made tangible through the Holy Spirit. This passage also highlights the personal nature of *Parousia*, bridging the gap between physical absence and spiritual closeness, offering believers continuous fellowship with Christ.

This passage speaks to the faithful in a number of ways: believers are called to embrace the assurance of Christ's indwelling presence, even when physical evidence seems absent. The passage also encourages bold and joyful living, rooted in the awareness of Christ's transformative work in their lives. Empowered by His presence, believers are commissioned to reflect Christ's essence in their communities, embodying the values of His kingdom in everyday life.

THE TRANSFORMATIVE AND RELATIONAL DIMENSIONS OF THE *PAROUSIA*

Parousia in the New Testament is not only a promise of future glory but a present unveiling of Christ's relational and transformative presence. It portrays the *Parousia* as restoring relationships, renewing hearts, and shaping the daily lives of those who trust in Him. Rather than focusing solely on eschatological speculation, the New Testament presents *Parousia* as a dynamic encounter with Christ's essence, inviting believers to experience His nearness in tangible and life-changing ways.

At its core *Parousia* is a profoundly relational reality, emphasizing the restoration of communion—both with Christ and within the community of faith. Throughout the New Testament it is portrayed not merely as an event of cosmic proportions but as the fulfillment of God's desire to dwell with His people. This relational aspect offers a source of hope, comfort, and joy as believers are assured of their union with Christ and their shared identity within the body of believers.

Encounters with Christ in the here and now—whether through His Word, the Holy Spirit, or the community of believers—are moments of *Parousia* that invite transformation. The New Testament contains many examples of such encounters. The disciples on the road to Emmaus (Luke 24:31–32) recognized Jesus in the breaking of bread, illustrating how Christ's presence becomes perceptible in everyday moments. This same kind of transformational encounter is seen in Paul's experience on the road to Damascus (Acts 9:3–5), where Christ's unveiled essence radically redirected his life and mission. These moments of revelation demonstrate how the *Parousia* of Christ is an invitation to align with divine purposes and to allow His presence to shape the way believers live, think, and act.

The New Testament calls believers to actively embrace the reality of *Parousia* in their daily lives. Rather than passively waiting for a distant fulfillment, they are encouraged to live in faithful anticipation, allowing Christ's transformative presence to inform their worship, mission, and relationships. This practical dimension of *Parousia* challenges believers to embody the values of Christ's kingdom—faithfulness, vigilance, and hope—while navigating the complexities of life in a fallen world.

Passages such as Matthew 24 encourage believers to remain watchful and engaged, not through anxiety or fear but through a confident expectation that Christ's presence is both sustaining and guiding them. The *Parousia* of Christ empowers them to engage in acts of love, justice, and service, reflecting His glory in their communities and workplaces.

Several key moments throughout the New Testament continue to illuminate the relational and transformative dimensions of the *Parousia*. Rather than being limited to a distant eschatological event, Christ's appearing is consistently shown to be near, personal, and life altering. His presence is revealed not only in dramatic encounters but also in the quiet rhythms of life, forming the hearts of those who see with faith. Jesus's promise in John 16:22—"Your hearts will rejoice, and no one will take your joy from you"—reinforces the enduring intimacy of this relationship. The *Parousia*, then, is not a singular moment but an unfolding reality in which Christ's essence confronts, comforts, and calls believers into deeper union with Him.

The New Testament presents *Parousia* within the framework of an "already-but-not-yet" tension—where Christ's presence is fully accessible now, yet believers anticipate its ultimate fulfillment in the future. This dual perspective encourages Christians to embrace the present reality of Christ's reign while eagerly expecting the consummation of His kingdom. By viewing *Parousia* through this lens, believers are empowered to live with joy, purpose, and unwavering hope. Christ's presence is not a distant promise but a present reality, shaping their identity and mission in the world. Whether through prayer, worship, or acts of service, they are invited to experience the richness of His unveiled essence in their daily walk.

The New Testament's portrayal of *Parousia* transcends speculative obsession with end-times events. Through passages such as Matthew 24, John 16, 1 Thessalonians 4, and 2 Thessalonians 2, *Parousia* emerges as a call to live with faith, hope, and joy in the assurance of Christ's reign. It is a relational invitation to draw nearer to Him, a transformative force that renews lives, and a practical framework that empowers believers to reflect His essence in every aspect of life.

To grasp this mystery more fully, however, we must return to the foundation from which these themes emerge. The theological vision of *Parousia* is deeply rooted in Jewish eschatological hope—a hope that anticipated divine intervention, restoration, and the ultimate dwelling of God with His people.

Eschatology—the study of ultimate things—serves as a vital lens through which the intersection of divine purpose and human destiny can be examined. In Jewish tradition eschatological expectations were central to the theological framework, deeply rooted in God's promises and the enduring hope for ultimate restoration. These expectations developed within diverse cultural, historical, and theological contexts, reflecting the resilience of Jewish faith amid trials of persecution, exile, and oppression.

At the core of Jewish eschatology was a profound hope in God's decisive intervention in history—an expectation of the vindication of the righteous, the judgment of the wicked, and the renewal of creation. This hope, articulated through apocalyptic literature, prophetic pronouncements, and covenantal theology, not only shaped the worldview of ancient Israel but also laid the foundation for the messianic hope ultimately fulfilled in Jesus Christ. Far from being a distant speculation about future events, Jewish eschatology provided comfort and a call to faithfulness in the present moment, offering assurance that God's redemptive purposes were at work even in times of hardship.

As we consider the roots of Christian hope, these eschatological themes illuminate how the *Parousia* of Christ fulfills and transforms Israel's longing for divine presence, justice, and restoration. The Jewish anticipation of a Messiah—an anointed figure who would establish God's reign—found its ultimate fulfillment in Jesus. However, His mission redefined these expectations, shifting the focus from a physical restoration of Israel to the spiritual unveiling of God's kingdom. In examining the rich tapestry of Jewish eschatological thought we uncover how the themes of divine presence, justice, and restoration find their fulfillment and transformation in the *Parousia* of Christ. Eschatology, then, is not only about what is to come but about what is already being unveiled through Christ, both now and in the age to come.

A DIVERSE YET UNIFIED HOPE IN JEWISH ESCHATOLOGY

Although Jewish eschatological expectations were diverse, the Jews shared a common anticipation of God's decisive action in history. At the heart of these hopes was the coming of the Messiah, envisioned as the agent of God's reign, the vindicator of the righteous, and the restorer of covenantal promises. Apocalyptic texts such as Daniel, 1 Enoch, and 4 Ezra depict celestial signs, the judgment of the wicked, and the resurrection of the faithful—dramatic cosmic events that signal the full arrival of God's kingdom on earth. These expectations, infused with both hope and urgency, resonated particularly during periods of exile, oppression, and Roman occupation, when the longing for divine intervention was most acute.

The New Testament writers, deeply immersed in this eschatological tradition, reframed these expectations through the lens of Jesus Christ's life, death, resurrection, and ascension. Instead of emphasizing a singular apocalyptic event they introduced a radical reinterpretation: the "already-but-not-yet" kingdom—a reign of God inaugurated by Christ's first appearing and continually revealed through His spiritual presence. This reinterpretation marked a profound theological shift—transforming the long-anticipated apocalyptic moment into a continuing unveiling of Christ's divine essence and reign, already at work in the lives of believers.

MESSIANIC EXPECTATIONS AND APOCALYPTIC IMAGERY

Few passages captured Jewish messianic hope as vividly as Daniel 7:13–14, where "one like a son of man" comes with the clouds of heaven to receive dominion, glory, and an everlasting kingdom from the Ancient of Days. This imagery profoundly influenced Jewish expectations of the Messiah as a figure of divine authority and eternal reign.

In the New Testament this vision is fulfilled in Christ's ascension and spiritual reign. Jesus explicitly identifies Himself with the "Son of

Man" in Matthew 28:18, proclaiming, "All authority has been given to me in heaven and on earth." The imagery of clouds, often symbolizing divine presence and majesty, further underscores Christ's transcendent role as the mediator of God's kingdom, bridging the realms of heaven and earth.

Jewish eschatology was saturated with promises of restoration, as seen in prophecies like Isaiah 65:17, which speaks of "new heavens and a new earth," and Ezekiel 37:26–28, where God promises an eternal covenant and His dwelling among His people. These prophecies originally envisioned a national and physical restoration—God's people regathered, the land restored, and the temple rebuilt—offering hope amid exile and foreign oppression.

The New Testament, however, reframes these promises through the work of Christ. In Revelation 21:1–3 "a new heaven and a new earth" are presented as the culmination of Christ's redemptive mission, where the *Parousia* signifies the complete renewal of creation. Ezekiel's vision of God dwelling among His people finds its fulfillment first in the incarnation of Christ—"the Word became flesh and dwelt among us" (John 1:14)—and then in the indwelling of the Holy Spirit, through whom the Church becomes God's living temple (Ephesians 2:22).

THE COVENANTS UNVEILED IN CHRIST

Jewish eschatological hope was deeply intertwined with covenantal theology, which emphasized God's unwavering faithfulness to His promises. Together these covenants shaped Israel's expectation for divine intervention, a restored kingdom, and the indwelling presence of God with His people. The covenants established with Abraham, Moses, and David each contributed to the anticipation of restoration and renewal.

"In Christ" these covenants are not only fulfilled but transcended. Regarding the Abrahamic Covenant, Jesus—as the promised "seed" of Abraham (Galatians 3:16)—extends God's blessings to all nations through His redemptive work, fulfilling the covenant's ultimate purpose. Regarding the Mosaic Covenant, Christ fulfills the righteous demands of the Law and inaugurates a new covenant, written on the hearts of believers (Jeremiah 31:31–34; Hebrews 9:15) and bringing internal transformation. And regarding the Davidic Covenant, Jesus reigns as the eternal King, establishing a kingdom that is not of this world (John 18:36) but is fully active and revealed in the present spiritual reality that far surpasses human expectations, unveiling the eternal purposes of God.

APOCALYPSE UNVEILED: THE SPIRITUAL REALITY OF THE *PAROUSIA*

Inspired by the Spirit the New Testament writers unveil the deeper spiritual truth behind Jewish apocalyptic imagery—not as a cosmic spectacle but as the revelation of Christ's living presence. Rather than portraying the *Parousia* as a distant and cataclysmic event, they present it as a transformative reality—active, relational, and redemptive—manifested in the lives of those who walk by faith.

The *Parousia* embodies the central New Testament tension of the "already-but-not-yet": the kingdom of Christ has come and continues to unfold. Believers now experience His presence through the Holy Spirit (Colossians 1:27), even as they await the full renewal of creation (Revelation 21:5). This dual perspective does not dilute the urgency of hope; it amplifies the call to live in the light of His unveiled essence, engaging in the ongoing work of His kingdom here and now.

Living in this tension, believers are not passive observers of divine history but active participants in God's redemptive story. To understand the *Parousia* in light of Jewish eschatology is to recognize that the ancient hope of divine intervention has not been discarded—it has been fulfilled and transformed in Christ. This reality calls believers to faithfulness, perseverance, and joyful anticipation, grounded not in speculation but in the certainty of Christ's present reign.

Through this lens the apocalyptic hopes of Israel are neither abandoned nor delayed—they are made alive in ways that surpass expectation. Christ's *Parousia* offers not merely the promise of future restoration but the living reality of transformation now: His is a reign that renews lives, reconciles relationships, and reshapes communities in the light of God's redemptive purpose. The veil has been lifted. In Christ the apocalypse is no longer a fearful horizon but a radiant unveiling of the world to come—already breaking into the present through the faithful.

This theological shift—away from catastrophic expectation and toward unveiled communion—brings the ancient covenants and prophetic visions into sharp focus. In what follows we turn to the heartbeat of Jewish hope: the covenants of Abraham, Moses, and David. These promises, long held by the people of Israel, find their convergence and fulfillment in the *Parousia* of Christ, not merely as theological completion but as spiritual transformation. It is in this convergence that the kingdom of God is seen not as a return to national prominence but as a spiritual reality breaking forth into the world through the lives of the redeemed.

THE REFRAMING OF JEWISH APOCALYPTIC IMAGERY IN THE NEW TESTAMENT

Jewish apocalyptic literature—with its celestial battles, heavenly courts, and cosmic upheavals—provided a powerful symbolic vocabulary for expressing divine intervention and hope amid oppression. Texts like Daniel, 1 Enoch, and 4 Ezra gave voice to Israel's longing for God's decisive action to restore creation and vindicate the faithful. These rich metaphors offered not only consolation in suffering but a framework for anticipating the coming kingdom of God.

The New Testament writers, deeply shaped by this apocalyptic tradition, reframed these images through the lens of Christ's life, death, resurrection, and *Parousia*. Rather than emphasizing external catastrophe, they unveil the deeper spiritual meaning of apocalyptic symbols as signs of Christ's transformative reign. The *Parousia* becomes not merely a climactic future event but the present unveiling of Christ's sovereign authority—a light breaking into darkness and reordering creation through His presence.

Cosmic disturbances—such as the darkened sun, falling stars, or the heavens rolled back like a scroll—do not forecast physical destruction but signify profound spiritual realignment. In Matthew 24:29–31 these symbols echo the prophetic language of Isaiah and Joel, announcing that a new order is being established under Christ's lordship. Revelation 6:12–14, where the sky recedes and the earth trembles, reveals not the annihilation of creation but the unveiling of divine reality—the lifting of the veil between heaven and earth.

In this reframed vision the apocalyptic language serves not to terrify but to reveal. The *Parousia* is the apocalypse—the *unveiling*—of Christ's essence, His authority breaking into the world through judgment, renewal, and presence. It calls believers to see through the imagery into the spiritual transformation already underway.

JUDGMENT AND VINDICATION IN THE NEW TESTAMENT PERSPECTIVE

This unveiling includes judgment, but not in the form of external vengeance. In Jewish tradition the Day of the Lord was expected to bring both reckoning and reward, as seen in the prophetic voices of Amos and Zephaniah. It was to be a day of decisive justice—punishing the wicked and delivering the righteous.

The New Testament transforms this expectation by recentering judgment on relational proximity to Christ. Rather than rendering judgment as retribution alone, it becomes a revelation of the heart—a divine discernment that separates those who walk in communion with Christ from those who remain self-directed. The *Parousia* thus becomes not just a judgment day but a continual process of spiritual clarification.

Jesus's parable of the sheep and the goats in Matthew 25:31–46 illustrates this reorientation. The decisive criterion is not religious affiliation or eschatological knowledge but love expressed in action: feeding the hungry, welcoming the stranger, or visiting the sick. Judgment in this light is not arbitrary sentencing—it is the natural outworking of one's life bearing the imprint of Christ's presence.

In this framework judgment is not postponed to the end of the age—it is woven into the *Parousia* now. Christ's unveiled presence calls every believer to live in relational alignment with His kingdom. It is both invitation and warning: live now in union with the King, and His life will flow through you; resist Him, and that absence will be your undoing.

THE RESTORATION OF CREATION AND THE FULFILLMENT OF APOCALYPTIC HOPE IN CHRIST'S *PAROUSIA*

The restoration of creation—a central longing in Jewish eschatology—finds its ultimate expression in the *Parousia* of Christ. Prophetic texts such as Isaiah 65:17–25 and Ezekiel 37:26–28 envisioned a renewed world in which God's eternal covenant would bring lasting peace, justice, and divine presence. These visions spoke to a people shaped by exile and longing, offering hope for a time when God would dwell among His people and make all things right.

Yet the New Testament reveals a deeper and more enduring fulfillment of these promises. In Christ the restoration is not merely physical or national but spiritual and cosmic. The kingdom of God is not postponed to a future age—it breaks into the present through

Christ's reign, transforming hearts and communities even now. The *Parousia* unveils this active, redemptive presence.

Revelation 21:1–5 captures this fulfillment: a new heaven and a new earth, not replacing the old but transfiguring it. The dwelling of God with humanity becomes the defining reality. No longer will the sun or moon be needed, for the Lamb will be its light. In this vision the restoration long anticipated in Jewish tradition is realized in the unveiled presence of Christ. The true renewal of creation is found not in the rebuilding of borders or the conquest of kingdoms but in the communion between God and His redeemed people.

Jewish apocalyptic hopes often imagined a Messiah who would deliver Israel from political oppression and restore national sovereignty. This figure, drawn from images like the "Son of Man" in Daniel 7 and the servant-king in Isaiah 11, was expected to wield divine authority to overthrow worldly powers. But the New Testament reorients these expectations around the person of Jesus—not as a military liberator but as the crucified and risen Lord whose kingdom transcends time, space, and human structures.

Rather than establishing a temporal dominion, Christ inaugurates a reign marked by inward transformation and eternal purpose. His life, death, resurrection, and ascension fulfill the deepest yearnings of Israel—not by reclaiming earthly rule but by opening the way to divine communion. Colossians 1:27 declares, "Christ in you, the hope of glory." In this single phrase Paul collapses the distance between apocalyptic expectation and spiritual fulfillment. What was once longed for in the future is now realized in the believer's present life through union with Christ.

This radical reframing does not discard Jewish eschatology but transfigures it. The *Parousia* becomes the moment—and the movement—through which Christ's unveiled presence restores creation from within. The hope of national deliverance is surpassed by the glory of spiritual adoption. The longing for a temple is fulfilled in the indwelling presence of the Spirit. And the anticipation of an age to come is joined with the invitation to live in the reality of that age now.

In this light the *Parousia* is not only a hope for the end of history—it is the unveiling of Christ's reign at the center of history. It is both promise and presence, both future and now. Through the lens of Christ, the ancient hopes of Israel are fulfilled in ways that no eye had seen or heart had imagined. And through the lives of believers, this restored creation begins to shine.

JEWISH ANTICIPATION OF A WARRIOR KING AND A PHYSICAL KINGDOM

During the Second Temple period Jewish eschatology was shaped by a profound longing for a Messiah who would establish a physical kingdom through divine power and military triumph. Centuries of foreign domination—from the Babylonian exile to Hellenistic rule and Roman occupation—deepened this collective hope for national liberation. The vision of a warrior king, reminiscent of David, resonated deeply within a people forged by suffering and sustained by covenantal promise. This messianic expectation was not merely political; it was theological, rooted in the sacred texts and prophetic visions that promised justice, peace, and restoration.

Key prophetic passages gave voice to this hope. Isaiah 9:6–7 declares, "For a child will be born for us, a son will be given to us, and the government will be on His shoulders. . . . He will reign on the throne of David and over His kingdom, to establish and sustain it with justice and righteousness from now on and forever." Here the Messiah is envisioned as a just and divinely empowered ruler, restoring the Davidic throne in perpetual righteousness.

Micah 5:2–5 expands this vision: "Bethlehem . . . , one will come from you to be ruler over Israel for me. His origin is from antiquity, from ancient times. . . . He will stand and shepherd them in the strength of the LORD. . . . His greatness will extend to the ends of the earth. He will be their peace." The Messiah is both a sovereign leader and a protective shepherd, one whose dominion will bring both global influence and divine shalom.

Other prophetic texts heightened expectations of dramatic intervention. Zechariah 14:3–4 envisions the Lord Himself fighting against the nations: "Then the LORD will go out to fight against those nations as he fights on a day of battle. On that day his feet will stand on the Mount of Olives." This apocalyptic scene underscored the belief that the Messiah's arrival would usher in cosmic upheaval, divine warfare, and the decisive establishment of God's kingdom on earth.

Together these prophetic visions fostered the expectation of a Messiah who would restore Israel's sovereignty, defeat its enemies, and inaugurate a new era of peace and righteousness. This vision would stand in stark contrast to the spiritual unveiling of the Messiah in the New Testament—an unveiling that would both fulfill and radically transform these ancient hopes.

JESUS'S REINTERPRETATION OF MESSIANIC HOPES

The Jewish longing for a warrior king was shaped as much by sociopolitical struggle as by theological promise. Under Roman occupation, with its crushing taxation, military oppression, and cultural domination, Jewish communities clung to the hope of a Messiah who would bring national deliverance. Apocalyptic texts like 1 Enoch and 4 Ezra offered vivid portraits of cosmic battles and divine judgment, fueling the belief that the Messiah would arrive in power to judge the nations, vindicate Israel, and inaugurate an age of peace and prosperity.

Yet Jesus of Nazareth radically redefined these expectations. His life, death, and resurrection revealed a kingdom "not of this world" (John 18:36), rooted not in political conquest but in spiritual renewal. His mission did not conform to the imagery of earthly revolt; instead, it unveiled a kingdom founded on grace, reconciliation, and the transformation of the human heart.

The messianic promises of the Old Testament were not abandoned but fulfilled in ways that surpassed every nationalistic expectation. Isaiah 9:6–7, once read as a call for political restoration, found deeper meaning in Christ, who reigns with justice and righteousness not through war but through the Spirit. Daniel 7:13–14 described "one like a son of man" receiving eternal dominion; Jesus identified Himself with this figure when He declared, "You will see the Son of Man seated at the right hand of Power and coming on the clouds of heaven" (Matthew 26:64). After His resurrection He affirmed this fulfillment: "All authority has been given to me in heaven and on earth" (Matthew 28:18). The clouds, rich with Old Testament symbolism, signal the unveiling of Christ's divine authority—His *Parousia*—now present and active in the world.

Even the Bethlehem prophecy of Micah 5:2–5 was reoriented through Him. While Jesus indeed fulfilled its geographic detail, He also embodied the Good Shepherd who would lead not merely a nation but all of humanity into communion with God.

Jesus's teachings further clarified the nature of His reign. Rather than announcing a geopolitical revolution, He revealed a kingdom that was spiritual, present, and transformative. "The kingdom of God is not coming with something observable. . . . For you see, the kingdom of God is in your midst" (Luke 17:20–21). With these words Jesus dismantled long-standing expectations and invited His followers to recognize the nearness of God's reign—already breaking in through Him.

In the Sermon on the Mount (Matthew 5:3–10) He offered the Beatitudes not as abstract moral platitudes but as the charter of the kingdom—an inversion of worldly power that exalted humility, mercy, and purity of heart. These values did not overthrow Rome; they redefined what it meant to be truly powerful, marking those who would inherit the earth and reflect the presence of the King.

THE SUFFERING SERVANT

Jesus's deepest redefinition of messianic hope came through His identification with the suffering servant. The triumphant warrior was revealed instead as the sacrificial Redeemer. Rather than taking up arms He took up the cross, bearing the sins of the world in an act of redemptive love.

The prophet Isaiah had foreseen such a Messiah: "He was pierced because of our rebellion, crushed because of our iniquities . . . and we are healed by his wounds" (Isaiah 53:5). This vision, once overlooked or misunderstood, became the centerpiece of Christ's identity. In Mark 10:45 Jesus affirmed His mission: "The Son of Man did not come to be served, but to serve, and to give his life as a ransom for many." His suffering was not a detour but the very path to messianic fulfillment—demonstrating that true victory comes not through domination but through self-giving love.

Through His death and resurrection Jesus redefined triumph and inaugurated a new covenant of grace. Liberation was no longer framed by the fall of earthly empires but by the defeat of sin and death. Restoration was not a national project but a global invitation to be reconciled to God.

To follow this Messiah is to walk the same path of sacrificial love. Believers are called not to conquer but to serve—to embody the kingdom through humility, mercy, and peace. In doing so they participate in the ongoing *Parousia* of Christ, becoming vessels through which His reign is revealed in the world.

SIGNS OF THE KINGDOM

The miracles of Jesus were not mere demonstrations of power; they were living signs that the kingdom of God had broken into the world. Each act of healing, provision, and forgiveness fulfilled messianic expectations, while revealing the deeper spiritual reality of God's restorative reign.

When Jesus gave sight to the blind and caused the lame to walk, He fulfilled the promises of Isaiah 35:5–6 and confirmed to John's messengers that the signs of the Messiah were present (Matthew 11:5). These were not just healings—they were windows into the transformative power of the kingdom. In feeding the multitudes Jesus revealed Himself as the Good Shepherd of Psalm 23, the One who leads His people to abundant provision and rest (Matthew 14:19–20). When He forgave sins, as in the healing of the paralytic (Mark 2:5–12), He revealed the heart of the kingdom: reconciliation with God and the restoration of broken humanity.

These miracles were not confined to the past. They call believers today to recognize Christ's ongoing presence and power through the Spirit. As they extend compassion, offer forgiveness, and meet needs in love, believers become participants in the same kingdom reality. Their lives become signs of the *Parousia*—living testimonies that the reign of Christ is not only coming but already here.

THE *PAROUSIA* AS THE ULTIMATE FULFILLMENT

While Jesus inaugurated the kingdom during His earthly ministry, its fullness continues to be unveiled through the ongoing revelation of His essence in the *Parousia*. This reframes messianic hope—not as a dramatic external conquest but as a continual spiritual unveiling of Christ's reign in the hearts of those who live by faith.

Following His resurrection Jesus proclaimed, "All authority has been given to me in heaven and on earth" (Matthew 28:18). His ascension marked the enthronement of the King, and His *Parousia* began—not with spectacle but with the quiet, sovereign rule that would transform the world from within. Stephen's vision in Acts 7:55–56 offers a glimpse into this reality: Christ, standing at the right hand of God, reigning in glory even amid earthly violence and injustice. This was no delayed promise. It was the manifestation of a kingdom already in motion.

The *Parousia* invites believers to live not as bystanders but as agents of this unfolding reality. It calls them to align their lives with Christ's transformative presence and to anticipate—not with passive waiting but with active participation—the full consummation of His reign. In this way every act of faith, every expression of love, and every embodiment of the kingdom becomes a signpost of His return and a reflection of His glory already at work.

In every aspect—covenantal, prophetic, and apocalyptic—Jesus fulfills and transforms the deepest hopes of Jewish eschatology. Yet His fulfillment does not arrive with political revolution or cosmic destruction but through the quiet power of divine presence unveiled in the *Parousia*. This presence, once anticipated in shadow and symbol, now radiates through the Spirit, inviting believers into a kingdom not made by hands but shaped by surrender, love, and transformation. As we move forward we now turn to the heart of this mystery: how the *Parousia* is not merely a fulfillment of the past but the ongoing revelation of Christ's glory—a living presence that transforms every moment, every life, and every corner of creation.

CHAPTER 8

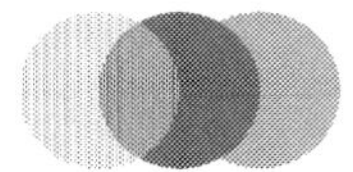

ESCHATOLOGICAL EXPECTATIONS IN JEWISH TRADITION

The concept of *Parousia* extends beyond a distant eschatological event; it is a profound revelation of Christ's glory, authority, and essence that permeates the lives of believers and the fabric of creation. Rooted in the rich theological framework of the New Testament, *Parousia* unveils Christ's presence as both an active reality and a future fulfillment. This section explores three foundational themes of *Parousia*: His glory, His authority, and the unveiling of His essence. Each contributes to a deeper understanding of the transformative power of Christ's presence.

At the heart of *Parousia* is the radiant glory of Christ, which is revealed in both His earthly incarnation and the ultimate renewal of creation. The apostle John captures this profound reality in his Gospel, declaring, "We observed his glory, the glory as the one and only Son from the Father, full of grace and truth" (John 1:14). This glory, once veiled in human form, is now accessible through the *Parousia*, transforming lives and illuminating the path to God's eternal purposes.

The New Testament presents Christ's glory as both a present experience and a future expectation. In Revelation 21:23 the ultimate fulfillment of this glory is envisioned in the New Jerusalem, where "the glory of God illuminates it, and its lamp is the Lamb." The brilliance of Christ's unveiled presence eradicates all darkness, signifying the complete restoration of God's dwelling with humanity. Yet this glory is not merely reserved for the age to come; it is actively experienced now as believers are transformed "from glory to glory" (2 Corinthians 3:18), drawing them into deeper communion with Christ.

Parousia, therefore, calls believers to recognize and reflect Christ's glory in their daily lives. His presence reshapes their character, renews their minds, and empowers them to radiate His light in a world longing for redemption. It is an invitation to live in the reality of His unveiled majesty, anticipating the day when His glory will fully permeate creation.

Parousia also serves as the ultimate revelation of Christ's sovereign authority—an authority that extends over all creation and stands as the foundation of the believer's faith. In Matthew 28:18 Jesus proclaims, "All authority has been given to me in heaven and on earth." This declaration affirms Christ's kingship, which, through *Parousia*, is continually unveiled in the present and will be fully realized in the consummation of His kingdom.

The apostle Paul echoes this truth, describing the *Parousia* as a moment when Christ's justice will be revealed to the world. In 2 Thessalonians 1:7–10 he writes that "this will take place at the revelation of the Lord Jesus from heaven with his powerful angels, when he takes vengeance with flaming fire on those who don't know God." Here Christ's authority is portrayed as both a source of judgment and a beacon of hope, bringing vindication to the faithful and ensuring the triumph of righteousness over evil.

This understanding of Christ's authority invites believers to live under His rule now, submitting every aspect of their lives to His sovereign will. *Parousia* challenges them to recognize that Christ's reign is not limited to a future event but is actively unfolding in the here and now, guiding their decisions, shaping their character, and empowering them to advance His kingdom on earth. His authority, therefore, becomes a source of confidence and strength, enabling believers to navigate the complexities of life with unwavering trust in His leadership.

Beyond the external manifestations of glory and authority, *Parousia* unveils the very essence of Christ within the lives of believers, inviting them into an intimate and transformative relationship with Him. Paul captures this reality in 2 Corinthians 3:18, stating, "We all, with unveiled faces, are looking as in a mirror at the glory of the Lord and are being transformed into the same image from glory to glory." This ongoing transformation reflects the essence of *Parousia*: Christ's presence progressively reshaping believers into His likeness.

The unveiling of Christ's essence is not confined to a distant moment in the future; it is an active process that occurs in the present as believers grow in their knowledge and experience of Him. Through the work of the Holy Spirit, they are sanctified, empowered, and conformed to His image, embodying His love, wisdom, and righteousness in their daily lives.

Parousia, in this sense, serves as a divine invitation to deeper communion with Christ, urging believers to move beyond mere external observance to an internal transformation that reflects His character. As they surrender to His presence they experience a profound renewal that touches every aspect of their being—mind, heart, and soul.

The theological themes of *Parousia*—Christ's glory, authority, and essence—offer a comprehensive framework for understanding the transformative nature of His presence. Through the lens of *Parousia*, believers are invited to behold His glory, submit to His sovereign rule, and experience the unveiling of His essence in their lives.

As they embrace this reality they are called to live with a heightened awareness of Christ's presence, allowing His transformative power to shape their identity, mission, and hope. *Parousia* is not merely an anticipation of the future but a present reality that continues to unfold, drawing believers into a deeper relationship with their Savior and empowering them to reflect His glory in the world.

In the following section we will explore how specific passages, such as 2 Thessalonians 2:8–9 and the apocalyptic visions of John, further illuminate the significance of *Parousia* in revealing Christ's ultimate victory and eternal reign.

THE BRIGHTNESS AND TRANSFORMATIVE POWER OF CHRIST'S *PAROUSIA*

The *Parousia* of Christ is often depicted in Scripture as a radiant and transformative reality, a divine unveiling that dispels darkness and reveals the fullness of God's truth. This profound concept is illuminated through key New Testament passages, particularly in Paul's letters and the apocalyptic visions of John. Through their writings the *Parousia* is presented not as a distant or purely future event but as an active and ongoing revelation that reshapes the hearts and minds of believers.

Paul's use of the Greek term *epiphaneia*, meaning "manifestation," "appearing," or "brightness," underscores the dazzling and transformative nature of Christ's *Parousia*. In 2 Thessalonians 2:8 he writes that "the Lord Jesus will destroy [the lawless one] with the breath of his mouth and will bring him to nothing at the appearance [*epiphaneia*] of his coming [*parousia*]." This powerful coupling of terms—*epiphaneia* and *parousia*—conveys the *Parousia* not merely as a return but as a radiant unveiling of divine glory. It is a force of illumination that exposes falsehood, banishes fear, and establishes the supremacy of Christ's truth over the forces of darkness.

The brightness of Christ's *Parousia* is not merely an external spectacle; it is an internal spiritual reality that profoundly affects those who experience it. This radiance reveals the depth of God's grace and love, drawing believers out of sin and into the fullness of His light. It is through this transformative power that followers of Christ are continually renewed and empowered to reflect His glory in their lives and to expose the "the lawless one."

The book of Revelation expands upon the grandeur of Christ's unveiled majesty, portraying Him as the exalted King and High Priest whose presence permeates all creation. In Revelation 1:12–16 John witnesses a breathtaking vision of the risen Christ, with eyes "like a fiery flame" and a face shining "like the sun at full strength." This powerful depiction communicates the overwhelming brilliance and authority of Christ, emphasizing that His *Parousia* is not confined to a future event but is a present and continuous reality.

If, as some scholars suggest, Revelation was written prior to the destruction of the temple and Jerusalem in AD 70, then certain visions, particularly those of judgment and upheaval, did have a predictive element for John's original audience. Yet even then these prophecies were not intended only to forecast events; they revealed the deeper spiritual reality of Christ's enthronement and the unraveling of the Old Covenant order. What was once predictive has now become part of an ongoing unveiling—Christ's *Parousia*—through which His presence continues to reshape both the Church and the cosmos in preparation for the new creation.

ONGOING SPIRITUAL TRANSFORMATION OVER SUDDEN PHYSICAL SPECTACLE

While the New Testament contains vivid descriptions of Christ's appearing, it consistently presents the *Parousia* as primarily a transformative, relational reality rather than a distant physical phenomenon. The emphasis is placed not on waiting for a dramatic conclusion of history but on participating in the ongoing work of Christ's presence in the here and now.

Paul writes in Philippians 1:6, "He who started a good work in you will carry it on to completion until the day of Christ Jesus." This verse underscores that the *Parousia* is not a singular event but a process of continual growth and sanctification. Christ's presence is actively shaping believers, molding them into His image and calling them to align their lives with His kingdom values.

The focus of *Parousia*, therefore, is on inward transformation, a process of becoming more like Christ in character, love, and faithfulness. The New Testament encourages believers to embrace this reality, living in daily expectation of God's transformative work rather than becoming preoccupied with speculative timelines and future signs.

The New Testament presents the *Parousia* within the framework of the "already but not yet" reality of God's kingdom. In Colossians 1:27 Paul speaks of "Christ in you, the hope of glory," affirming that believers experience Christ's presence now while eagerly awaiting the full realization of His kingdom. This tension invites Christians to live with a dual perspective, recognizing the present power of Christ's rule in their lives while holding fast to the promise of its complete fulfillment in the future.

Believers are called to embody the values of the coming kingdom in their daily lives, acting as agents of renewal and reconciliation in a world still awaiting the full revelation of God's purposes.

THE HOLY SPIRIT AS THE MEDIATOR OF CHRIST'S *PAROUSIA*

Integral to the experience of *Parousia* is the work of the Holy Spirit, who serves as the agent through whom Christ's presence is revealed and experienced. Jesus assured His disciples in John 16:13, "When the Spirit of truth comes, he will guide you into all the truth." This guiding presence of the Spirit allows believers to perceive and experience Christ's *Parousia* in their lives, leading them into deeper understanding, communion, and transformation.

After Christ's physical departure the disciples were able to "see" Him in a new and profound way through the indwelling presence of the Holy Spirit. In John 16:16–33 Jesus explained to His followers that, although He would no longer be physically present, the Spirit would make His presence real to them in powerful ways. This shift from physical sight to spiritual perception remains a central reality of *Parousia* today: believers are invited to experience Christ's presence through the Spirit's work in their hearts and lives.

The Spirit's role in unveiling Christ's essence allows believers to experience His presence in ways that transcend the limitations of the physical world, fostering a relationship that is deeply personal and transformative. The indwelling of the Holy Spirit empowers believers to live in the reality of Christ's *Parousia*, guiding them toward deeper faith, obedience, and intimacy with God. Through the Spirit they are sanctified, strengthened, and called to reflect Christ's character in their daily interactions.

The ongoing revelation of Christ through the Spirit calls believers to actively engage in the mission of God's kingdom. Prayer, worship, and acts of service become avenues through which the *Parousia* is made manifest in the lives of believers. As they yield to the Spirit's work they become living testimonies of Christ's presence, embodying His love and truth in a world longing for redemption. *Parousia* is not a passive waiting but an active participation in the unfolding plan of redemption. Believers are invited to live out the reality of Christ's presence in their relationships, communities, and the broader world, reflecting His love and justice in tangible ways. As we embrace this calling we become conduits of the transformative power of *Parousia*, bringing light and hope to a world in need.

The *Parousia*, as revealed in Scripture, is a profound and multifaceted reality that encompasses the brightness of Christ's presence, the transformative work of the Spirit, and the ongoing call to live in anticipation of His kingdom. It is not merely a future event but an invitation to experience Christ's authority, glory, and essence in the present.

Through the insights of Paul and the apocalyptic visions of John, believers are reminded that Christ's *Parousia* dispels darkness and lawlessness, transforms lives, and calls them into active participation in God's redemptive mission. As they walk in the light of His presence they are empowered to reflect His glory, embody His kingdom, and await with hope the day when His fullness will be revealed.

CHRIST'S TRANSFORMATIVE PRESENCE IN THE CHURCH AND IN BELIEVERS

The *Parousia*, understood as the continuous unveiling of Christ's essence, is profoundly relational in nature. It is not simply an event to be anticipated but an active and transformative presence that shapes the lives of individual believers and the collective body of the Church. This relational dynamic provides a foundation for deepening personal faith, cultivating spiritual maturity, and embracing the believer's identity in Christ.

John 1:12 declares, "To all who did receive him, he gave the right to be children of God." This passage captures the essence of the relational aspect of the *Parousia*, revealing that receiving Christ is not a one-time occurrence but an ongoing transformative journey. Believers are invited into an intimate relationship with God, one that continually reshapes their identity and purpose.

Receiving Christ's presence is more than a passive acceptance; it is an active, daily engagement that redefines believers' understanding of themselves and their purpose. The *Parousia*, as an ongoing revelation, calls believers to embrace their identity as children of God, allowing His transformative presence to permeate every aspect of life.

While this transformation begins at the individual level, it extends into the shared life of the Church—the gathered community of believers united by faith in Christ. As members of God's family, believers are called to reflect Christ's essence together, expressing unity, love, and service within the Church community. This communal reflection of the *Parousia* fosters a culture of belonging and spiritual growth. Believers are invited to daily receive Christ's presence through prayer, Scripture, and obedience, allowing His transformation to shape both their character and their relationships. Members of the Church, as Christ's body, are called to embrace one another as partners in a unified whole, embodying His love in mutual care, humility, and mission.

SANCTIFICATION THROUGH CHRIST'S PRESENCE

Paul's prayer in 1 Thessalonians 3:13 expresses the dual aspect of the *Parousia*, both as a present process and a future hope: "May He make your hearts blameless in holiness before our God and Father at the coming (*Parousia*) of our Lord Jesus with all his saints." This verse highlights the transformative power of Christ's presence in both personal sanctification and communal holiness.

The *Parousia* continually purifies and refines believers, calling them to align their hearts and actions with Christ's holiness. This inner transformation leads to an authentic and blameless walk before God, demonstrating His sanctifying work in their lives. As individuals are sanctified, the unity of the Church is strengthened. The collective body of Christ becomes a visible representation of His presence in the world, reflecting the values of His kingdom—love, justice, and righteousness.

The Church, empowered by the ongoing unveiling of Christ's essence, is called to act as both a recipient and a vessel of His transformative presence. This mission requires believers to embody and share Christ's essence in every aspect of life. As ambassadors of Christ, believers represent His presence in the world. Paul's words, "We are ambassadors for Christ, since God is making his appeal through us," remind the Church of its calling to reflect Christ's love, grace, and truth in their interactions and witness (2 Corinthians 5:20).

The Holy Spirit is the empowering agent of the *Parousia*, equipping believers to fulfill their mission through worship, service, and evangelism. "You will receive power when the Holy Spirit has come on you, and you will be my witnesses." This empowerment ensures that the Church remains a dynamic force for transformation in the world (Acts 1:8).

SPIRITUAL PREPAREDNESS AND VIGILANCE IN LIGHT OF THE *PAROUSIA*

The Synoptic Gospels and Revelation offer vital teachings on spiritual preparedness, underscoring the necessity of vigilance and faithful anticipation of Christ's unveiled presence. The parable of the ten virgins (Matthew 25:1–13) serves as a poignant illustration of spiritual readiness. The wise virgins who kept their lamps filled with oil symbolize those who maintain an ongoing, living connection to Christ. Readiness, therefore, is not passive waiting but an active, relational engagement with Christ through faith, worship, and obedience. Believers must cultivate an attitude of readiness through an intimate, ongoing relationship "in Christ." This readiness will transform a believer's attitude to one of Spiritual vigilance, leading to a life marked by the fruit of the Spirit (Galatians 5:22–23) and preparing believers to fully embrace Christ's unveiled presence.

Revelation offers a vision of Christ's unveiled presence in all its glory. John describes Christ's majestic appearance, inspiring awe and reverence among believers. The vision of the New Jerusalem reveals the ultimate culmination of the *Parousia*—God dwelling fully with His people (Revelation 1:12–16; 21:3–5). These passages invite believers to deepen their intimacy with Christ through worship and surrender. Christ's unveiled presence motivates believers to align their lives with His kingdom values of holiness, justice, and love. Allow Christ's unveiled presence to shape your personal devotion and inspire corporate worship. Believers can align daily life with the values of the New Jerusalem, embodying Christ's character in every sphere of influence.

The relational dimensions of the *Parousia* call believers to embrace Christ's unveiled presence as an active and ongoing reality. Whether through personal transformation, communal sanctification, or active participation in the Church's mission, believers are invited to experience and reflect the transformative power of His presence.

This profound reality challenges believers to action. Believers are called to continually receive Christ's presence in their lives, deepening their identity as children of God. They are called to pursue holiness both individually and collectively, embodying the values of Christ's kingdom. They are called to serve as ambassadors of His presence, empowered by the Holy Spirit to reflect His light in the world. And they are called to remain spiritually vigilant and prepared, living in anticipation of the fullness of His unveiled glory.

Through the *Parousia* believers are summoned to an ever-deepening relationship with Christ—one that transforms not only their lives but also the world around them, as they reveal His essence in every aspect of life.

The *Parousia*, as revealed in the New Testament, serves as the bridge between the theological and eschatological themes of the Old and New Testaments, connecting God's redemptive plan to its culmination in the person and work of Jesus Christ. It fulfills the covenantal promises given to Abraham, the prophetic visions of the coming Messiah, and the eschatological hope of divine intervention to restore creation. Rooted in Jewish expectations yet expanded through Christ's life, death, resurrection, and ascension, *Parousia* unveils the fullness of God's glory and authority. It is both the fulfillment of ancient promises and the ongoing reality of God's presence in the lives of believers.

LIVING THE *PAROUSIA*: THE CHURCH'S MISSION AND IDENTITY

The New Testament presents *Parousia* not merely as a distant event on the horizon of history but as a present and transformative reality. It calls believers to live with an acute awareness of Christ's unveiled presence, empowering them to reflect His essence in their daily lives while anticipating the full realization of His kingdom.

Living in the reality of *Parousia* requires a continual openness to Christ's transformative work. It reshapes the believers' identity and actions, calling them to embody the values of God's kingdom: love, justice, and holiness. The unveiled presence of Christ in believers fosters a life of worship, service, and mission, ensuring that faith is not static but a dynamic engagement with God's ongoing work.

Parousia embodies the theological tension of living between the "already" of Christ's reign and the "not yet" of its ultimate fulfillment. Believers experience His presence now—guiding, comforting, and transforming them—while also longing for the day when all things will be made new. This dual perspective shapes Christian living, instilling both urgency and hopeful expectation in worship, discipleship, and mission.

The *Parousia* is an invitation for the Church to fully embrace Christ's unveiled presence and actively participate in His redemptive mission. This participation is both personal and communal, reflecting Christ's light in a world longing for hope and transformation.

As the body of Christ, the Church is called to reflect His glory through worship, unity, and faithful living. The *Parousia* empowers believers to embody Christ's love and reconciliation, serving as a living testimony to the transformative power of His presence.

Parousia drives the Church's mission forward, inspiring it to proclaim the gospel and demonstrate God's justice and compassion in tangible ways. As the unveiled presence of Christ continues to work through the Spirit, the Church is called to actively engage in the world, testifying to the hope and renewal found in Him. Individual believers are called to reflect Christ's presence in all interactions, embodying His love and grace.

Throughout the New Testament key passages illustrate the multifaceted nature of *Parousia* as both an immediate and a future reality. Matthew 24 emphasizes vigilance and readiness for Christ's unveiled presence. First Thessalonians 4 highlights the hope of reunion with Christ and the unity of believers in His presence, while 2 Thessalonians 2 portrays the triumph of Christ's presence over darkness and evil. And John 1:12 and 1 Thessalonians 3:13 reveal the relational and transformative dimensions of *Parousia* in shaping the believer's life.

The unveiling of Christ's essence through the *Parousia* carries profound theological implications, shaping how believers understand and experience God's redemptive plan. *Parousia* reveals the faithfulness of God in fulfilling His covenantal promises and prophetic declarations, uniting Old Testament expectations with New Testament fulfillment in Christ. It assures believers that God's redemptive work, which began with Abraham, finds its completion in Christ's presence. Experiencing Christ's unveiled presence deepens personal devotion and transforms corporate worship. Believers respond with gratitude, awe, and obedience, aligning their lives with the ongoing work of Christ and celebrating His presence in their midst.

The *Parousia* defines the Church's mission and identity, calling believers to act as ambassadors of Christ's kingdom. It challenges the Church to embody His justice, love, and holiness, serving as a living foretaste of the New Jerusalem. *Parousia* is not a passive waiting but an active, lived experience. It invites believers to engage in Christ's transformative work through prayer, service, and witness, living in expectation while fully participating in God's mission.

Believers recognize Christ as the fulfillment of God's promises, trusting in His continued faithfulness. Christ's presence transforms your spiritual life and guides your worship. Believers are called to live as representatives of Christ's kingdom, actively engaging in His redemptive work and thus participating in the unfolding of God's plan, embracing His unveiled presence in all aspects of life.

This chapter has revealed that the *Parousia* is far more than an end-times event; it is a transformative reality that reshapes the believer's relationship with Christ, the Church's mission, and the trajectory of God's redemptive plan. Through the *Parousia* Christ's essence is continually unveiled, calling believers to reflect His presence, live with purpose, and participate in the renewal of all things.

As believers embrace the dual reality of the *Parousia*—living in Christ's presence now while anticipating the fullness of His kingdom—they are empowered to reflect His glory, embody His love, and advance His mission in the world. Through worship, mission, and faithful living they testify to the ongoing reality of Christ's unveiled presence, offering hope and transformation to a world longing for redemption.

Ultimately, the *Parousia* stands as both a present truth and a future hope, an invitation to experience the fullness of Christ's presence today and to eagerly anticipate the glorious fulfillment of God's redemptive plan.

PARALLELS TO MODERN EXPECTATIONS OF A PHYSICAL SECOND COMING

Modern Christian eschatology often echoes the Jewish anticipation of a physical kingdom and visible messianic reign. Certain theological traditions, particularly premillennialism, emphasize a literal interpretation of Christ's future return to establish an earthly reign.

Revelation 20:1–6 describes a thousand-year reign of Christ, interpreted in premillennial thought as a future physical kingdom on earth: "They came to life and reigned with Christ for a thousand years." This view envisions a singular future event marked by visible divine intervention and justice, mirroring ancient Jewish expectations. Both premillennial Christian theology and Second Temple Jewish eschatology anticipate a tangible physical restorative transformation of the world whereby divine power is visibly manifested. The hope for God's direct intervention to rectify injustices and establish His rule resonates across both perspectives.

While the anticipation of Christ's return is vital, an overemphasis on a physical reign can obscure the spiritual realities that Jesus emphasized. In John 18:36 Jesus clarified, "My kingdom is not of this world." A fixation on external events risks neglecting the inward transformation His reign brings.

Apocalyptic texts often use symbolic language to convey spiritual truths, and a purely literal interpretation can diminish their deeper meanings. For example, Revelation's cosmic imagery is best understood as depicting Christ's sovereign authority rather than predicting specific future events.

Throughout His ministry Jesus redefined Jewish eschatological expectations by unveiling the kingdom of God as a present spiritual reality rather than a distant geopolitical event. His teachings shifted the focus from national restoration to personal transformation, emphasizing humility, mercy, righteousness, and spiritual rebirth as marks of true kingdom citizenship.

In His parables Jesus revealed the "already-but-not-yet" nature of the kingdom, illustrating both the patience of God's redemptive plan and the call for believers to participate in it through faithful living. His metaphors, such as the vine and the branches, emphasized intimate union with Him as the source of spiritual fruitfulness and kingdom life.

The cross and resurrection further redefined messianic victory, not as conquest but as liberation. Jesus declared that by being "lifted up" He would draw all people to Himself (John 12:32), signaling that His death would mark the judgment of the world and the casting out of its ruler. His mission, as proclaimed in Luke 4 and fulfilled in His ministry, brought spiritual healing, freedom, and restoration, revealing the true nature of divine kingship.

In light of His teachings, the *Parousia* should not be reduced to a distant dramatic event. Rather, it is an ongoing unveiling of Christ's reign, a spiritual reality believers are called to live in now. This transformation is both personal and communal: abiding "in Christ," reflecting His values, and anticipating the full restoration to come. Before we can understand the fullness of the *Parousia*, however, we must first address some common assumptions that have shaped—and at times distorted—its meaning.

ADDRESSING COMMON ASSUMPTIONS

A prevalent assumption surrounding the second coming is the expectation of grand, visible, cosmic upheavals. Many envision the event in terms of literal celestial disturbances and cataclysmic signs, often shaped by popular interpretations of apocalyptic imagery. Yet such perspectives risk overshadowing Christ's own emphasis on the present spiritual reality of the kingdom and its inward transformation.

In Matthew 24:29–31 Jesus says, "The sun will be darkened, and the moon will not shed its light; the stars will fall from the sky, and the powers of the heavens will be shaken. Then the sign of the Son of Man will appear in the sky." While often interpreted literally, this language draws upon a rich tradition of Jewish apocalyptic symbolism. These cosmic signs are not merely descriptions of physical events but expressions of profound spiritual shifts. The darkening of the heavens and the falling of stars symbolize the collapse of worldly powers and the unveiling of Christ's authority. His reign brings about a reordering of reality—transforming the world from the inside out.

The prophetic books of the Old Testament, such as Joel and Amos, employ similarly vivid imagery. These visions of judgment and renewal were never meant to serve as precise blueprints for the future but as theological portraits of God's decisive intervention. Joel 2:1–2 and Amos 5:18–20 use the motif of celestial disturbance to announce the Day of the Lord—a time of upheaval not to be feared by the faithful but to be understood as the inauguration of God's transformative work. In the same way the celestial signs in Matthew 24 illustrate the spiritual impact of Christ's coming and the establishment of His kingdom, not through external spectacle but through divine revelation.

Recognizing the symbolic nature of apocalyptic literature allows for a spiritually richer and theologically more consistent understanding of the *Parousia*. Rather than pointing to a singular future spectacle, these symbols highlight the ongoing, present unveiling of Christ's reign—a kingdom breaking into history and reshaping it from within.

ALIGNING THE SECOND COMING WITH BIBLICAL THEOLOGY

An undue fixation on physical signs and future predictions often leads believers to overlook the transformative realities already inaugurated through Christ's first coming. Jesus's words in Luke 17:21, "The kingdom of God is in your midst," challenge the expectation of a distant reign by affirming the kingdom's active presence wherever Christ is received.

While many in the Jewish tradition expected the restoration of a physical kingdom, the true fulfillment of those hopes is found in the spiritual reality Christ has brought—transcending time, space, and political boundaries. This is the mystery now revealed: that Christ's indwelling presence transforms hearts, communities, and the world.

The New Testament affirms this unfolding reality. Paul declares in Colossians 1:27 that the hope of glory is not in a future spectacle but in "Christ in you." Likewise, in 1 Corinthians 15:51–52 Paul speaks of the transformation that occurs "in a moment," not just as a final event but as an ongoing process conforming believers to Christ's image.

The *Parousia*, then, is not merely an endpoint on a timeline—it is the culmination of Christ's redemptive mission. It is His unveiled presence progressively transforming creation and revealing the glory of God through His people.

This reality is rooted deeply in Jewish eschatological hope. The "Day of the LORD," as described in Isaiah 2:12–17 and Zephaniah 1:14–18, represents a time of divine judgment, purification, and restoration. These prophetic visions reach their spiritual fulfillment in the ongoing work of Christ, who purifies and renews not only hearts but all of creation. As Paul writes in Romans 8:19–21, "The creation eagerly waits with anticipation for God's sons to be revealed. . . . The creation itself will also be set free from the bondage to decay." The unveiling of Christ's presence is both the means and the goal of cosmic renewal.

In this light the vision of the New Jerusalem becomes more than a future hope—it is the eschatological symbol of fulfilled communion. In Revelation 21:2–3 the holy city comes down from heaven as a bride adorned for her husband, revealing God's eternal presence among His people. This is not merely the promise of a future city but the picture of perfect, unbroken fellowship—Christ's unveiled glory as the eternal light and life of a renewed creation.

LIVING IN THE "ALREADY-NOT-YET" REALITY

The tension between what has already come and what is not yet fully revealed lies at the heart of the believer's experience of the *Parousia*. Christ reigns now, but His reign is not yet fully realized. This tension invites us into a life of faithful anticipation and meaningful participation in the unfolding kingdom.

The messianic expectation of a conquering king is redefined through the cross. Christ's triumph comes through humility, sacrifice, and love. The apocalyptic promises of deliverance and judgment are fulfilled not through military conquest or geopolitical shifts but through the Spirit's quiet, transformative power working in the hearts of those who believe.

To live in the present reality of the *Parousia*, believers must embrace the unveiled presence of Christ and allow His essence to reshape their priorities and relationships. We are called to reflect His kingdom values through daily acts of justice, mercy, and love. The Holy Spirit empowers us to embody the kingdom—not through striving or spectacle but through a surrendered life that reveals Christ's glory.

As we navigate the complexities of eschatological expectation, the vision of the New Jerusalem offers a compelling image of the *Parousia*'s final fulfillment. It is the culmination of God's redemptive work: the restoration of creation, the renewal of hearts, and the eternal communion between God and His people. This future vision compels us not to retreat from the world but to live in it as citizens of another kingdom—embodying Christ's essence as we await the fullness of His appearing.

CONCLUDING REFLECTION

In light of Jewish eschatological expectations, the *Parousia* reorients the believer's gaze. It invites us to see beyond temporal kingdoms, celestial signs, and popular speculation—to behold the mystery that Christ is already present and His kingdom is already advancing. The true hope of Israel—the restoration of all things, the reign of righteousness, and the indwelling of God with His people—has begun in Christ and continues through His Spirit. The *Parousia* is not a distant disruption but a divine unveiling. As His presence is revealed in us and through us, we participate in the redemptive movement of God, anticipating the day when all things will be made new.

CHAPTER 9

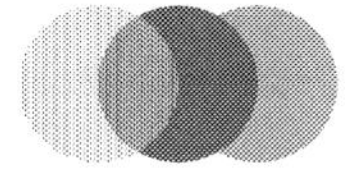

THE *PAROUSIA* AS A HERMENEUTIC

The *Parousia*, understood as the spiritual unveiling of Christ's essence, calls believers to experience His transformative presence in the present while eagerly anticipating its ultimate fulfillment in eternity. This dual nature—the "already" and the "not yet"—necessitates a thoughtful and biblically sound interpretative approach to navigate its present realities and eschatological implications. An approach to interpreting Scripture is called a hermeneutic. Put differently, hermeneutics can be defined as the art and science of interpreting Scripture. A good hermeneutic serves as the bridge between ancient contexts and contemporary application. Reading Scripture through the lens of the *Parousia* allows believers to align our understanding of the *Parousia* with Scripture's overarching theological vision.

While previous discussions have emphasized the *Parousia's* theological and practical impact on individuals and the Church, this chapter shifts focus to the interpretive principles that illuminate its deeper spiritual truths. Through a Christ-centered hermeneutic believers are equipped to discern the unfolding reality of Christ's presence and its ultimate consummation within the grand narrative of Scripture.

Interpreting the *Parousia* requires an engagement with the diverse literary styles of the Bible—metaphor, parable, prophecy, and historical narrative—each offering unique insights into God's redemptive plan.

Jesus Himself provided the foundation for this approach through His teaching methods. Throughout His ministry He employed metaphor, parable, and symbolic language to reveal profound spiritual realities. These tools were not meant to obscure meaning but to invite faith-filled individuals to perceive the deeper dimensions of God's kingdom. Similarly, a Christ-centered hermeneutic enables believers to recognize the *Parousia* as an ongoing revelation of Christ's presence—one that transforms our personal lives and enriches our faith communities.

This chapter will first outline the essential hermeneutical principles that guide a faithful interpretation of the *Parousia*. It will then explore practical applications of these principles to key biblical texts and conclude with an examination of how Jesus's teaching methods provide a spiritually rich approach to understanding the *Parousia*. Ultimately, the goal is to equip believers with the interpretive tools necessary to deepen our awareness of Christ's unveiled presence and inspire us to embody His essence in a world longing for redemption.

FOUNDATION FOR HERMENEUTIC: THE TEACHING METHODS OF JESUS

Interpreting the *Parousia* through a spiritual lens offers a profound way to honor the theological richness and literary diversity of Scripture. The Bible frequently employs symbolic and metaphorical language, emphasizing spiritual realities that challenge readers to look beyond surface interpretations and discern the deeper divine truths embedded within the text. This interpretive approach reveals the *Parousia* not merely as an eschatological event to anticipate but as a present and transformative experience of Christ's ongoing presence.

The foundation for this approach is found in the teaching methods of Jesus Himself. Throughout His ministry Jesus consistently used physical imagery to communicate profound spiritual truths, redirecting His audience's focus from visible, temporal realities to the unseen and eternal. In John 18:36 Jesus declares, "My kingdom is not of this world," shifting the emphasis from earthly dominion to the spiritual nature of His reign. This statement, as we have seen, challenges conventional expectations of a political Messiah and reveals the deeper reality of His kingdom as a spiritual realm that transcends worldly power structures.

Similarly, in Luke 17:20–21 Jesus states, "The kingdom of God is in your midst," inviting His followers to recognize the presence of God's reign both within their hearts and within their community. This teaching underscores that the *Parousia* is not confined to a future event but is already unfolding in the lives of believers who embrace Christ's presence. The kingdom is not a distant promise but an immediate reality, shaping the way believers live and interact with the world around them.

By adopting a hermeneutical framework that prioritizes spiritual interpretation, believers are empowered to perceive the *Parousia* as an ongoing and dynamic reality rather than merely a distant physical event. This perspective fosters a deeper communion with Christ and a greater alignment with His mission, encouraging believers to embody His essence in their daily lives. Understanding the *Parousia* in this way transforms Christian living, moving it beyond passive anticipation into active participation in the unfolding of God's redemptive plan. Through this approach the unveiling of Christ's presence becomes a guiding force, shaping worship, mission, and the believer's relationship with God and others.

KEY HERMENEUTICAL PRINCIPLES: CONTEXT, GENRE, SCRIPTURAL HARMONY, CHRIST-CENTRICITY

A faithful interpretation of the *Parousia* requires adherence to several foundational hermeneutical principles, each of which provides crucial insights into its meaning and application within the broader narrative of Scripture. These principles guide believers in understanding the *Parousia* not merely as a future event but as an ongoing spiritual reality that reveals Christ's presence and transformation in their lives.

The principle of context emphasizes the necessity of interpreting Scripture within its immediate literary, historical, and theological setting to grasp its intended meaning accurately. For example, in Hebrews 9:28 the imagery of the High Priest appearing a second time draws directly from Jewish temple practices, underscoring the spiritual redemption accomplished through Christ. Rather than pointing to a physical return in the sense of earthly expectation, this passage highlights the spiritual fulfillment of Christ's atonement, revealing the completeness of His redemptive work. This contextual approach ensures that interpretations remain faithful to the original intent of the passage, while aligning with the overarching themes of Scripture, safeguarding against misapplications or distortions.

Recognizing the genre of a biblical passage is another essential interpretive principle, as different literary forms convey truth in distinct ways. Apocalyptic literature, such as the book of Revelation, employs rich symbolism to communicate profound spiritual realities. In Revelation 5:6, for instance, the image of the Lamb represents Christ's sacrificial essence rather than a literal depiction of events. Similarly, the New Jerusalem described in Revelation 21:2 serves as a metaphor for the spiritual dwelling of God among His people rather than a physical city awaiting construction. By considering genre believers can avoid overly literal interpretations that risk distorting the intended theological message and instead focus on the deeper spiritual truths embedded within the text.

Another crucial principle is the understanding that Scripture interprets Scripture. Individual passages must be examined within the broader biblical narrative to allow Scripture to clarify and illuminate itself. Jesus's statement in John 18:36, "My kingdom is not of this world," finds further clarity in Luke 17:21, where He affirms that "the kingdom of God is in your midst." Together these passages depict the *Parousia* as an unveiling of Christ's presence in the spiritual realm rather than a geopolitical event confined to human expectations. This interpretive approach ensures theological consistency and protects against isolated readings that may lead to misinterpretation or doctrinal imbalance.

At the heart of biblical interpretation lies the principle of Christ-centricity, which asserts that Christ is the ultimate key to understanding Scripture. All interpretations must align with His life, teachings, and mission. In Matthew 5:17 Jesus affirms, "I did not come to abolish [the Law] but to fulfill," establishing Himself as the fulfillment of Old Testament expectations. Through this lens the *Parousia* is best understood as the ultimate revelation of Christ's essence, fulfilling both prophetic hopes and the New Testament's vision of redemption. Similarly, in John 8:12 Jesus declares, "I am the light of the world," echoing the prophecy of Isaiah 42:6, where the Servant of the Lord is described as a light to the nations. This light represents spiritual illumination, inviting believers into the transformative reality of Christ's unveiled presence, which continues to shape and empower our lives.

The interpretive principles of context, genre, scriptural harmony, and Christ-centricity provide a robust framework for understanding the *Parousia* as both a present reality and a future hope. By grounding their interpretation in these foundational principles, believers can develop a richer and more accurate perspective of the *Parousia's* significance, moving beyond a simplistic expectation of future events to an active engagement with Christ's ongoing presence.

Embracing these hermeneutical principles allows believers to experience the unfolding revelation of Christ's essence in our daily lives and empowers us to actively embody His presence in the world. As we deepen our understanding of the *Parousia*, we are called to align our lives with God's redemptive mission, reflecting the transformative power of Christ's kingdom in our relationships, communities, and personal spiritual journeys. In doing so we become living testimonies of the *Parousia*, revealing Christ's light and love to a world in need of His redemptive presence.

HERMENEUTICS AS A SPIRITUAL DISCIPLINE

Interpreting Scripture is not merely an intellectual endeavor; it is a profound spiritual discipline that fosters deeper communion with Christ. Through the application of Christ-centered hermeneutical principles, believers are invited to move beyond superficial readings of the Bible to uncover the divine realities embedded within its text. This interpretive process allows us to discern the ongoing unveiling of Christ's presence and align our lives with His transformative mission. By engaging with Scripture in this way, believers develop a richer understanding of the *Parousia*—not merely as a distant future event but as a present and active spiritual reality shaping our faith and daily walk with God.

Applying hermeneutical principles to the *Parousia* equips believers with the ability to discern spiritual truths, aligning our understanding with the deeper dimensions of God's kingdom. Scripture consistently invites believers to look beyond the literal and recognize the *Parousia* as the continuous revelation of Christ's presence in our lives. This understanding encourages believers to align themselves with Christ's mission, moving from passive anticipation to active participation in His transformative work. By embracing the *Parousia* as a dynamic, ongoing reality, believers are called to embody Christ's essence in their daily interactions, relationships, and spiritual pursuits.

Furthermore, this alignment enables believers to participate fully in God's kingdom, allowing the unveiled presence of Christ to shape our worship, our service to others, and our overarching mission in the world. Through these insights we as believers are empowered to engage with Scripture in ways that enrich our faith and equip us to advance Christ's redemptive work in a world longing for His presence.

A Christ-centered hermeneutic reveals that the *Parousia* is fundamentally about Christ's ongoing spiritual presence and revelation rather than a distant, singular physical event. This understanding challenges believers to cultivate an awareness of Christ's active presence through the Holy Spirit, integrating this reality into our daily lives. In John 14:16–17 Jesus assures His disciples of the indwelling of the Holy Spirit, promising that He will remain with them and within them, offering a foretaste of eternal communion with God. This passage highlights the transformative nature of the *Parousia* as an ongoing spiritual reality, calling believers to experience faith not as a distant hope but as a lived encounter with Christ's presence in the here and now.

Viewing the *Parousia* as a present spiritual reality profoundly deepens the believer's engagement with both worship and mission. Worship moves beyond mere anticipation of future fulfillment and becomes a celebration of Christ's unveiled presence now, shaping the way believers respond to Him in prayer, praise, and service. Mission, likewise, becomes an active partnership with God, as believers reveal His essence through their love, service, and proclamation of the gospel. Revelation 21:3 presents the image of the New Jerusalem, describing God's dwelling among His people. This image points not only to the future culmination of God's kingdom but also to the present reality of the Church as His dwelling place. This perspective challenges believers to live as citizens of the New Jerusalem today, embodying God's holiness, love, and justice in their communities and spheres of influence.

Apocalyptic symbols found in Scripture, such as the New Jerusalem and the marriage of the Lamb, are not merely distant eschatological hopes; they are spiritual truths actively unfolding in the present. Believers are called to engage in the ongoing work of God's kingdom by living as His Spirit's dwelling place and reflecting His glory to the world. In Revelation 21:23 the New Jerusalem is described as being illuminated by the glory of God and the Lamb, signifying that Christ's essence is the true light sustaining His people. This imagery calls believers to embody Christ's light, serving as beacons of hope and transformation within their communities. By embracing these spiritual realities believers participate in the unfolding of God's redemptive plan and experience the *Parousia* as a continuous unveiling of Christ's transformative presence.

Ultimately, interpreting the *Parousia* through a Christ-centered hermeneutical approach invites believers into a deeper awareness of Christ's ongoing work within us and the world around us. By applying these principles to our understanding of Scripture, believers are not only equipped to discern spiritual truths but are also inspired to actively reflect Christ's glory and advance His mission. This approach fosters a dynamic faith that embraces both the "already" and the "not yet" aspects of God's kingdom, encouraging believers to live in joyful anticipation while fully engaging in the present realities of Christ's unveiled presence.

CHRIST'S USE OF METAPHOR AND PARABLES

Throughout His ministry, as we have seen, Jesus employed metaphors and parables to reveal profound spiritual truths, inviting His followers to embrace the deeper realities of God's kingdom. These teaching methods provide a valuable framework for interpreting the *Parousia* in a spiritually meaningful way, enabling believers to perceive its ongoing and transformative presence in their lives.

Jesus often used tangible images to communicate profound spiritual realities, inviting reflection and transformation through metaphor. In John 15:1–8 He presents the metaphor of the vine and the branches to illustrate the intimate connection between Himself and His followers. He emphasizes the necessity of abiding in Him to bear spiritual fruit, highlighting that, apart from Him, believers can do nothing. This metaphor serves as a powerful reminder that the *Parousia* is not merely a future event but an ongoing experience of Christ's presence, nurturing believers and shaping our spiritual growth. Similarly, in John 4:10–14 Jesus introduces the imagery of living water, describing the sustaining and renewing work of the Holy Spirit. In this passage He tells the Samaritan woman that "whoever drinks from the water that I will give him will never get thirsty again." This metaphor underscores the *Parousia* as an ever-present source of spiritual nourishment, satisfying the deepest needs of the soul and continually refreshing those who remain in Christ.

In John 10:10 Jesus provides another key insight into the nature of His mission by proclaiming, "I have come so that they may have life and have it in abundance." Here He redefines abundant life not in terms of material wealth or worldly success but as the unveiling of His essence within believers, transforming them into reflections of His glory. This abundant life is characterized by spiritual renewal, intimate communion with Christ, and the ongoing experience of His indwelling presence through the Holy Spirit.

In addition to metaphors, Jesus conveyed the hidden yet transformative nature of God's kingdom through parables, which served as revelatory tools to disclose spiritual realities to those with hearts open to receive them. The parable of the mustard seed, found in Matthew 13:31–32, portrays the kingdom of God as starting from the smallest beginnings yet growing into something vast and expansive. This story reassures believers that God's kingdom, though sometimes imperceptible in its growth, will ultimately permeate all of creation with its influence. In another parable, that of the wheat and the weeds recorded in Matthew 13:24–30, Jesus illustrates the coexistence of good and evil within the world, emphasizing the patience and faithfulness required as believers await the final revelation of God's justice. Through this parable Jesus teaches that the *Parousia* is an unfolding process, with ultimate fulfillment yet to come, while urging believers to remain steadfast in our faith.

Jesus consistently redirected the focus of His teachings from physical expectations to spiritual realities, revealing the transformative nature of God's kingdom through His words and actions. His frequent use of symbolic language—parables, metaphors, and prophetic imagery—was not only illustrative but essential; the symbolic reinforces the spiritual, inviting deeper discernment of divine truths that transcend physical categories.

In John 6:26–63 He declares Himself to be the Bread of Life, contrasting physical nourishment with the spiritual sustenance found in Him. He tells the crowd, "The one who eats my flesh and drinks my blood has eternal life," inviting them into a deeper, ongoing communion with Him that transcends physical sustenance. This teaching reveals that the *Parousia* is not a distant event to be awaited but a present reality to be embraced through faith and intimacy with Christ.

Likewise, in the Sermon on the Mount (Matthew 5:21–48) Jesus reinterprets the Mosaic Law, revealing its deeper spiritual intent. He calls His followers to a higher standard of righteousness—one that is not merely external but rooted in the heart. This teaching affirms the spiritual nature of the *Parousia* as a transformative force that shapes believers from within, leading us into a life that reflects the holiness and character of Christ.

By examining Christ's use of metaphor and parable, believers can gain a richer understanding of the *Parousia* as a present and unfolding reality. Jesus's teachings invite us to experience the ongoing unveiling of His presence in our lives, empowering us to live in alignment with His kingdom values. These spiritual truths, once hidden, are now revealed through the illuminating work of the Holy Spirit, calling believers to embrace the *Parousia* not just as a future hope but as an ever-present and transformative experience shaping our faith, relationships, and mission.

CONCLUSION

The hermeneutical principles explored in this chapter provide believers with the tools to interpret the *Parousia* as the spiritual unveiling of Christ's essence, aligning with the nature of His kingdom and mission.

By embracing these interpretive approaches believers can shift their focus from viewing the *Parousia* as a distant hope to experiencing it as a present, transformative reality that shapes their identity, worship, and mission.

Central to this unveiling is Christ's dual role as the ultimate atoning sacrifice and the eternal High Priest. His work transcends the physical rituals of the Old Covenant, ushering in the spiritual assurance of salvation and reconciliation for all who believe. Hebrews 9:28 provides a profound insight into how Christ's first and second appearances fulfill and surpass the sacrificial system, offering a deeper understanding of the *Parousia* as an ongoing reality.

As the unveiling of Christ's essence continues, it invites believers to reconsider traditional expectations surrounding the second coming. In the next chapter we will explore how the *Parousia* provides clarity to longstanding eschatological questions. Rather than viewing Christ's appearing as an abrupt singular event, we will uncover how Scripture reveals it as the culmination of His ongoing presence and transformative work. This perspective offers believers the confidence to embrace the fullness of our salvation now, living as visible manifestations of Christ's kingdom in a world yearning for redemption.

CHAPTER 10

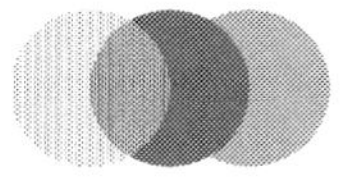

HEBREWS 9:28: THE SECOND COMING MYSTERY RESOLVED

The eschatological unveiling of Christ's essence, as previously explored, invites believers to embrace the present reality of His transformative presence. This reality finds its theological foundation in Christ's high priestly work, which serves as the bridge between the Old Covenant's physical rituals and the New Covenant's eternal spiritual realities. As Hebrews 9:28 declares, "Christ, having been offered once to bear the sins of many, will appear a second time, not to bear sin, but to bring salvation to those who are waiting for him." This pivotal passage sheds light on the true nature of Christ's second appearing—not as a future physical return but as the ongoing spiritual unveiling of His completed work within our lives. Far more than a mere proof text for the doctrine of Christ's return, Hebrews 9:28 serves as a gateway to understanding the profound transition from the temporary and symbolic rituals of the Old Covenant to the eternal spiritual realities fulfilled *in Christ.*

CHRIST AS THE ULTIMATE HIGH PRIEST

This verse encapsulates the transformative essence of Christ's high priestly work and reorients believers toward His continuous spiritual presence and power. To fully grasp this perspective it is essential to recognize the typology of the high priest's role within the Jewish sacrificial system.

In the Old Testament the Day of Atonement provided a significant ritual wherein the high priest entered the Most Holy Place twice. His first entrance was to make atonement for his own sins, while the second was to present the blood of the sacrificial offering on behalf of the people. The priest's reappearance from the Most Holy Place signified that God had accepted the sacrifice, bringing assurance of forgiveness and reconciliation to the community. The author of Hebrews, writing to a Jewish audience well acquainted with these traditions, presents Christ as the ultimate High Priest who both fulfills and transcends these rituals. His first appearance, culminating in His sacrificial death, bore the sins of humanity and inaugurated the New Covenant. His second appearance, rather than signifying a future physical return, symbolizes the spiritual unveiling of His finished work—an ongoing revelation that affirms the acceptance of His sacrifice and the assurance of salvation for all who eagerly await Him.

Paul's theology of being "in Christ" complements this high priestly imagery by emphasizing the believer's participation in the ascended Christ's essence. Through this mystical union believers experience Christ's second appearing as a continual unveiling of His presence within us. This perspective aligns seamlessly with the overarching message of Hebrews, which contrasts the transient physical rituals of the Old Covenant with the eternal spiritual realities now made available "in Christ."

The significance of Hebrews 9:28 for the topic at hand lies in its role as a key verse in theological discussions regarding the second coming of Christ. Traditionally, it has been interpreted as a reference to a future physical return of Christ. However, an alternative perspective presents His appearing "a second time" within the context of His priestly work and the believer's union with Him "in Christ." This interpretation shifts the focus from a distant, anticipated event to the immediate and ongoing experience of Christ's presence in the life of the believer.

The high priestly role of Christ, as detailed in Hebrews 9:11–14, presents Him as the greater High Priest who entered the heavenly tabernacle. Unlike the earthly high priests whose ministry was confined to the physical temple, Christ entered the true Most Holy Place in the heavenly realm, offering His own blood as the ultimate and final atonement for sin. In the Old Covenant system the high priest's first entrance into the Most Holy Place symbolized atonement, but it was a limited and repetitive act. Christ's first appearing, by contrast, transcended this ritual, as He entered the heavenly sanctuary once for all, securing eternal redemption.

The Day of Atonement provides an essential backdrop for understanding the significance of Christ's work. The priest's reemergence from the Most Holy Place assured the people that the sacrifice had been accepted and that atonement had been accomplished. Similarly, in Hebrews 9:28 Christ's second appearance is likened to this act, but it carries a spiritual assurance of salvation and reconciliation rather than a physical manifestation. His first appearing was the culmination of the sacrificial system, while His second appearing is the realization of its effects, inviting believers to live in the fullness of our redemption through our ongoing union with Christ.

Christ's role as the ultimate atoning sacrifice fulfills the high priestly typology in its entirety. While the earthly high priests performed symbolic atonement through repetitive sacrifices, Christ's single perfect offering secured eternal redemption and inaugurated the spiritual realities of the New Covenant. His first appearing marked the transition from the physical shadows of the Old Covenant to the spiritual substance of the New. This appearance was not merely a historical event but the initiation of a transformative relationship with believers, drawing us into His priestly work through our union "in Christ."

Paul's emphasis on being "in Christ" further illuminates this concept by illustrating how believers are active participants in Christ's priestly work. We are not passive recipients of salvation but are called to live in the ongoing reality of Christ's unveiled presence, experiencing His transformative power daily. Through this lens Christ's first appearance signifies the beginning of a union that progressively shapes believers into His likeness, while His second appearance confirms the ongoing revelation of this reality within us.

A typological analysis of Christ's high priestly work reveals significant insights. The Levitical rituals provide a vital context for understanding Christ's second appearing. The high priest's reemergence from the Most Holy Place served as a visible assurance to the community that atonement had been accepted. This typological framework is essential for interpreting Christ's second appearing as a spiritual assurance rather than a future physical descent.

Additionally, the eternal completion of Christ's work stands in contrast to the repeated nature of the high priest's sacrifices. As Hebrews 9:12 and 26 declare, Christ's sacrifice was offered "once for all," demonstrating that His second appearance is not an additional act but the affirmation of His eternal efficacy. His reemergence, experienced spiritually by believers "in Christ," serves as a reminder of the completeness of His atoning work, empowering us to live in the reality of our reconciliation with God.

In essence, the second appearing of Christ mirrors the Day of Atonement's ritual but shifts its significance to the spiritual realm. The ongoing *Parousia*, experienced in the life of the believer, affirms the sufficiency of Christ's redemptive work and calls us to a deeper awareness of our spiritual inheritance. Through this lens the *Parousia* is not a singular future event but an ever-present unveiling of Christ's essence, transforming believers and empowering us to walk in the fullness of His salvation.

Christ's priestly work redefines eschatological expectations, and the ongoing revelation of His presence shapes the believer's journey of faith. Understanding Christ's high priestly work provides clarity on the theological implications of living in the reality of Christ's unveiled essence.

CHRIST'S SECOND APPEARING

In Hebrews 9:28 the author presents a profound theological truth, stating that Christ "will appear a second time, not to bear sin, but to bring salvation to those who are waiting for him." This verse draws from the rich imagery of the high priest's second appearance during the Day of Atonement. Just as the high priest emerged from the Most Holy Place to signify that God had accepted the atonement and forgiven the people, Christ's second appearing reveals the completion of His atoning work. However, unlike the high priest's physical emergence, Christ's second appearing unfolds as a spiritual reality: the ongoing revelation of His essence to those who are united with Him "in Christ." This interpretation challenges the common expectation of a physical return and invites believers to experience the transformative reality of His unveiled presence.

The rituals performed by the high priest in the Old Testament provide a typological foundation for understanding Christ's appearances. The high priest's first entrance into the Most Holy Place was to make atonement for his own sins, paralleling Christ's first coming, in which He fulfilled the role of the "Lamb of God, who takes away the sin of the world!" (John 1:29). Christ's resurrection appearances further affirmed that God had accepted His sacrifice, much as the high priest's emergence in cleansed robes signified his readiness to intercede for the people.

After His resurrection Christ told Mary Magdalene, "Don't cling to me, . . . since I have not yet ascended to my Father" (John 20:17), reflecting the transitional nature of His first appearance. Later, when Christ invited His disciples to touch Him and ate with them, He demonstrated that His work as the holy and acceptable High Priest was complete.

Just as the high priest's second appearance marked the assurance of forgiveness for the people, Christ's second appearing, described in Hebrews 9:28, does not involve addressing sin but signifies the unveiling of salvation for those eagerly awaiting Him. This second appearing is not an event confined to the future; rather, it is a present spiritual reality experienced through faith by those who are "in Christ." As believers die to the world and are raised to new life "in Him," they participate in the unveiling of His essence, as Paul declares in Colossians 3:1–4: "If you have been raised with Christ, seek the things above, where Christ is, seated at the right hand of God. . . . Your life is hidden with Christ in God."

The salvation referenced in Hebrews 9:28 has to do with the completion of the redemptive process for believers, aligning with the spiritual transformation experienced through our union with Christ. Paul's declaration in Galatians 2:20—"I have been crucified with Christ, and I no longer live, but Christ lives in me"—reinforces the idea that the *Parousia* is the transformative indwelling of Christ, a present and ongoing reality for those united with Him through faith.

Understanding the broader context of Hebrews is essential to grasping this interpretation. The author(s) addressed Jewish believers who were well acquainted with high priestly imagery and contrasted the temporary, physical acts of the Levitical priests with the eternal, spiritual work of Christ. Throughout the epistle the superiority of Christ's priesthood is emphasized, showing how He fulfills and transcends the law by inaugurating a new and better covenant. The temporary and repetitive sacrifices of the Old Covenant are shown to be mere shadows of the true and eternal atonement provided through Christ's once-for-all sacrifice.

Paul's frequent use of the phrase "in Christ" across his epistles further affirms this spiritual reality, emphasizing that the ascended Christ's essence becomes the believer's source of life and transformation. This understanding of the *Parousia* as an unveiling of Christ's essence rather than a physical return aligns with the thesis of this work, presenting profound implications for eschatology and Christian theology. Rather than focusing on a future physical expectation, believers are called to live in the reality of Christ's completed work, actively engaging with His ongoing presence and allowing it to shape our worship, relationships, and mission.

ADDRESSING ALTERNATIVE INTERPRETATIONS OF CHRIST'S RETURN

While this interpretation offers a fresh perspective, it is necessary to address alternative views that emphasize a literal, physical return of Christ. Many sincere believers hold that the language of Hebrews and other eschatological texts points to a future, tangible second coming. However, the spiritual and symbolic framework of Hebrews invites us to consider a deeper reality already at work.

Rather than anchoring hope in a delayed event, the epistle to the Hebrews consistently highlights the present and ongoing manifestation of Christ's completed work. Hebrews 10:1 declares that "the law has only a shadow of the good things to come, and not the reality itself of those things." This reinforces the spiritual thrust of the letter, emphasizing that Christ's ministry transcends the limitations of earthly rituals and now manifests in the transformative realities of His presence in the believer's life.

This perspective does not necessarily deny the possibility of a final consummating act of Christ's reign. Instead, it reframes the "second appearing" described in Hebrews 9:28 as an already unfolding spiritual unveiling—a *Parousia* that is not delayed but is dynamically present in those who live by faith and await Him in hope. In this light Christ's second appearing is not confined to the future but is accessible now through the Spirit, fulfilling the redemptive aim of His first coming.

CONCLUSION

Furthermore, a spiritual interpretation of Hebrews 9:28 finds continuity with New Testament eschatology as a whole. In John 17:22–23 Christ prays, “I have given them the glory you have given me, so that they may be one as we are one.” This passage highlights the present reality of Christ’s unveiled essence through unity with believers, further reinforcing the idea that the *Parousia* is a spiritual unveiling rather than a future event to be passively awaited.

By unveiling Christ’s essence as a present and active reality, Hebrews 9:28 challenges believers to live in the fullness of His accomplished work. The *Parousia* is not a distant hope but a transformative truth, inviting the Church to embody His presence and reflect His glory in a world longing for redemption. As believers grow in our understanding of the *Parousia*, we are called to embrace our identity “in Christ,” participating in the divine work of reconciliation and renewal.

This exploration of the *Parousia* naturally transitions into the next chapter, which delves into the relational meaning of the atonement of Christ and the *Parousia*. Our focus shifts to understanding how Christ’s unveiled presence brings not only salvation but also accountability. The transformative essence of the *Parousia* invites believers to live with a renewed sense of purpose and responsibility, reflecting the relational nature of God’s redemptive work. Through Christ’s atonement judgment is no longer an external fear but a relational reality that calls believers into deeper communion with Him, guiding our lives according to His righteousness and grace.

CHAPTER 11

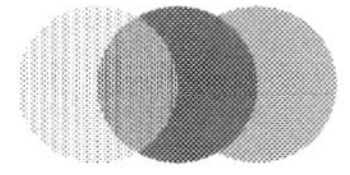

JUDGMENT AS RELATIONAL REALITY IN CHRIST'S ATONEMENT

The unveiling of Christ's essence through the *Parousia* brings not only the revelation of His presence but also the fulfillment of divine judgment, which plays a crucial role in the believer's journey of sanctification. At the heart of this understanding lies the Day of Atonement, a central aspect of Jewish liturgical life that foreshadowed Christ's ultimate high priestly work. Through His atonement, divine judgment is no longer a cause for fear and condemnation but a means of drawing believers into God's rest, where we experience the fullness of life "in Christ."

The concept of God's rest, as expounded in Hebrews 4, serves as a cornerstone for understanding the *Parousia*, revealing rest not merely as a cessation of labor but as a deeper spiritual renewal—one that is fully realized "in Christ." In Him believers find our true inheritance, transitioning from striving under the Law to resting in His completed work. As the ultimate High Priest, Christ's atonement secures both divine judgment and reconciliation, making participation in this rest a present reality while pointing toward its ultimate fulfillment.

The unveiling of divine judgment is an *epiphaneia* moment, where the reality of Christ's presence breaks through and demands a response. To stand before the unveiled Christ is to experience both judgment and transformation simultaneously—for His essence, once revealed, calls for an alignment of all things to His righteousness. Just as light exposes what is hidden in darkness, Christ's *Parousia* reveals the true condition of every heart. "For the word of God is living and effective and sharper than any double-edged sword, penetrating as far as the separation of soul and spirit, joints and marrow. It is able to judge the thoughts and intentions of the heart" (Hebrews 4:12).

For those who are in Christ, this divine judgment is not about condemnation (Romans 8:1) but about the necessary unveiling that leads to sanctification. Each moment of conviction, correction, and spiritual renewal is an *epiphaneia* of Christ's essence at work within the believer, drawing them deeper into conformity with Him.

PENTECOST: THE FIRST UNVEILING OF THE *PAROUSIA*

In the history of redemption few moments are as misunderstood or underappreciated in their theological weight as Pentecost. While often seen as the birth of the Church or the empowering arrival of the Spirit, Pentecost was something even more profound: it was the first great unveiling of the *Parousia*. In that moment the exalted Christ was not only preached but revealed. Through the Spirit His essence was made manifest in those who believed. This was not just the beginning of mission; it was the beginning of manifestation. The kingdom had come. Christ had come. The *Parousia* had begun.

The unveiling of Christ's essence in the *Parousia* not only reveals divine judgment but also initiates a transformation within believers that conforms them to His image. This unveiling is not merely an abstract theological concept but a lived reality that began unfolding in the earliest believers.

The most striking example of this transformative revelation is Pentecost, where Christ's presence was made manifest through the Spirit and His disciples were caught up in a moment of *epiphaneia*—a moment when the essence of Christ was revealed in and through those who received Him by faith. Rather than merely initiating a new religious movement, Pentecost marked the visible, Spirit-empowered manifestation of Christ's reign, breaking into the world through transformed lives.

Peter's words to the crowd on this day in Jerusalem carried a weight beyond mere explanation. Some, seeing the disciples' ecstatic behavior, assumed that they were drunk. But Peter redirected their attention to the prophetic words of Joel (Joel 2:28–32), who had spoken of a time when God would pour out His Spirit upon all flesh, leading to a radical transformation by which people would prophesy, see visions, and experience divine dreams.

This was no abstract metaphor. The prophecy spoke of a moment when the veil between the seen and the unseen would be pulled back, allowing humanity to glimpse divine reality through the Spirit. This, Peter proclaimed, was happening before their very eyes. The Spirit had been poured out, and those who had received it were now standing in the revelation of Christ's exaltation, caught up in the wonder of His unveiled presence.

Many traditions have interpreted Pentecost and the *Parousia* as two separate events: Pentecost as the empowering work of the Spirit and the *Parousia* as a future return of Christ. But Peter's words in Acts, grounded in Joel's prophecy, defy such division. What the crowd witnessed was not simply a downpayment on future glory; it was glory itself breaking into history. The Spirit's outpouring was not a sign of Christ's absence but the manifestation of His reigning presence. As Jesus had promised, "You will see me. . . . I am in my Father, you are in me, and I am in you" (John 14:19–20). The world did not see, but the Church did. This was the essence of the *Parousia*: the unveiled Christ dwelling within His people.

What they experienced was not simply an emotional or spiritual high but the transformative unveiling of Christ's enthronement. Peter's sermon made this clear: "God has raised this Jesus; we are all witnesses of this. Therefore, since he has been exalted to the right hand of God and has received from the Father the promised Holy Spirit, he has poured out what you both see and hear" (Acts 2:32–33). The Spirit's outpouring was evidence of Christ's *presence*, revealing that His reign had begun and was now manifesting itself through those who were in Him. This was not a distant expectation but a reality unfolding in their very being. The *Parousia* was not something they were awaiting; it was something they were experiencing.

The response of the disciples reflected the magnitude of this unveiling. They spoke in other languages, prophesied, and were so overwhelmed that onlookers mistook their spiritual rapture for intoxication. But their condition was not drunkenness—it was *epiphaneia*, a state of divine manifestation. They were not merely preaching about Christ; they were experiencing the reality of His presence, seeing with unveiled eyes the truth of His exaltation. Their prophetic speech was not about a coming kingdom in the distant future but about a kingdom that had already begun to break forth, one that was taking shape within them by the power of the Spirit.

Joel's prophecy pointed to three specific manifestations of the Spirit's work—prophecy (*naba*), visions (*chizzayon*), and dreams (*chalom*)—each representing a different facet of divine revelation. To prophesy was to be caught up in the inspired utterance of divine truth, to speak with the Spirit's breath filling one's words. This was not the prophetic voice of warning alone but of revelation, a proclamation of the unveiled Christ.

To see visions was to perceive spiritual realities beyond the physical realm, to behold with clarity what had previously been hidden. The disciples at Pentecost were seeing the truth of Christ's kingship not with their natural eyes but with the eyes of the Spirit, just as Paul would later describe in his letters—the unveiling of Christ's glory transforming those who beheld it (2 Corinthians 3:16–18).

Dreams, in the prophetic sense, carried the weight of divine mystery, the overwhelming wonder of encountering the fullness of God's purposes through symbolic revelation. These were not simply random or poetic dreamscapes but spiritual awakenings in which eternity pressed into time, revealing divine truth through the language of mystery, metaphor, and awe.

These signs were not given as isolated spiritual experiences but as markers of the unveiling presence of Christ. The disciples were not waiting for the *Parousia*; they were immersed in it. The Spirit's outpouring was not merely empowerment for mission—it was the means by which the exalted Christ was making Himself known, revealing His essence within His people. What had been hidden in ages past was now being disclosed.

The significance of this moment cannot be overstated. It was not merely the dawn of a new religious movement but the fulfillment of what Jesus had promised—that He would come to His people through the Spirit, that they would know Him, and that He would reveal Himself to them (John 14:16–20). From that moment forward the revelation of Christ's presence would not be restricted to visions given to a select few but would be available to all who received the Spirit. The prophecy of Joel was not simply fulfilled in that moment; it was set in motion as an ongoing reality, unfolding in every believer who walks by the Spirit and beholds the unveiled presence of Christ.

Many have interpreted Pentecost and the *Parousia* as separate events, as though the Spirit's outpouring were merely an initial sign, while the *Parousia* remained a distant occurrence. Yet Peter's words defy this division. The Spirit's arrival was not a temporary phenomenon, nor was it a substitute for Christ's presence—it was the very means by which Christ was unveiling Himself to His people. Jesus had said, "In a little while the world will no longer see me, but you will see me. . . . On that day you will know that I am in my Father, you are in me, and I am in you" (John 14:19–20). The world could not perceive what was happening at Pentecost, but those who had faith received the Spirit and were seeing Christ. The veil was being lifted.

Paul would later describe this transformation in unmistakable terms: "We all, with unveiled faces, are looking as in a mirror at the glory of the Lord and are being transformed into the same image from glory to glory" (2 Corinthians 3:18). The unveiling of Christ's essence was not a single event in time but an ongoing revelation in those who belong to Him through faith. The Spirit was the *Parousia* in motion, the active presence of Christ transforming His people. It was not an external event they were waiting for but a reality they were living.

This was the mystery that had been hidden for generations: "Christ in you, the hope of glory" (Colossians 1:26–27). Pentecost was not a foreshadowing of some future unveiling—it was the unveiling itself, the revelation that Christ's presence had already come and that His essence was now being revealed through the Spirit in those who were His. The disciples had not been given a mere taste of the kingdom; they had entered into its fullness. They had beheld the exalted Christ, not with their physical eyes but with eyes that had been opened by the Spirit. And in that beholding they had begun to be transformed.

Pentecost revealed the pattern of the *Parousia*: not as a spectacle but as transformation, not as a cosmic rupture but as a spiritual unveiling. The world expected thunder; God sent wind and flame. The Church expected return; Christ came in Spirit and truth. The *Parousia* had begun, not in the clouds but in the hearts of those made new. It continues now wherever Christ is revealed through faith, wherever the Spirit bears witness to His reign, and wherever lives are transformed into His likeness. Christ has come. Christ is here. The kingdom has arrived.

IMAGOFORMITY

This transformation is not instantaneous but an ongoing, Spirit-led process—a progressive shaping into the fullness of Christ's likeness. Just as divine judgment serves to expose, refine, and realign all things to His righteousness, so too does it act as the catalyst for what I call *Imagoformity*—a term that emphasizes the dynamic journey by which believers are continually formed into the image (*imago*) of Christ through the sanctifying work of the Spirit. Unlike the static concept of the *Imago Dei*, which refers to humanity's original creation in God's image, Imagoformity highlights the ongoing, relational process of becoming conformed to Christ's essence over time.

This process is deeply intertwined with judgment, for it is through the *epiphaneia*—the appearing—of Christ's presence that every believer is refined and sanctified. Each encounter with divine judgment is not merely a reckoning with past failures but an invitation into deeper transformation. In this way judgment is not punitive but revelatory, unveiling what is necessary for believers to walk in the fullness of Christ's life.

Paul captures this dynamic in 2 Corinthians 3:18: "We all, with unveiled faces, are looking as in a mirror at the glory of the Lord and are being transformed into the same image from glory to glory; this is from the Lord who is the Spirit." This verse reveals that transformation into Christ's image is a process of increasing glory, an ongoing work of the Spirit rather than an event completed in a moment. Thus, Imagoformity is not just a theological concept but a lived reality—a call to participate in the ever-deepening unveiling of Christ's presence within us. It is in the refining fire of divine judgment that believers are stripped of all that is not of Christ, allowing His righteousness to be fully formed within them.

THE ATONING WORK OF CHRIST

Just as the Day of Atonement in Jewish tradition symbolized both judgment and purification, so too does the atoning work of Christ in the *Parousia* serve to both judge and transform. The priestly work of Christ is not merely about absolution but about formation—shaping believers into the fullness of His image, calling them to live in increasing alignment with their new identity in Him. This process, which finds its culmination in glorification, is the very essence of Imagoformity.

The Jewish observance of the Day of Atonement (Yom Kippur) offers a profound foreshadowing of Christ's work of atonement and judgment. This annual ritual, described in Leviticus 16, involved the high priest entering the Most Holy Place to sprinkle the blood of the atoning sacrifice upon the mercy seat. This sacred act symbolized the covering and removal of the people's sins, highlighting the necessity of mediation and divine acceptance.

However, as Hebrews 9:12–14 explains, Christ's atonement far surpasses this ritual, for He entered the heavenly sanctuary "once for all," offering His own blood to secure eternal redemption. His work fulfilled and transcended the temporary nature of the Levitical priesthood, establishing a lasting and complete atonement that grants believers access to God's presence.

The concept of Sabbath rest is deeply intertwined with the Day of Atonement, signifying the ultimate end of striving and the believer's entrance into God's presence. Just as the high priest's emergence from the Most Holy Place signaled the acceptance of the sacrifice, Christ's resurrection serves as the divine assurance of God's complete acceptance of His atoning work.

Hebrews 4:9–10 emphasizes that "a Sabbath rest remains for God's people. For the person who has entered his rest has rested from his own works, just as God did from his." This passage underscores that entering God's rest is both a present experience and a future hope, inviting believers to partake in the completeness of God's redemptive work through the *Parousia*. Christ's resurrection affirms that those united with Him partake in this rest, not through their own efforts but through faith in His finished atonement.

The cross stands as the ultimate expression of divine judgment, wherein the sins of the world were borne by Christ. In this climactic event judgment is transformed from a declaration of condemnation to an act of renewal and sanctification. As 2 Corinthians 5:21 declares, "He made the one who did not know sin to be sin for us, so that in him we might become the righteousness of God."

In Romans 8:1–2 Paul affirms the liberating reality of Christ's work by proclaiming, "There is now no condemnation for those who are in Christ Jesus." The cross not only demonstrates God's judgment upon sin but also provides the assurance of divine acceptance, much as the high priest's emergence from the Most Holy Place assured the people of God's forgiveness. Through the cross Christ's atoning work is validated and believers are drawn into the full scope of salvation, encompassing justification, sanctification, and glorification.

SAUL'S CONVERSION

One of the clearest biblical examples of *epiphaneia* in judgment is found in the conversion of Saul of Tarsus on the road to Damascus. This moment encapsulates the dual reality of divine judgment and transformative grace, revealing how the unveiling of Christ's essence radically reorients the life of a believer.

Saul, a zealous persecutor of the Church, was blinded by a sudden *epiphaneia*—the radiant presence of the risen Christ. "As he traveled and was nearing Damascus, a light from heaven suddenly flashed around him. Falling to the ground, he heard a voice saying to him, 'Saul, Saul, why are you persecuting me?'" (Acts 9:3–4).

This was an *epiphaneia* of judgment—a direct confrontation with the unveiled Christ, whose presence exposed the true nature of Saul's actions. The same man who had thought he was serving God by persecuting Christians now found himself blinded, stripped of his power, and left utterly dependent on the mercy of the One he had opposed. But this *epiphaneia* of judgment was also an *epiphaneia* of grace. Saul, later Paul, was not left in blindness, nor was he condemned.

Instead, through divine mercy he was led into the transformative process of sanctification.

This mirrors the universal experience of believers in the *Parousia*. The presence of Christ unveils what is false and demands a response, yet it also extends the invitation to transformation. "For God who said, 'Let light shine out of darkness,' has shone in our hearts to give the light of the knowledge of God's glory in the face of Jesus Christ" (2 Corinthians 4:6).

Through Paul's story we see that judgment in the *Parousia* is not meant to destroy but to reveal and transform. It is the necessary unveiling that confronts, convicts, and ultimately re-creates.

JUDGMENT FOR THE SAKE OF UNION

Union with Christ is central to understanding judgment within the framework of atonement. Through this mystical union believers experience a new identity, one that is deeply rooted in Christ's righteousness. Judgment, once a cause for fear, becomes a process of sanctification and transformation, drawing them more deeply into God's Sabbath rest. Paul's words in Galatians 2:20 capture this profound transformation: "I have been crucified with Christ, and I no longer live, but Christ lives in me." The believer's participation in Christ's life ensures that judgment serves not as an indictment but as an invitation to walk in the fullness of His grace and truth.

Christ's resurrection stands as the ultimate assurance of rest and the fulfillment of the believer's hope in the *Parousia*. As Romans 6:4 states, "We were buried with him by baptism into death, in order that, just as Christ was raised from the dead by the glory of the Father, so we too may walk in newness of life." The resurrection is not merely a historical event but the continuous unveiling of Christ's victorious life in and through His people. It signifies the believer's participation in Christ's triumph over sin and death, empowering us to live as witnesses of His transformative power. The resurrection is the essence of the

Parousia—the ongoing revelation of Christ's life and righteousness in the lives of believers.

Judgment, within the framework of the *Parousia*, is not a distant future event; rather, it is an ongoing spiritual reality experienced by those who are "in Christ." The transformative work of the *Parousia* reveals Christ's essence in the lives of believers, continually refining and sanctifying them. In John 5:24 Jesus declares, "Truly I tell you, anyone who hears my word and believes him who sent me has eternal life and will not come under judgment but has passed from death to life."

This passage affirms that judgment for those who believe is not a condemnation but a passage into eternal life, signifying an ongoing transformation rather than a singular end-time event. Similarly, 1 Peter 4:17 asserts, "For the time has come for judgment to begin with God's household," emphasizing that divine judgment is an active process that begins within the community of believers.

For those who walk in Christ, judgment is not a single moment of reckoning but a continuous unveiling—a progressive *epiphaneia* that transforms the believer into the image of Christ. Each moment of spiritual correction, conviction, and renewal is an encounter with the living presence of Christ, whose *Parousia* is actively at work within His people. As Paul from experience writes, "We all, with unveiled faces, are looking as in a mirror at the glory of the Lord and are being transformed into the same image from glory to glory; this is from the Lord who is the Spirit" (2 Corinthians 3:18).

This ongoing process of unveiling is what makes divine judgment relational rather than merely forensic. The judgment of God is not about weighing external actions on a scale but about exposing the heart to the transforming light of Christ. This is why the fire of divine judgment is often described as refining rather than destructive; "Look, I have refined you, but not as silver; I have tested you in the furnace of affliction" (Isaiah 48:10). Rather than viewing judgment as something to be feared, believers should embrace it as the unveiling of Christ's presence within them, leading them from glory to glory as they are purified by His love.

Through the *Parousia* Christ's presence unveils divine judgment as an active and daily experience. Each moment of conviction, repentance, and spiritual growth reflects the reality of His essence working within believers. Judgment, in this context, is not punitive but revelatory—it is a continual unveiling of Christ's transformative presence, drawing believers more deeply into His likeness. This process transcends future anticipation and instead invites believers to live in alignment with God's divine essence in the present. As believers yield to this process we are shaped by Christ's presence, experiencing the refining fire of divine love that purifies our hearts and minds.

The experience of divine judgment through the *Parousia* leads believers into the fullness of God's Sabbath rest. This rest, as described in Hebrews 4, is not merely a cessation from physical labor but an invitation to enter into the completed work of Christ. It signifies freedom from striving under the Law and an embrace of the peace and assurance found in His finished work. The unveiling of Christ's essence through judgment highlights the present reality of salvation—a transformative journey that moves believers from death to life, from striving to resting in God's completed atonement.

The final unveiling of Christ's essence—the ultimate *epiphaneia*—is God's rest itself. In the end, divine judgment serves only one purpose: to prepare the believer for the fullness of God's presence. Every moment of refining, every unveiling of Christ's essence in the believer, is drawing them toward the completeness of rest in Him.

This is why the *Parousia* is not merely an event but a process, a divine unfolding that leads believers out of striving and into being, out of self-effort and into union with Christ. The judgment of God, rightly understood, is not a barrier to rest but the gateway into it. The writer of Hebrews understood this when he wrote, "A Sabbath rest remains for

God's people. For the person who has entered his rest has rested from his own works, just as God from his" (Hebrews 4:9–10).

Through the ongoing *epiphaneia* of Christ's presence, believers experience true Sabbath rest, no longer defined by human toil but by divine grace. This is the final transformation, when all striving ceases and the unveiled glory of Christ is fully and eternally known.

Transformation through union with Christ is an essential aspect of the *Parousia*, illustrating that those who are "in Christ" are not merely justified but are actively being conformed to His image. In 2 Corinthians 3:18 Paul writes, "We all, with unveiled faces, are looking as in a mirror at the glory of the Lord and are being transformed into the same image from glory to glory."

This passage underscores the progressive nature of spiritual transformation, where judgment serves as a refining process that leads believers into greater conformity with Christ's image. Similarly, Ephesians 2:6 proclaims, "He also raised us up with him and seated us with him in the heavens in Christ Jesus," affirming that believers already share in the reality of Christ's exaltation and victory.

SABBATH REST

This transformation is intricately tied to the concept of God's Sabbath rest. Just as the Sabbath signifies divine completion and fulfillment, life "in Christ" invites believers to cease striving and to embrace the spiritual renewal found in Him. The *Parousia* reveals that believers are called to reflect Christ's essence, embodying the spiritual fulfillment of God's rest and serving as a testament to His transformative presence in the world. Through our daily lives believers manifest the reality of the *Parousia* by embodying Christ's love, holiness, and grace in our relationships and communities.

However, this rest is not passive; it is deeply active and dynamic. It calls believers to live in the freedom of Christ's grace, to participate in

His mission, and to display His glory in all areas of life. By living in this rest believers engage with the transformative power of Christ's presence, demonstrating that the *Parousia* is not merely an eschatological event but an ongoing reality that shapes our identity and purpose. In doing so we anticipate the ultimate fulfillment of the *Parousia* in eternity, when the fullness of Christ's essence will be revealed and all creation will enter into God's perfect rest.

THE WORK OF THE SPIRIT

The Holy Spirit serves as the divine agent through whom the transformative judgment of the *Parousia* is revealed. Through the Spirit's convicting, sanctifying, and empowering work Christ's essence is continually unveiled in the lives of believers. As Jesus declares in John 16:8–11, "When he comes, he will convict the world about sin, righteousness, and judgment." This conviction is not merely about condemnation but serves as the means by which believers are led into the fullness of God's Sabbath rest.

The Spirit's role in judgment is restorative, drawing believers into deeper communion with Christ and aligning our lives with His righteousness. Paul affirms this in Romans 8:11, stating, "If the Spirit of him who raised Jesus from the dead lives in you, then he who raised Christ from the dead will also bring your mortal bodies to life through his Spirit who lives in you."

Paul is not referring to a distant future resurrection of the body; rather, he speaks of a present reality. If the Spirit that raised Jesus from the dead now dwells in believers, then our mortal bodies—these present bodies—are continuously being transformed and receiving life through the Spirit, who unveils Christ's presence within us through the *Parousia*. This life-giving work of the Spirit ensures that the sanctifying process, which began through Christ's atonement, continually unfolds in believers, preparing us to fully reflect His essence.

Far from being a passive process, the Spirit's work calls believers to actively engage with Christ's presence. Conviction leads us to rest in His completed work, while also empowering us to reflect His glory in the world. As the indwelling Spirit continually renews and strengthens us, believers become living testimonies of the transformative reality of the *Parousia*. We are not left to our own efforts but are equipped by the Spirit to embody Christ's righteousness and love in our daily lives, revealing the ongoing work of sanctification that judgment brings.

This transformative judgment of the *Parousia* calls believers to live as image bearers of Christ, reflecting His character and love to the world. Paul captures this calling in Colossians 3:10, reminding believers that we are "being renewed in knowledge according to the image of [our] Creator." Similarly, in Ephesians 4:22–24 he urges us to "put on the new self, the one created according to God's likeness in righteousness and purity of the truth." The *Parousia* is not merely an external event to be anticipated but a present reality in which believers participate by embodying Christ's essence.

Living as image bearers of Christ means embracing the transformative power of God's rest and reflecting the peace and joy that come from life "in Christ." This calling extends beyond individual transformation to include the communal life of the Church, which corporately serves as the visible representation of Christ's presence on earth. The process of sanctification is dynamic and ongoing, inviting believers to grow continually in Christlikeness, aligning our thoughts, desires, and actions with His mission. Through this transformation believers not only experience personal renewal but also become agents of redemption in our relationships, workplaces, and communities.

The reality of judgment and rest in the *Parousia* offers believers a profound invitation to enter into the depth of Christ's transformative power. Hebrews 4:9 highlights this reality, stating that "a Sabbath rest remains for God's people." This rest is not simply a cessation of labor but signifies the completion of Christ's atonement, where believers cease striving under the Law and instead live in the freedom of His grace. Just as God rested after His work in creation, Christ's finished work invites believers into a spiritual Sabbath in which their efforts to achieve righteousness are replaced by resting in His accomplished work.

The judgment revealed through the *Parousia* brings a refining and sanctifying work that deepens the believer's understanding of God's grace. As the Spirit convicts of sin, righteousness, and judgment (John 16:8–11), believers experience transformation that draws us closer to God's purpose and aligns us with His kingdom. This conviction is not meant to bring fear or condemnation but to restore and renew, calling believers to participate in the unfolding reality of God's redemptive work.

Ultimately, the *Parousia* reveals that judgment and rest are intertwined, forming the foundation of the believer's identity "in Christ." Judgment refines and sanctifies, while rest offers the assurance of God's completed work, allowing believers to live confidently in His grace. This dual reality is both present and future. It is experienced now in the life of faith and awaits its ultimate fulfillment in eternity.

CONCLUSION

In summary, the *Parousia* unveils the spiritual reality of judgment through Christ's high priestly work, fulfilling the typology of the Day of Atonement. Judgment within the *Parousia* is not confined to a future event but is an ongoing, transformative process experienced by those who are "in Christ." Rather than condemnation, judgment serves as a means of sanctification, drawing believers into God's Sabbath rest and aligning us with His divine essence. The Holy Spirit plays a central role in this process, guiding believers through sanctification and empowering us to live as reflections of Christ's glory. Through this transformative journey believers are called to embody Christ's presence, participating in His mission to redeem the world and anticipating the ultimate fulfillment of His kingdom.

As we deepen our understanding of the transformative relational *Parousia*—the ongoing unveiling of Christ's presence that both reveals His essence and reshapes His people—we now turn our attention to the resurrection. In the next chapter we will see how the resurrection stands as the ultimate revelation of Christ's glory and the cornerstone of the believer's hope. It is through the resurrection that we experience the fullness of life "in Christ," not as a future expectation but as a present and transformative reality, conforming us to His likeness and preparing us for the consummation of His kingdom.

CHAPTER 12

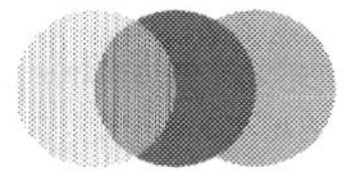

THE RESURRECTION UNVEILS THE ESSENCE OF CHRIST

In this chapter we explore how the resurrection of Jesus Christ stands as the supreme unveiling of His essence, marking the central moment in which the *Parousia* becomes unmistakably manifest. The resurrection is not only proof of life after death; it is the revelation of Christ's divine nature, His victory over sin and death, and the inauguration of the new creation. In rising from the grave, Christ embodies the fullness of God's truth, love, and righteousness, not only as a historical event but as a living, ongoing reality that continues to shape the world and the Church.

Building upon the theological foundations established in previous chapters, this chapter highlights the resurrection as the pivotal expression of the transformative relational *Parousia*. Through it Christ's presence is not only affirmed but actively revealed, His glorified body becoming the sign of what is now possible for those who are in Him. This unveiling does not end with the empty tomb; it continues through the ascension, the outpouring of the Spirit, the testimony of Scripture, and the Church's faithful witness. To understand the *Parousia* rightly we must begin with the resurrection, not only as a precursor to future glory but as the present and eternal manifestation of it.

THE RESURRECTION AS *EPIPHANEIA*

The scriptural articulation of Christ's essence is unveiled through His identity as the eternal Word of God, the Lamb of God, and the radiance of God's glory. Through this lens the *Parousia* becomes a call to active engagement with His presence, transforming eschatological hope into present reality and inspiring believers to embody His love and truth in the world.

The continual unveiling of Christ's glory lies at the heart of the *Parousia*, illuminating the nature of God's presence and mission. The revelation of Christ's glory began with the Incarnation, when the eternal Word entered human history, bridging the divine and human realms. As John 1:14 proclaims, "The Word became flesh and dwelt among us. We observed his glory, the glory as the one and only Son from the Father, full of grace and truth." The Incarnation marks the inauguration of the *Parousia*, the beginning of God's revealed presence through the person of Jesus Christ.

In taking on flesh Christ made visible the fullness of God's truth and love, embodying the divine mission to reconcile creation to Himself. This revelation was not confined to those who walked beside Him in history; through faith it now extends across time and space to all who receive Him, inviting participation in His ongoing presence. As John 1:12 affirms, "To all who did receive him, he gave them the right to be children of God, to those who believe in his name." Receiving Christ is more than intellectual acknowledgment; it is a transformative act of faith that aligns the believer with Christ's essence and grants us the authority and responsibility to reflect His character. This transformative revelation redefines the believer's understanding of God and draws us into an intimate relationship that reshapes our human identity and purpose.

Yet the fullest unveiling of Christ's essence did not occur in the Incarnation alone but in conjunction with His resurrection—the moment when His divine nature was revealed in power. The resurrection was not merely a return to life but an *epiphaneia* of His glorified essence, breaking through the constraints of mortality. Paul stated this to the Roman believers when he wrote that Jesus was "appointed to be the powerful Son of God according to the Spirit of holiness by the resurrection of the dead" (Romans 1:4).

JOHN 12:32

This unveiling of Christ's essence is also expressed in His own words in John 12:32: "As for me, if I am lifted up from the earth I will draw all people to myself." The Greek construction of this verse highlights a profound theological reality. The lifting up (ὑψωθῶ, *hypsōthō*) is not only Christ's crucifixion but also His exaltation in resurrection and glory. The cross, far from being merely an instrument of suffering, was the means by which Christ's essence was unveiled to the world. His death was not an end but a moment of profound self-revelation, demonstrating the depth of divine love and the power of redemptive sacrifice.

The verb "draw" (ἑλκύσω, *helkysō*) signifies not compulsion but revelation—a force so transformative that it alters the perception of those who respond to it. This drawing is the unveiling of Christ's relational essence, when those who recognize His exaltation are drawn into divine communion with Him. This theme aligns with the resurrection as the great *epiphaneia*: Christ's presence revealed in power, no longer hidden in mortality but exalted in glory. The phrase "to myself" (πρὸς ἐμαυτόν, *pros emauton*) emphasizes this relational nature, demonstrating that the resurrection is not just an event to be believed but a reality to be entered.

In this way John 12:32 serves as a bridge between the crucifixion, the resurrection, and the ongoing *Parousia*—the continual unveiling of Christ's essence that transforms believers. Just as the disciples encountered the risen Christ and were forever changed, so too are believers today drawn into His glorified presence, experiencing the transformative power of the *Parousia*.

POST-RESURRECTION ENCOUNTERS

The resurrection removed the final veil, revealing Christ not just as the suffering servant but as the glorified Son, victorious over death. The disciples, who had once walked with Him in the flesh, now encountered Him in a new dimension—one that both confirmed His identity and transformed their understanding of His presence.

Recognizing Christ's essence is an ongoing spiritual journey marked by deep union with Him. To be "in Christ" is to enter into a profound spiritual relationship, whereby His essence transforms the believer's life from within. This union calls for active participation in reflecting His light and embodying His love in the world. The author of Hebrews affirms this reality, stating in Hebrews 1:3, "The Son is the radiance of God's glory and the exact expression of his nature."

This verse underscores the divine nature of Christ's essence, fully revealed through His life, death, resurrection, and ongoing work. As believers grow in our relationship with Him, we are progressively conformed to His image, becoming visible reflections of His glory to the world. Receiving Christ's essence empowers believers to live as His image bearers, participating in His mission to bring light to a world shrouded in darkness.

The first witnesses to the resurrection were transformed not merely by seeing an empty tomb but by experiencing the *epiphaneia* of the risen Christ. Each post-resurrection encounter reveals a progressive unveiling of His glorified essence. At the tomb Mary Magdalene initially mistook Jesus for the gardener and was unable to recognize Him until He spoke her name (John 20:11–18). This was an *epiphaneia* moment—a sudden realization that the One she grieved was indeed alive and that His essence transcended mere physical recognition.

Luke 24:13–35 says that the hearts of the disciples walking on the road to Emmaus burned as Jesus explained the Scriptures to them, yet they did not recognize Him until the breaking of the bread—another *epiphaneia* that revealed His presence in communion.

John writes that Thomas refused to believe until he could touch the wounds. But when Christ appeared before him his doubt was shattered in an instant of divine unveiling, and he declared, "My Lord and my God!" (John 20:24–29). And the disciples at the Sea of Galilee, in a moment reminiscent of their first calling, recognized Jesus only after He had provided a miraculous catch of fish, reminding them that His presence had never left them (John 21:1–14).

Each of these encounters was not just a confirmation of resurrection but an unveiling of Christ's essence. Each disciple was forever changed by the *epiphaneia* of the risen Christ. Likewise, every believer must experience their own resurrection *epiphaneia*, where Christ is revealed not merely as a historical figure but as the living presence that transforms their being.

The revelation of Christ's essence is not a static event but an unfolding, dynamic reality experienced in the lives of believers throughout history. As Paul declares in 2 Corinthians 5:17, "Therefore, if anyone is in Christ, he is a new creation; the old has passed away, and see, the new has come!" This transformation into a "new creation" reflects the ongoing unveiling of Christ's essence within the believer. Through the *Parousia* believers are continually renewed and sanctified, enabling us to embody the reality of God's kingdom in our daily lives. The work of the Holy Spirit plays a central role in this revelation, illuminating Scripture, empowering spiritual growth, and guiding believers into deeper communion with Christ. The Spirit ensures that the *Parousia* is not limited to a distant eschatological event but is a present and unfolding experience of Christ's presence in the believer's life.

KNOWING CHRIST

This unfolding reality of the resurrection is not only historical but deeply personal. The power of resurrection is not just something to be affirmed. It must be unveiled within. As Paul said, "My goal is to know him and the power of his resurrection and the fellowship of his sufferings, being conformed to his death" (Philippians 3:10).

Paul's words reveal that knowing Christ is not about intellectual assent but about experiencing the *epiphaneia* of His resurrection power. Just as Christ was unveiled in glory, so too must believers be transformed by His presence, progressively becoming reflections of His essence. This is why he said to the Corinthian believers, "We all, with unveiled faces, are looking as in a mirror at the glory of the Lord and are being transformed into the same image from glory to glory; this is from the Lord who is the Spirit" (2 Corinthians 3:18). This transformation is the very essence of the *Parousia*—not a distant event but a living reality in which believers continually experience *epiphaneia* moments that conform them to Christ's image.

As the *Parousia* continues to unfold, believers are called to embrace the fullness of Christ's essence, allowing His transformative presence to shape our thoughts, actions, and relationships. This ongoing revelation not only transforms individuals but also strengthens the collective witness of the Church. The Church, as the body of Christ, stands as a living testament to His presence and power, reflecting the reality of the *Parousia* to the world. The dynamic nature of this unveiling challenges believers to actively engage with Christ's presence, continually growing in our understanding and expression of His essence.

EXOUSIA

In the transformative reality of the *Parousia*, believers are granted spiritual authority—*exousia*—enabling us to live as children of God and to reflect Christ's essence in our daily lives. This authority, given through grace, is not merely a positional designation but a dynamic empowerment that aligns believers with the divine nature of Christ and equips us to advance His kingdom on earth. John 1:12 affirms this truth, stating, "But to all who did receive him, he gave them the right to be children of God, to those who believe in his name."

Receiving Christ is more than an acknowledgment of His existence; it is an invitation into an entirely new identity as God's children, entrusted with the responsibility to reflect His character and fulfill His mission. The transformative nature of this divine authority is further emphasized in 2 Corinthians 3:18, which declares, "We all, with unveiled faces, are looking as in a mirror at the glory of the Lord and are being transformed into the same image from glory to glory." Through the *Parousia* believers undergo an ongoing transformation as Christ's essence is progressively unveiled within us, conforming us to His image and empowering us to embody His glory.

This continual unveiling of Christ's presence serves as the catalyst for spiritual transformation, shaping believers into His likeness and equipping us to reflect His character and love. The transformative process initiated by the *Parousia* is not a singular moment but a continual journey of renewal and conformity to Christ. In 1 John 3:2 the apostle writes, "We know that when he appears, we will be like him because we will see him as he is." The *Parousia*, therefore, is the unveiling that enables believers to behold Christ's essence and, in doing so, to become like Him. This transformation is an active process that calls believers to a deeper engagement with Christ's presence, resulting in lives that radiate His love, grace, and holiness.

The authority granted through the *Parousia* is not limited to personal transformation but extends to the believer's mission in the world. Christ's Great Commission in Matthew 28:18–20 reveals the scope of this authority: "All authority has been given to me in heaven and on earth. Go, therefore, and make disciples of all nations." The authority of Christ, shared with believers, empowers us to advance His kingdom through discipleship, teaching, and the embodiment of His presence. As image bearers of Christ, believers are called to carry His authority into the world, demonstrating the transformative power of the *Parousia* in our daily lives and interactions. This shared mission affirms that the *Parousia* is not a distant hope but a present, active reality shaping the Church's engagement with the world.

THE LIGHT AND THE TEMPLE

The apocalyptic vision of the New Jerusalem in Revelation offers a vivid depiction of Christ's essence as both the spiritual light and the temple, emphasizing His centrality in God's eternal plan. Revelation 21:23 declares, "The city does not need the sun or the moon to shine on it, because the glory of God illuminates it, and its lamp is the Lamb." This imagery presents Christ as the ultimate source of divine illumination, revealing His truth and holiness to all who dwell "in Him." The light of Christ is not merely a physical phenomenon but a profound spiritual reality that guides believers into the fullness of God's presence. This revelation underscores the truth that Christ's essence is the foundation of the believer's spiritual journey, continually illuminating our path and shaping our understanding of God's kingdom.

If the resurrection was the first great unveiling of Christ's glorified essence, then the final *epiphaneia* is the moment when all creation beholds Him fully. As we have seen, Revelation 21:23 declares, "The city does not need the sun or the moon to shine on it, because the glory of God illuminates it, and its lamp is the Lamb."

In that day the veil will be removed for all—not just for the disciples, not just for the Church, but for all of creation. The *Parousia* reaches its consummation when every knee bows and every tongue confesses that Christ is Lord, not merely by compulsion but by the undeniable *epiphaneia* of His unveiled glory.

Yet even now this unveiling has already begun. Those who live in the resurrection power of Christ experience the *Parousia* as a present reality; each day is a step closer to the full realization of His unveiled essence. As the apostle John says, "Dear friends, we are God's children now, and what we will be has not yet been revealed. We know that when he appears, we will be like him because we will see him as he is" (1 John 3:2). To see Him as He is—that is the final *epiphaneia*, and in that moment the transformation will be complete. The *Parousia*, which began in the resurrection, will be fully realized in the unveiled presence of Christ when all things are made new.

In addition to being the light, Christ is also the temple of the New Jerusalem, signifying the culmination of God's redemptive plan. Revelation 21:22 states, "I did not see a temple in it, because the Lord God the Almighty and the Lamb are its temple." Christ's body, once declared in John 2:19–21 to be the true temple, is revealed in its ultimate spiritual fulfillment in the New Jerusalem, where God and humanity are united in perfect communion. This vision highlights the reality that believers, through our union with Christ, participate in the spiritual dwelling of God, as expressed in Ephesians 2:19–22, where believers are described as being "built together for God's dwelling in the Spirit." This communal aspect of the *Parousia* emphasizes that the Church, as the body of Christ, embodies His presence and mission in the world.

The destruction of the Jerusalem temple in AD 70 was not merely a historical catastrophe; it was a theological watershed, marking the definitive end of the Old Covenant system and the establishment of Christ as the true and eternal temple. Jesus had already foretold this event in Matthew 24:1–2, linking the temple's fall to the judgment of an age that refused to recognize the true dwelling of God among men. In Hebrews 8:13 the writer affirms that the Old Covenant was becoming "obsolete and growing old" and was "about to pass away." The temple's destruction signified the culmination of that transition, reinforcing that the place of divine encounter had shifted from a physical structure to the resurrected Christ and His body, the Church.

Historical accounts further affirm this theological reality. The Roman General Titus, upon surveying the destruction of Jerusalem, reportedly marveled at the city's fortifications and acknowledged that such a stronghold should not have been taken by human effort alone. According to Josephus (*The Wars of the Jews*, Book 6, Chapter 9), Titus recognized the fall of Jerusalem as an act of divine will. This acknowledgment aligns with Christ's sovereign declaration that no stone of the temple would remain upon another. Though Titus originally sought to preserve the temple, it was destroyed against his orders, demonstrating that Rome's power—though immense—was ultimately subject to God's plan. The destruction of the earthly temple forced a necessary transition, whereby worship was no longer centered in a physical location but found its true fulfillment in the heavenly New Jerusalem, where the Lamb Himself is the temple.

CONCLUSION

The unfolding revelation of Christ's essence through the *Parousia* is not a future event to be passively anticipated but an active, present reality that continually transforms believers and aligns us with God's redemptive purposes. Through the resurrection the *Parousia* unveils Christ's divine essence, progressively revealing His glory, authority, and transformative presence.

Without the resurrection Christ's essence would remain concealed, and the empowering work of the Holy Spirit would not be realized in believers. Romans 6:5 underscores this profound reality: "For if we have been united with him in the likeness of his death, we will certainly also be in the likeness of his resurrection." Through the resurrection believers are empowered to live in the fullness of Christ's life, experiencing the transformative power of the *Parousia* as we are conformed to His likeness and prepared for the consummation of His kingdom.

This ongoing unveiling calls believers to active participation in Christ's mission, reflecting His glory, embodying His essence, and proclaiming His victory to a world in need of redemption. The resurrection does not merely point to a future hope but invites believers to walk in the present reality of Christ's resurrection power, living as witnesses to the reality of His kingdom. The power of Christ's resurrection to reveal His essence as an ongoing relational transformation is evident in the believer's daily walk with Him.

As we transition to the next chapter, the focus shifts toward reinterpreting Christian theology and eschatology through the lens of the *Parousia*. Understanding Christ's essence as the foundation of the believer's identity and mission provides a transformative framework that reframes traditional theological concepts and deepens our comprehension of God's redemptive plan. In this light the *Parousia* calls the Church and individual believers to a renewed perspective that embraces the fullness of Christ's presence and His ongoing work in the world.

CHAPTER 13

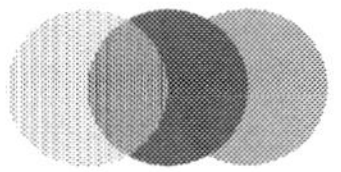

A NEW LENS FOR CHRISTIAN ESCHATOLOGY

The *Parousia*, as the ongoing spiritual unveiling of Christ's essence, redefines the theological and eschatological framework through which believers understand their relationship with God and their role in His redemptive plan. Building upon the revelation of Christ's essence and the transformative nature of judgment outlined in previous chapters, the *Parousia* emerges not as a singular future event but as an active, unfolding reality in the life of the Church and of individual believers. This unveiling challenges traditional paradigms, shifting the focus from passive anticipation to active participation in Christ's presence and mission.

To grasp the true beginning of this eschatological unveiling, we must return to a pivotal moment in history—the destruction of Jerusalem in AD 70. This cataclysm was not the end of the world but the end of an age: the Old Covenant era gave way to the New, and the *Parousia* moved from prophecy to manifestation. The implications of this event transformed worship, mission, and the very identity of God's people. What follows is an exploration of that moment as the opening of the New Age in Christ.

THE FALL OF JERUSALEM: A TURNING POINT IN THE UNVEILING OF THE *PAROUSIA*

The siege of Jerusalem in AD 70, as we have seen, was a moment of unparalleled devastation, but beneath the chaos and destruction lay a divine unveiling. As flames engulfed the temple, the once-magnificent house of worship—long seen as the dwelling place of God's presence—was reduced to rubble. Jesus had foretold this moment decades earlier, warning His disciples that not one stone would remain upon another (Matthew 24:1–2). The destruction was not merely the consequence of Roman conquest; it was the final, dramatic sign that the Old Covenant system had reached its end and that the fullness of Christ's presence was now being revealed through the New Covenant reality.

Within the besieged city famine and desperation drove the people into madness. Josephus, an eyewitness, recorded scenes so horrific that even hardened Roman soldiers recoiled in horror. The people of Jerusalem had placed their hope in the sanctuary of the temple, believing it to be indestructible, yet now the sacred space burned, and the cries of the people echoed through the streets. As mentioned in the precious chapter, even the Roman General Titus believed that the destruction was an act of God (Josephus, *The Wars of the Jews*, Book 6, Chapter 9).

Though many believed that God had forsaken Israel, this event was actually the fulfillment of His plan to unveil His greater presence. The old system of sacrifices and priestly mediation was no longer necessary—the true temple had already been raised "in Christ." The dwelling of God was now with His people, not in stone and mortar but in spirit and truth (John 4:23–24). The *Parousia* was not manifesting as cataclysmic, world-ending destruction, but rather as the progressive revelation of Christ's reign through His body, the Church.

The destruction of the temple marked a necessary transition, ensuring that the gospel would no longer be confined to one people, one land, or one structure. Worship was no longer about location; the true temple was the risen Christ, and those united with Him were now part of the New Jerusalem (Revelation 21:22).

Paradoxically, this judgment also marked the birth of something new—not only the visible end of the Old Covenant age but also the dawning of the New Covenant age. In the same way that Christ's resurrection unveiled His eternal presence, the fall of Jerusalem unveiled the reality that His kingdom was not of this world but within those who believed (Luke 17:21).

For many the temple had become an idol, a symbol of national pride and security, obscuring its true purpose—to foreshadow the presence of God fully revealed "in Christ." The *Parousia*—the unveiling of Christ's essence—necessitated the removal of all earthly representations of God's dwelling, so that the greater spiritual reality could be seen. This aligns with Paul's revelation in Colossians 1:27 that the mystery once hidden is now revealed: "Christ in you, the hope of glory."

The physical loss of Jerusalem signified the spiritual reality that Christ's kingdom had come, just as He had promised. No longer did worship require a journey to a holy city; rather, wherever believers gathered the presence of Christ was made manifest. The temple's destruction served as the final, irreversible sign that the world had entered into a new era of worship, one centered entirely on Christ's unveiled essence in the believer's life.

The *Parousia*, then, was not about passively awaiting a distant future return but about living in the reality of Christ's rule breaking into history, reorienting worship, and drawing all nations into His kingdom. The old had passed away, and the new had indeed come (2 Corinthians 5:17).

SPIRITUAL GROWTH THROUGH THE *PAROUSIA*

Believers experience spiritual growth as we encounter the unveiled essence of Christ, a transformative process that shapes us into children of God and aligns our lives with His divine nature. The transformative power of the *Parousia* enables believers to step into their identity as God's children, empowered to reflect His glory and walk in His mission.

John 1:12 declares, "But to all who did receive him, he gave them the right to be children of God, to those who believe in his name."

Receiving Christ is not a mere intellectual affirmation but an entrance into a new reality wherein believers are granted spiritual authority and identity through our union with Him. This transformation is a dynamic, ongoing process, as described in 2 Corinthians 3:18, which states, "We all, with unveiled faces, are looking as in a mirror at the glory of the Lord and are being transformed into the same image from glory to glory."

The process of spiritual growth is not a mere accumulation of theological knowledge but a progressive series of *epiphaneia* moments—encounters wherein Christ's essence is unveiled in deeper measure, leading to transformation. Each revelation of Christ's presence draws believers into greater conformity with His image, shaping our identity as children of God.

This reality is seen in the life of the apostle Paul. Despite his being well versed in Jewish theology, his *epiphaneia* on the road to Damascus (Acts 9:3–6) shattered his former understanding and reoriented his entire theological framework. His knowledge of the Law and the Prophets was redefined in the light of Christ, leading him to proclaim, "I consider everything to be a loss in view of the surpassing value of knowing Christ Jesus my Lord" (Philippians 3:8). Spiritual growth, therefore, is not merely intellectual assent but divine unveiling—an ongoing epiphaneia whereby the *Parousia* becomes real in the believer's life.

Through the *Parousia* believers are progressively conformed to Christ's image, moving from one degree of glory to another. No longer defined by our limitations, we are infused with the divine life of Christ, empowered to embody His essence and participate in His redemptive work in the world. The authority granted through the unveiling of Christ's presence enables believers to reflect His character and walk confidently in our calling.

The *Parousia* is not a distant event on the horizon but an ongoing spiritual reality facilitated by the Holy Spirit, who guides believers into all truth and empowers us to experience the fullness of Christ's presence. Jesus affirms this in John 16:13, where He states, "When the Spirit of truth comes, He will guide you into all the truth." And Paul echoes this truth in Galatians 2:20, emphasizing the intimate union believers share with Christ: "I no longer live, but Christ lives in me." This profound union ensures that the *Parousia* remains an active and dynamic reality, shaping every aspect of the believer's daily walk.

Many believers have been taught to think of eschatology as a distant hope, a waiting for Christ's return in some future event. But the biblical pattern of *epiphaneia* challenges this view, showing that the unveiling of Christ's essence is already happening in the lives of those who walk by faith.

The New Testament consistently presents the *Parousia* as an ongoing experience, not merely a climactic event. The disciples did not simply wait for a future revelation—they encountered progressive *epiphaneia* moments that deepened their understanding of Christ's presence: At Pentecost (Acts 2:1–4) the Holy Spirit's outpouring was an *epiphaneia* of divine indwelling, shifting the disciples' expectations of Christ's reign from external kingship to internal transformation.

At Stephen's martyrdom (Acts 7:55–56) he saw the heavens opened and Christ standing—an *epiphaneia* of Christ's present authority that redefined his understanding of death and resurrection. And at Paul's vision of the third heaven (2 Corinthians 12:2–4), he experienced an *epiphaneia* that unveiled spiritual realities beyond human perception, reinforcing the ongoing nature of divine revelation.

These encounters demonstrate that eschatology is not about waiting for an external event but about living in the reality of Christ's ever-increasing revelation. The *Parousia* unfolds through *epiphaneia*, transforming both personal faith and the collective witness of the Church.

The life of Stephen provides a powerful example of how the *Parousia* is realized in the believer's life. As recorded in Acts 7:55–56, at the moment of his martyrdom Stephen, "full of the Holy Spirit, gazed into heaven. He saw the glory of God, and Jesus standing at the right hand of God. He said, 'Look, I see the heavens opened and the Son of Man standing at the right hand of God!'" This experience was not a distant vision of a future return but an immediate revelation of Christ's ascended essence, strengthening Stephen in his moment of greatest trial. His experience affirms that the *Parousia* is not an abstract theological concept but a present reality, accessible to all who live by faith and remain steadfast "in Christ."

Paul further reinforces this reality in Colossians 1:27, stating, "Christ in you, the hope of glory." The *Parousia*, therefore, signifies the fulfillment of Christ's indwelling presence, empowering believers to live victoriously as reflections of His glory. Through the Spirit's ongoing work Christ's essence is continuously unveiled, providing believers with strength, peace, and transformative power as we navigate our spiritual journey.

CHRIST'S KINGDOM AS A PRESENT REALITY

The unveiling of Christ's essence through the *Parousia* establishes His kingdom as an active and present reality in the lives of believers. This kingdom is not dependent on external circumstances but is realized through faith and submission to Christ's rule. Colossians 1:13 affirms this truth, stating, "He has rescued us from the domain of darkness and transferred us into the kingdom of the Son he loves." Believers are not waiting for the kingdom to arrive; we are living in it now, experiencing the righteousness, peace, and joy that come through the Holy Spirit (Romans 14:17).

Jesus proclaimed in Luke 17:21, "The kingdom of God is in your midst," revealing that His kingdom is not of this world but is a spiritual reality manifested in the hearts and lives of those who believe. The *Parousia* reveals Christ's rule as an internal reality, transforming believers from within and empowering us to serve as active participants in His reign. Our union "in Christ" anchors us in this kingdom, making us co-heirs with Him and calling us to manifest His presence in the world.

Participation in Christ's kingdom is not optional or passive—it is a present and urgent calling that demands active, Spirit-empowered engagement through faith. Romans 14:17 clarifies that "the kingdom of God is not eating and drinking, but righteousness, peace, and joy in the Holy Spirit." Believers do not merely wait for this kingdom to arrive; we are summoned to live in it now through spiritual transformation and willing submission to Christ's reign, finding our purpose and fulfillment in His presence. Abiding in Christ, as emphasized in John 15:4–5, illustrates the essential connection believers have with their King. Jesus declares, "Remain in me, and I in you. . . . The one who remains in me and I in him produces much fruit, because you can do nothing without me." This abiding relationship ensures that the kingdom is not only experienced in the present but bears fruit in the lives of believers, demonstrating Christ's power and presence to the world.

The *Parousia* invites believers to embody the principles of Christ's kingdom, serving as conduits of His love, righteousness, and peace in a world desperate for redemption. As Christ's essence is unveiled within us, we become living testimonies of His kingdom, reflecting His light and proclaiming His victory. The present reality of the kingdom empowers believers to walk in the confidence of Christ's authority, knowing that His reign is not something we await but something we actively participate in now.

The expansion of Christ's kingdom is not achieved through political conquest or worldly power but through the transformative power of His presence within believers. Through our union with Christ we become instruments of His grace, advancing His kingdom by living lives that reflect His essence. This reality challenges traditional eschatological views that position the kingdom solely in the future, calling believers to embrace the *Parousia* as an immediate and ongoing unveiling of Christ's rule.

The *Parousia* redefines eschatology by shifting the focus from passive anticipation of a distant, physical return to an active participation in the ongoing spiritual unveiling of Christ's presence and reign—a revelation that will reach its fullness at the consummation of all things. This paradigm shift not only transforms theological perspectives but also deeply influences the practical expressions of worship, mission, and personal transformation. Understanding the *Parousia* as a continuous spiritual reality invites believers to embrace our role as participants in Christ's unveiled essence, living as agents of His kingdom in the present.

ESCHATOLOGY AS PRESENT ENGAGEMENT

The vision of Stephen in Acts 7 serves as a profound example of eschatology as a present and transformative reality. In the moment of his martyrdom, Stephen, "full of the Holy Spirit," gazes into heaven and proclaims, "Look, I see the heavens opened and the Son of Man standing at the right hand of God!" (Acts 7:55–56). This revelation of Christ's ascended presence underscores that the *Parousia* is not limited to a future physical return but is an ongoing spiritual unveiling. For Stephen the *Parousia* was an immediate experience that empowered him with divine strength and assurance, allowing him to face death with unwavering faith and confidence in Christ's reign.

This perspective challenges the traditional eschatological framework, which often centers on waiting for a climactic physical event. Instead, believers are called to recognize Christ's present reign and to align our lives with His ongoing work in the world. Paul's words in Philippians 3:20–21 affirm this engagement: "Our citizenship is in heaven, and we eagerly await a Savior from there, the Lord Jesus Christ." This awaiting, however, is not passive; it is an active posture of living under the transformative power of Christ's presence and reflecting His kingdom in every aspect of life.

Eschatology, therefore, is not simply an expectation of what is to come but an invitation to experience the reality of Christ's reign now. As Paul states in Philippians 1:21, "For me, to live is Christ and to die is gain." This understanding calls us as believers to embrace our heavenly citizenship in the present, experiencing the assurance, strength, and purpose that flow from our participation in Christ's ongoing unveiling.

THE TRANSFORMATIVE IMPACT OF THE *PAROUSIA* ON WORSHIP

Recognizing the *Parousia* as an ongoing spiritual event reorients eschatology itself, revealing that the end is not merely about what will happen *then* but about who is unveiled *now*. This realization fundamentally transforms worship. Worship becomes a present acknowledgment of Christ's reign and an active participation in the unfolding of eschatological reality. It is no longer an act of mere anticipation but a celebration of the inbreaking future, manifest now in the presence of Christ through the Spirit.

This understanding is vividly captured in Revelation 5:13, which declares, "Every creature in heaven, on earth, under the earth, on the sea, and everything in them say, 'Blessing and honor and glory and power be to the one seated on the throne, and to the Lamb, forever and ever!'" Such worship is eschatological in nature—it reflects heaven's present song, which believers are drawn into as the veil is lifted.

True worship, then, is not about rituals or longing for what has yet to occur but about stepping into an *epiphaneia* encounter—a moment when Christ's essence is unveiled and His presence is experienced in real time. Worship, in this light, becomes not only an expression of faith but an act of revelation. It participates in the *Parousia*, unveiling the reality that Christ is enthroned now.

This vision is grounded in Scripture. Isaiah's throne room encounter (Isaiah 6:1–8) was not merely personal; it was eschatological—a heavenly revelation that transformed his mission on earth. John's vision in Revelation 1:12–18 was likewise a present-tense unveiling of eschatological glory, leading him to fall at Christ's feet in worship.

Jesus affirmed that worship is a response to revelation, declaring: "True worshipers will worship the Father in Spirit and in truth" (John 4:23). To worship in Spirit and truth is to participate in the unveiled presence of Christ; it is eschatology experienced rather than merely awaited. In this way worship becomes a living engagement with the *Parousia*.

Corporate worship, then, is not just symbolic. It is a microcosm of the age to come, a present-tense participation in the heavenly assembly, where believers unite with the hosts of heaven in exalting Christ. Worship is not confined to ritual or location but arises from the awareness of Christ's indwelling presence, transforming both the individual and the gathered body.

In short, the *Parousia* reshapes eschatology from a deferred hope into a lived reality, and worship becomes its primary expression. As believers behold Christ's unveiled glory, they are transformed by His truth and empowered to carry His mission into the world.

THE URGENCY AND PURPOSE OF MISSION IN LIGHT OF THE *PAROUSIA*

The ongoing nature of the *Parousia* redefines eschatology, not as a countdown to a climactic event but as a present and unfolding revelation of Christ's reign. This eschatological unveiling infuses mission with renewed urgency and eternal purpose. The Great Commission is not only a command to prepare for Christ's appearing but also an invitation to participate in the eschaton made visible now.

Jesus declares in Matthew 28:18–20, "All authority has been given to me in heaven and on earth. Go, therefore, and make disciples of all nations." This commission flows directly from His enthronement and is undergirded by His abiding presence: "I am with you always, to the end of the age." In light of the *Parousia*, this statement is not a promise of future companionship but the declaration of an eschatological reality that is already unfolding.

The urgency of mission, then, is not driven by fear of a looming judgment or a distant second coming but by the present unveiling of Christ in the world. Every moment of *epiphaneia* calls for a response. Those who see the unveiled Christ cannot remain passive; they are compelled to proclaim what they have seen and known.

This was the pattern of the early Church. After Paul's Damascus road *epiphaneia* he did not wait for further confirmation but immediately began preaching Christ (Acts 9:20). Likewise, after Peter, James, and John had witnessed the Transfiguration Jesus did not instruct them to look ahead to some future kingdom—He directed them to listen to Him and follow.

The *Parousia*, rightly understood, demands active participation. Christ's essence is being revealed now, and believers are invited to bear witness to this eschatological unveiling. The Great Commission is not just about evangelism; it is about revealing the already reigning Christ to a world still veiled in darkness. As Paul writes, "For God who said, 'Let light shine out of darkness,' has shone in our hearts to give the light of the knowledge of God's glory in the face of Jesus Christ" (2 Corinthians 4:6). Mission, in this view, is an act of eschatological disclosure.

To live on mission is to live as an *epiphaneia*-bearer, carrying the light of the unveiled Christ into the world. Understanding the *Parousia* as a present and ongoing reality empowers believers to engage in mission with boldness and clarity. It transforms the Church's eschatology from future awaiting to present revealing.

Believers are not simply waiting for Christ to establish His kingdom; they are already living in it. The *Parousia* reframes mission as the visible manifestation of God's reign through His people. It is not a task to be completed but a foretaste of the age to come—a living witness that the kingdom has already arrived in the face of Christ and is advancing through those who bear His light.

THE CALL TO PERSONAL TRANSFORMATION

The *Parousia* also calls believers to focus on their personal spiritual growth and alignment with Christ's image—as Paul declares in Ephesians 4:13, "until we all reach unity in the faith and in the knowledge of God's Son, growing into maturity with a stature measured by Christ's fullness." This transformation is not a future expectation but a present reality, made possible by the unveiling of Christ's essence in the believer's life.

The *Parousia* invites believers to experience ongoing renewal and sanctification, shaping us into reflections of Christ's glory. This transformation is not an isolated endeavor but a communal reality in which the Church collectively reflects Christ's presence to the world. It calls believers to maturity, unity, and a shared commitment to embodying Christ's love and truth. Living in the reality of the *Parousia* means embracing the process of becoming more like Christ, allowing His essence to shape our thoughts, actions, and character. It challenges believers to move beyond superficial faith and to enter into a deeper, more authentic relationship with Christ, marked by continual growth and transformation.

The *Parousia* offers a new lens through which believers can view their theology, eschatology, and personal transformation. It calls for a shift from passive anticipation to active engagement with Christ's ongoing revelation and mission. The destruction of the temple in AD 70 confirmed that the old order had passed away, reinforcing that the presence of Christ is now unveiled in His people rather than in physical structures. This understanding compels believers to recognize the immediacy of His kingdom, the transformative power of worship, and the urgency of discipleship.

As the journey continues into the next chapter, the focus will turn to how the essence of Christ is unveiled within believers, shaping our identity and mission in profound ways. Understanding the *Parousia* as an ongoing reality invites believers to fully embrace our calling to reflect His essence and advance His kingdom in our daily lives.

CHAPTER 14

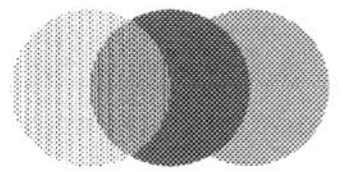

SEEING CHRIST: THE SPIRITUAL UNVEILING OF HIS ESSENCE TO BELIEVERS

To live by faith is to live with new eyes. The *Parousia* is not an abstract theological reality; it is a lived experience for those who have been given eyes to see. As Jesus told His disciples, "Blessed are your eyes because they do see, and your ears because they do hear. For truly I tell you, many prophets and righteous people longed to see the things you see but didn't see them" (Matthew 13:16–17). This blessing of spiritual sight is not reserved for a distant future but is available now through the Spirit.

Throughout the New Testament to see Christ is to know Him, to recognize His glory, and to be transformed by His presence. From Paul's declaration that "God . . . has shone in our hearts to give the light of the knowledge of God's glory in the face of Jesus Christ" (2 Corinthians 4:6) to the promise that "we all . . . are being transformed . . . from glory to glory" (2 Corinthians 3:18), Scripture makes clear that spiritual vision is the foundation of discipleship and transformation.

This chapter builds on earlier discussions of Christ's essence and judgment by narrowing the lens: here we explore how Christ reveals Himself *to* believers and how this vision shapes their lives. We will examine how post-resurrection appearances serve as a model for spiritual recognition, how the Spirit illuminates the eyes of the heart, and how the act of seeing Christ is inseparably linked with becoming like Him.

The *Parousia* is not only a cosmic or historical unveiling but is also deeply personal. As Christ is revealed more fully to the believer, the believer is drawn into deeper union, greater transformation, and clearer vision. To see Christ is to participate in His life. And in that seeing the eyes of faith behold what the eyes of the world cannot: the glory of the unveiled King.

THE MEANS OF SEEING—REVELATION, FAITH, AND THE SPIRIT

Spiritual sight is not achieved by intellect or effort; it is granted by revelation. From the beginning Christ's essence has been hidden from natural perception and unveiled only through divine initiative. The Gospels are filled with examples of people who looked directly at Jesus but did not recognize Him, while others—often the lowly, the poor, and the contrite—saw clearly who He was. Seeing Christ is not the product of religious training or human willpower; it is the result of a heart awakened by the Spirit and aligned by faith.

Paul captures this mystery when he writes, "The god of this age has blinded the minds of the unbelievers to keep them from seeing the light of the gospel of the glory of Christ" (2 Corinthians 4:4) but then affirms that "God who said, 'Let light shine out of darkness,' has shone in our hearts to give the light of the knowledge of God's glory in the face of Jesus Christ" (2 Corinthians 4:6). Here Paul presents revelation not as a moment of mental clarity but as a divine act of new creation. God speaks light into darkness, and what is revealed is Christ Himself.

This act of unveiling is both sudden and ongoing. The eyes of faith are opened at conversion, but spiritual clarity deepens as believers walk in communion with the Spirit. Paul prays that the "eyes of your heart may be enlightened" (Ephesians 1:18), showing that revelation is not a one-time experience but a progressive unveiling.

Faith is the posture by which this vision is received. As Hebrews 11:1 declares, "Now faith is the reality of what is hoped for, the proof of what is not seen." In the kingdom of God faith is not blind; it is what truly sees. The one who believes is the one who perceives. This is why those who rejected Jesus could not see Him for who He was, though He stood before them in plain sight, while the humble and trusting recognized His glory.

It is the Spirit who opens this vision. Jesus said that the Spirit would take what belongs to Him and reveal it to His disciples (John 16:14). The Spirit is not only the agent of revelation but the indwelling presence of Christ who illuminates the believer's inner life. To walk by the Spirit is to walk with open eyes, to behold the unveiled Christ in the present moment and be transformed by that vision.

Thus, seeing Christ is not reserved for a distant age or a climactic future. The unveiling has already begun. The *Parousia* is at work in the life of every believer who, by faith, sees Jesus not merely as a historical figure but as the ever-present Lord whose glory is shining in and through them.

The truth that Christ is spiritually seen through revelation, faith, and the Spirit becomes all the more vivid when we observe how His followers came to recognize Him after the resurrection. These encounters offer more than historical testimony—they reveal the spiritual pattern by which Christ makes Himself known. In every instance Jesus is unveiled not to the curious or casual observer but to those whose hearts are open, humbled, and ready to believe. What was true for them is true for us. Their pattern becomes our path.

THE PATTERN OF UNVEILING—POST-RESURRECTION ENCOUNTERS

The resurrection of Jesus did not simply reverse death; it redefined how He would be seen. After rising from the dead Jesus appeared to His followers not in displays of grandeur or power but through quiet unveilings, moments of recognition when faith and revelation converged. These encounters form a pattern for how Christ is seen by believers even now, in the age of the *Parousia*.

Mary Magdalene was the first to encounter the risen Christ, but at first she did not recognize Him. She mistook Him for a gardener—until He called her by name (John 20:14–16). Her eyes were opened not by sight alone but by relational intimacy. It was when she heard His voice that she saw Him for who He truly was. This encounter reveals that Christ is not known by outward appearance but by personal revelation.

On the road to Emmaus two disciples walked with Jesus for miles, discussing the Scriptures and the events of the past days. Though their hearts burned within them, they did not know it was Jesus walking beside them—until He broke the bread (Luke 24:30–31). Their eyes were opened in the context of communion, Word, and shared table. Again the pattern is clear: recognition comes not from physical observation but from spiritual revelation tied to trust, relationship, and divine timing.

Thomas, perhaps the best-known doubter, demanded physical evidence to believe. Yet when Jesus stood before him, inviting him to touch His wounds, Thomas responded not with empirical examination but with worship: "My Lord and my God!" (John 20:28). Jesus responded, "Because you have seen me, you have believed. Blessed are those who have not seen and yet believe" (John 20:29). This beatitude affirms that spiritual vision is the greater blessing. The ones who truly see are those who believe.

In each of these post-resurrection moments the unveiling of Christ is not passive but is deeply relational, rooted in faith and animated by grace. The same Christ who walked beside these early believers now dwells within us. The *Parousia* continues through these encounters, not as dramatic apparitions but as daily revelations to the eyes of faith. We see Christ in the Word, in communion, in fellowship, and in the stillness of prayer. We see Him not because He becomes visible but because we have been made able to see.

These appearances after the resurrection are not relics of the past; they are invitations. As Christ was made known to them, so He is made known to us. Their pattern of recognition becomes our pattern of transformation. The risen Christ is still revealing Himself, and the ones who see Him are the ones whose hearts are attuned by faith and opened by the Spirit.

Each post-resurrection encounter revealed more than Christ's identity—they revealed what happens when He is truly seen. Eyes opened by faith become hearts transformed by glory. The *Parousia* is not merely the unveiling of Christ for observation; it is the unveiling of Christ for transformation. To see Him is to be changed by Him. In this next section we turn from the recognition of Christ to the renewal that comes through beholding—the transformation of vision into likeness.

THE TRANSFORMATION OF VISION—BEHOLDING AND BECOMING

Seeing Christ is not a static act; it is transformative. The spiritual unveiling of His essence does not leave the believer unchanged. Scripture teaches that to behold the Lord is to become like Him. In the economy of the Spirit, sight is formation. Revelation is not merely for admiration—it is for transfiguration.

Paul makes this clear in one of the theologically richest declarations in the New Testament: "We all, with unveiled faces, are looking as in a mirror at the glory of the Lord and are being transformed into the same image from glory to glory; this is from the Lord who is the Spirit" (2 Corinthians 3:18).

In this passage Paul draws on the image of Moses, whose face was veiled after encountering God's glory. But now "in Christ" the veil is removed. Believers no longer receive reflected glory from a distance;

they behold the glory of Christ directly, and that vision reshapes them. As the Spirit unveils Christ the believer is transformed into His image—not through effort but through exposure.

This transformation is vividly foreshadowed in the Transfiguration (Matthew 17:1–9) when Jesus took Peter, James, and John up a high mountain and was transfigured before them. His face shone like the sun, and His clothes became dazzling white. They saw His glory with their eyes, and they heard the Father's voice say, "This is my beloved Son, with whom I am well-pleased. Listen to Him!" (Matthew 3:17).

They fell on their faces in reverence and fear, not because they were seeing something terrifying but because they were seeing the true essence of Christ. This moment was not just an external vision; it was an internal awakening. Though Jesus instructed them to remain silent until after His resurrection, the event left a permanent mark on their lives. These three—Peter, James, and John—would go on to become foundational leaders in the early Church. They were not made perfect, but they were reoriented by what they saw and heard.

The Transfiguration reveals the link between beholding and calling. Jesus showed His glory not to the crowds but to those He would entrust with His mission. In seeing Christ's unveiled essence they glimpsed not only who He is but who they were being called to become.

The transformation that occurs is not simply moral improvement or religious maturity. It is the restoration of the image of God in us, according to the likeness of the Son. Paul affirms that "those he foreknew he also predestined to be conformed to the image of his Son" (Romans 8:29). This is not a future hope but a present reality, unfolding now through the ongoing *Parousia* of Christ within.

The more clearly we see Him, the more fully we reflect Him. This is the mystery of sanctification by sight. The eyes of the heart become the agents of transformation. Faith leads to vision, and vision leads to glory—not our glory but His radiating through us as we become vessels of the unveiled Christ.

In this light discipleship is not primarily about behavior management or intellectual assent but about exposure to Christ's essence until that essence is formed in us. The *Parousia* is not the glory we watch for—it is the glory we *participate* in. It is the great unveiling of Christ that not only reveals who He is but who we are becoming in Him.

If transformation begins with vision, the life of faith becomes a life of focus. Beholding Christ is not a passive moment but an intentional practice—one that must be sustained, renewed, and guarded. As the unveiled essence of Christ continues to be revealed believers are called not only to *see once* but to *keep seeing*. In the next section we explore the daily discipline of fixing our eyes on Jesus, the ongoing unveiling that anchors the believer's walk.

FIXING OUR EYES ON JESUS—THE PRACTICE OF SPIRITUAL SIGHT

The journey of faith is powered not by willpower but by vision. What we behold shapes who we become. This is why Scripture continually calls believers to turn their gaze not inward, not outward, but upward, to Jesus Himself. The writer of Hebrews exhorts us with these words: "Let us run with endurance the race that lies before us, keeping our eyes on Jesus, the pioneer and perfecter of our faith" (Hebrews 12:1–2).

This command is not metaphorical. It is deeply spiritual. To fix our eyes on Jesus is to orient the heart toward His continual unveiling and to walk through life with a sustained awareness of His presence, His glory, and His leadership. This is not merely about visualizing Jesus but about recognizing His ongoing reign and interpreting every part of life through the lens of His revealed essence.

Faith in this sense becomes the spiritual faculty of sight. It is the lens through which we perceive what cannot be seen with physical eyes. The believer's vision is not defined by circumstance or appearance but by the reality of Christ enthroned in glory. To walk by faith is to walk with eyes that are trained on Jesus, even when storms rage, even when the path is unclear, and even when all else fades (Matthew 8:23–27).

This spiritual sight is not effortless. It must be cultivated. Distractions abound, and the world constantly offers false images to fix our eyes upon—success, fear, self, power, or comfort. These distort the image of Christ and dim the radiance of His unveiled presence. But to those who choose the narrow way of attentiveness, Christ becomes clearer with each step. As Paul says, "Set your minds on things above, not on earthly things. For you died, and your life is hidden with Christ in God" (Colossians 3:2–3). What is hidden to the world is visible to the faithful.

Practicing spiritual sight means creating space for the Spirit to reveal Christ anew. It means returning daily to the Word, where the light of His face shines. It means entering prayer not merely to ask but to behold. It means gathering with the body of Christ not merely for instruction but for encounter. In these ordinary moments the extraordinary unveiling continues.

This practice is also communal. Just as Peter, James, and John beheld Christ together on the mountain, believers today are called to see Him together in worship, fellowship, and shared mission. There is a corporate vision of Christ that sharpens the individual gaze. The Church becomes a temple of unveiled glory—not because we see perfectly but because we see together.

To fix our eyes on Jesus is not a one-time act but the defining practice of the *Parousia*-shaped life. It is the posture of those who believe that the glory of Christ is already breaking into the present age. It is the way we run the race. It is how we are transformed. It is how we endure.

Fixing our eyes on Jesus is not only the practice of faith—it becomes the posture of life in the age of the *Parousia*. As the veil is removed and Christ's glory is revealed, believers are not merely spectators of a spiritual reality but participants in a new creation. In this final section we reflect on what it means to live with eyes open—to carry the vision of Christ into daily life and into the world He came to transform.

CONCLUSION—LIVING WITH EYES WIDE OPEN

To live with eyes wide open is to live as one awakened, not by fear or obligation but by glory. It is to walk through the world with a steady gaze on the unseen, a heart attuned to the Spirit, and a life shaped by the ongoing unveiling of Christ. This is not the life of spiritual elites or mystics but the birthright of every believer who has encountered the risen Lord and now sees by faith.

Spiritual vision does not remove us from the world; it redefines how we engage with it. We no longer interpret life through the lens of scarcity, striving, or survival. We interpret everything through the unveiled glory of Christ, the One who reigns now, speaks now, and is transforming the world through those who see Him. As Paul affirms, "We walk by faith, not by sight" (2 Corinthians 5:7), not because faith is blindness but because faith sees what the world cannot.

This vision reshapes our relationships, our work, our struggles, and our hopes. We begin to see others not as obstacles or assets but as fellow image-bearers, each one a person in whom the glory of Christ might one day be revealed. We begin to see suffering not as defeat but as the soil in which eternal glory takes root. We begin to see the Church not as a gathering of imperfect people but as the very body through which Christ continues to unveil His presence.

Living with eyes wide open means embracing the *Parousia* not just as doctrine but as daily reality. It means refusing to sleepwalk through life. It means stepping into each day asking not only "What must I do?" but "What is Christ revealing?" This is the posture of expectation that does not wait for the end of the world but recognizes that the world is already being remade "in Christ."

And so we live, not waiting for Christ to return to a broken world but rejoicing that He is already reigning within it. We see Him not as absent but as present, not as distant but as near. The *Parousia* opens our eyes wide, and in the seeing we are changed. The veil is lifted. The glory shines. And we, with unveiled faces, behold the Lord and become like Him.

CHAPTER 15

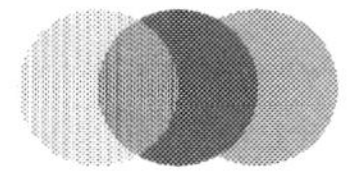

THE *PAROUSIA* IN THE REVELATION OF JOHN

The book of Revelation stands as the climactic culmination of biblical eschatology, weaving together apocalyptic imagery, prophetic declarations, and profound spiritual truths. As the grand finale of Scripture's narrative, it presents the *Parousia* as central to God's redemptive purposes. Within its vivid and symbolic language Revelation calls believers to perceive the deeper spiritual realities at work, emphasizing the ongoing presence of Christ and the transformative renewal that flows from His unveiled essence. The book of Revelation is not a prediction manual, as it is often portrayed. Instead, it is a prophetic unveiling of Jesus Christ, one that aligns with the broader thesis of this work by portraying the *Parousia* not only as a future consummation of God's purpose but as a present, active reality shaping the Church, the believer, and the cosmos itself.

Revelation offers a sweeping depiction of Christ's eternal reign, His ultimate triumph over darkness, and the renewal of all creation. It reveals how the *Parousia* unfolds progressively in the lives of believers, even as it anticipates the complete realization of God's kingdom. The book's powerful imagery serves as a profound declaration of the transformative power of Christ's essence—a reality that is both present and future, drawing creation into the fullness of divine restoration.

THE NEW HEAVEN AND THE NEW EARTH

The *Parousia* in the book of Revelation reveals the essence of Christ through the renewal of all creation, portraying the fulfillment of God's redemptive work. This spiritual renewal unfolds in two significant aspects: the vision of the new heaven and the new earth and the union of believers with the ascended Christ.

Revelation 21 introduces the ultimate vision of renewal with the words, "Then I saw a new heaven and a new earth, for the first heaven and the first earth had passed away, and the sea was no more. I also saw the holy city, the new Jerusalem, coming down out of heaven from God, prepared like a bride adorned for her husband. Then I heard a loud voice from the throne: 'Look, God's dwelling is with humanity, and he will live with them'" (Revelation 21:1–3).

This passage presents a compelling picture of spiritual transformation, in which the cosmos itself is renewed in Christ. The absence of the sea—a common biblical symbol of chaos, separation, and instability—signifies the full restoration of harmony and unity under Christ's reign. The new creation is not merely a physical reconstruction of the heavens and the earth but a profound spiritual renewal, reflecting the reconciliation of all things "in Christ" and the complete unveiling of His essence throughout creation.

Paul's declaration in 2 Corinthians 5:17 provides a theological parallel to this cosmic renewal: "If anyone is in Christ,' he is a new creation; the old has passed away, and see, the new has come!" Just as individual believers experience transformation through their union with Christ, so too does creation itself undergo renewal through His presence. The new creation described in Revelation aligns the entirety of existence with the divine will, making all things a reflection of God's redemptive work.

The vision of the new heaven and new earth demonstrates that the *Parousia* is not an isolated event confined to the distant future but an ongoing and unfolding reality. The transformative presence of

Christ actively reshapes creation, drawing all things into their intended fulfillment in God's eternal purposes.

UNION WITH THE ASCENDED CHRIST

The spiritual renewal portrayed in Revelation is deeply rooted in the believer's union with the ascended Christ. Paul's theology of union with Christ offers a framework for understanding this transformation, emphasizing that through faith believers participate in His divine nature and are progressively conformed to His image. The apostle affirms this truth in 2 Corinthians 5:17, highlighting that those who are in Christ become a new creation—a reality that is not only personal but extends to the entire cosmos.

Revelation's vision of the New Jerusalem descending from heaven reinforces this idea of union, in which the city symbolizes the dwelling place of God with humanity. This divine presence permeates every aspect of creation, ensuring that believers are no longer estranged from God but intimately united with Him through Christ's unveiled essence. The *Parousia*, therefore, is not merely the anticipation of Christ's return but the continual unfolding of His presence in and through believers.

Through this ongoing unveiling, believers are called to live in the reality of our spiritual renewal, experiencing the transformative power of Christ's essence in our daily lives. This dynamic process brings us into deeper communion with the ascended Christ, aligning our existence with the eternal purposes of God. The renewal of creation, then, is not only an eschatological hope but a present reality that invites believers to actively participate in God's redemptive work.

THE SYMBOLISM OF THE NEW JERUSALEM

The vision of the New Jerusalem in the book of Revelation stands as a profound symbol of the *Parousia*, embodying the spiritual reality of God's eternal presence with humanity. It reveals the culmination of

God's redemptive work, wherein Christ's unveiled essence permeates every aspect of existence. In this vision believers are invited to understand their present participation in the unfolding *Parousia* while anticipating its ultimate fulfillment.

Revelation 21:22–23 presents a striking image of the New Jerusalem: "I did not see a temple in it, because the Lord God the Almighty and the Lamb are its temple. The city does not need the sun or the moon to shine on it, because the glory of God illuminates it, and its lamp is the Lamb." The absence of a physical temple signifies the direct and unmediated presence of God, with Christ as the very essence of light and holiness. His unveiled presence dispels all darkness, guiding and transforming His people into reflections of His glory.

This imagery reveals that the New Jerusalem is not constructed of earthly stone but composed of divine presence—it is Christ Himself unveiled as the dwelling of God with humanity, radiating the life, truth, and holiness of Christ to all creation. Theological reflection on this passage reveals that believers, through our union with Christ, experience this divine light in our daily lives. The unveiled *Parousia* illuminates the believer's path, progressively conforming us to the image of Christ and empowering us to walk in the fullness of His presence.

The vision of the New Jerusalem aligns closely with Paul's teaching in Ephesians 2:22, where he writes, "You are also being built together for God's dwelling in the Spirit." The ongoing construction of God's spiritual dwelling highlights the transformative work of the *Parousia* in believers. Through the indwelling of the Holy Spirit, believers collectively become the living embodiment of the New Jerusalem, experiencing Christ's presence as an ever-unfolding reality.

The New Jerusalem, therefore, represents more than a future promise; it is the present reality of the Church's spiritual union with Christ. As believers are transformed by His essence we become living testimonies of His glory, bearing witness to His ongoing work in the world. This spiritual dwelling shapes not only individual identity but also the corporate mission of the Church, calling it to actively participate in God's redemptive plan through holiness, love, and justice.

THE BRIDE ADORNED FOR HER HUSBAND

In Revelation 21:2 the New Jerusalem is described as "a bride adorned for her husband," illustrating the intimate union between Christ and His Church. This bridal imagery finds its parallel in Paul's depiction of the Church in Ephesians 5:25–27, where Christ "loved the church and gave himself for her to make her holy, cleansing her with the washing of water by the word. He did this to present the church to himself in splendor, without spot or wrinkle." The imagery of the bride conveys the deep relational aspect of the *Parousia*, emphasizing how Christ's unveiled essence is revealed in the purity, love, and holiness of His people.

The adornment of the bride signifies the culmination of God's redemptive work, whereby the Church fully reflects Christ's essence and glory. The *Parousia*, therefore, is not an isolated event but an ongoing process in which believers are continually sanctified and prepared for our ultimate union with Christ. This understanding calls the Church to embrace its identity as the bride, living in faithful devotion and expectancy and displaying the beauty of Christ's character to the world.

THE PRIESTHOOD OF BELIEVERS

Revelation also affirms the identity of believers as priests, emphasizing our active participation in the ongoing unveiling of Christ's essence and His mission. The priestly role of believers is central to the *Parousia*, as we are entrusted with the sacred responsibility of reflecting Christ's presence and mediating His kingdom to the world.

The concept of believers as priests is presented in Revelation 1:6, where Christ is said to have "made us a kingdom, priests to his God and Father." This priesthood is not confined to ritualistic worship but extends into every aspect of life, whereby believers are called to bear witness to Christ's reign. Believers' lives become a living testimony of His transformative relational work, unveiling His essence through acts of love, justice, and proclamation.

The priestly ministry of believers finds its ultimate expression in Revelation 12:11, which declares that they "conquered him [the devil] by the blood of the Lamb and by the word of their testimony." This victory is rooted in Christ's atoning work and reveals the transformative power of the *Parousia* in our lives. As priests, believers mediate Christ's essence to the world, unveiling His kingdom through our faithful witness and sacrificial love. The believers' priesthood empowers us to embody the realities of Christ's reign, actively participating in His mission of reconciliation and renewal.

SYMMETRY WITH THE BOOK OF HEBREWS

The priestly imagery in Revelation closely aligns with the theology presented in the book of Hebrews, which portrays Christ as the ultimate High Priest who intercedes for believers. Revelation builds upon this foundation by extending Christ's priestly ministry to those united with Him, highlighting their active role in God's redemptive work. Hebrews 9:28 affirms this continuity, stating that "Christ, having been offered once to bear the sins of many, will appear a second time, not to bear sin but to bring salvation to those who are waiting for him." As stated in Chapter 9, "appear a second time" is related to the high priest's emergence from the Most Holy Place, signifying God's acceptance of the offer for sin for those who are waiting for the appearance of the high priest. Likewise, Christ appears to those who perceive the *Parousia*.

Believers, therefore, are not passive recipients of salvation but active participants in Christ's ongoing work of redemption. As priests in His kingdom, we are called to reflect His presence, intercede for the world, and advance His kingdom through faithful service. This understanding of the priesthood reinforces the thesis that the *Parousia* is an ever-unfolding reality wherein Christ's essence is continually revealed in the lives and ministries of His people.

Revelation and Hebrews together provide a holistic picture of the Church's priestly mission, emphasizing that believers are integral to the unveiling of the *Parousia*. Through their participation in Christ's priestly work they embody His presence and advance His kingdom in anticipation of its ultimate fulfillment.

CHRIST'S REIGN AND MISSION

The book of Revelation presents Christ's reign not merely as a distant future hope but as a present spiritual reality that unfolds progressively through the *Parousia*. This reign serves as both the foundation and the culmination of God's redemptive plan, inviting believers to actively engage in His mission, embodying His essence in the world and witnessing to His transformative power. Revelation declares that Christ's reign is already established through His ascension and is being unveiled continuously, leading creation toward its ultimate restoration.

The declaration in Revelation 11:15—"The kingdom of the world has become the kingdom of our Lord and of his Christ, and he will reign forever and ever"—proclaims the consummation of Christ's sovereign rule. This pronouncement does not merely point to a future event but affirms the present reality of His reign, progressively unveiled through the *Parousia*. Christ's authority permeates the lives of believers and our communities, drawing us into alignment with His kingdom values of righteousness, peace, and joy (Romans 14:17).

The *Parousia* manifests this reign in a dynamic and spiritual manner, in which Christ's presence is actively transforming hearts and minds. Believers are called to live as citizens of His kingdom, not confined by physical boundaries but empowered by His unveiled presence. This spiritual reign challenges believers to embrace our identity "in Christ" and reflect His essence in our relationships, decisions, and daily walk.

Revelation affirms that believers, united with Christ, are commissioned to participate in His redemptive mission. Our witness is an outflow of the *Parousia*, as we embody Christ's victory over sin and death and testify to His transformative power in the world. Revelation 12:11 declares, "They conquered him [the devil] by the blood of the Lamb and by the word of their testimony." This passage underscores that the believer's role is both a privilege and a responsibility—rooted in the unveiled reality of Christ's presence and fueled by the ongoing revelation of His essence.

Through our witness believers advance God's kingdom, living as tangible expressions of His love and truth. Our mission is not one of passive waiting but of active participation, unveiling Christ's presence in every sphere of life. As agents of reconciliation and ambassadors of the kingdom, we are called to reveal the *Parousia* through our lives, words, and works, offering the world a glimpse of Christ's glory and grace.

IMPLICATIONS FOR WORSHIP AND ESCHATOLOGY

The revelation of Christ's *Parousia* reshapes the believer's understanding of worship and eschatology, calling us to engage with Christ's unveiled presence in profound and transformative ways. Worship becomes more than an act of anticipation; it is a present celebration of Christ's reign, and eschatology shifts from distant expectation to present participation in God's unfolding plan.

In Revelation 5:13 the universal chorus of worship declares, "Every creature in heaven, on earth, under the earth, on the sea, and everything in them say: Blessing and honor and glory and power be to the one seated on the throne, and to the Lamb, forever and ever!" This vision encapsulates the essence of true worship, which is a response to the unveiled presence of Christ, recognizing His authority and glorifying His essence.

Through the *Parousia* worship becomes an acknowledgment of Christ's ongoing reign, uniting believers with the heavenly host in adoration and submission. This transformation in worship calls the Church to shift its focus from longing for a future event to celebrating the present reality of Christ's unveiled essence. In spirit and truth (John 4:23–24) worshipers encounter Christ, experiencing His transformative relational presence and aligning our hearts with His mission.

ESCHATOLOGY AS PRESENT ENGAGEMENT

Revelation reframes eschatology not as a passive waiting for future fulfillment but as an active participation in the current work of Christ's kingdom. The *Parousia* invites believers to engage in God's redemptive work now, living out the realities of His reign and embodying His kingdom values in a world in need of renewal. The unveiled presence of Christ empowers us to embrace a missional lifestyle, demonstrating the power of His essence in tangible ways.

Rather than focusing solely on end-times speculation, Revelation calls the Church to recognize the immediacy of Christ's presence and mission. The *Parousia* shifts eschatology from a distant hope to a lived reality, equipping believers to reflect Christ's glory in our lives and communities while eagerly anticipating the consummation of God's redemptive plan.

While many passages in Revelation have been historically interpreted as predictive of future geopolitical events, this chapter understands them instead as prophetic symbols, unveiling ongoing spiritual and celestial dynamics that have always shaped the life of the Church and the world. These visions reveal the cosmic conflict between Christ and all who oppose Him, not just in the distant future but in every age. The message is not confined to decoding timelines but is intended to awaken the Church to live faithfully under the rule of the Lamb now.

The book of Revelation presents the *Parousia* as the ongoing unveiling of Christ's essence, offering a transformative relational vision that shapes every aspect of the believer's life. It reveals what is presently occurring. First there is spiritual renewal—the *Parousia* initiates the renewal of creation, culminating in the reconciliation of all things through Christ's essence (Revelation 21:1–3). The second part of the vision is priestly identity: believers, as a kingdom of priests (Revelation 1:6), actively participate in the unveiling of Christ's presence and mission, advancing His kingdom in the world.

The *Parousia* reveals Christ's reign as a present spiritual reality, challenging believers to embody His values and live as citizens of His kingdom (Revelation 11:15). Finally, the *Parousia* transforms worship and eschatology: worship shifts from anticipation to celebration of Christ's presence, and eschatology becomes an active engagement with His ongoing mission (Revelation 5:13).

Revelation's vision affirms that the *Parousia* is not confined to a future event but is an ongoing and dynamic revelation of Christ's essence in the present. Believers are called to embrace our identity as participants in God's redemptive work, living as reflections of His glory and instruments of His grace.

As the Church engages with the unveiled presence of Christ, it is the Holy Spirit who facilitates this ongoing transformation and mission. The Spirit empowers believers to perceive the *Parousia*, guiding us into deeper communion with Christ and enabling us to live in alignment with His essence. The next chapter will explore the indispensable role of the Holy Spirit in revealing Christ's presence, empowering the Church, and equipping believers to reflect His glory in our daily lives. Through the Spirit's work the *Parousia* becomes a lived reality, fostering spiritual growth, unity, and the advancement of God's kingdom in the world.

CHAPTER 16

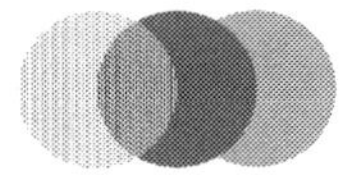

THE HOLY SPIRIT'S PLACE WITHIN THE *PAROUSIA*

The *Parousia*, as the ongoing unveiling of Christ's essence, is made accessible and experiential through the work of the Holy Spirit. The Spirit serves as the divine agent through whom Christ's presence is revealed, believers are transformed, and the Church is empowered to embody His mission in the world. Without the Spirit's work the reality of Christ's essence would remain distant and theoretical; instead, the Spirit brings the *Parousia* into a present, tangible experience. Through the Spirit's ministry believers are invited to participate in the transformative power of Christ's presence, aligning our lives with His character and purposes.

The Holy Spirit's role in facilitating the *Parousia* is central to the believer's experience of Christ. As Jesus declared in John 16:13–14, "When the Spirit of truth comes, he will guide you into all the truth.... He will glorify me, because he will take from what is mine and declare it to you." The Spirit's primary work is to glorify Christ by unveiling His essence to believers, guiding them into a deeper awareness of His presence and truth. This ongoing revelation draws believers into the transformative process of the *Parousia*, in which Christ's glory is progressively revealed within us. Paul affirms this in 2 Corinthians 3:17–18, stating that "where the Spirit of the Lord is, there is freedom," and that believers "are being transformed into the same image from glory to glory." Through the Spirit's continual unveiling believers experience true spiritual liberty and a progressive conformity to the image of Christ.

The Holy Spirit not only reveals Christ's essence but also provides believers with direct access to Him. Ephesians 2:18 declares, "Through Him we both have access in one Spirit to the Father." This access is not merely positional but deeply relational and transformative, drawing believers into greater communion with Christ and empowering us for His mission. The Pentecost event recorded in Acts 2 marks the Spirit's outpouring as the initiation of the *Parousia* within the Church. It signifies the active revelation of Christ's presence within His people, underscoring that the *Parousia* is not a static doctrine but a dynamic reality unfolding through the Spirit's ongoing work.

The practical implications of the Spirit's ministry in unveiling Christ's essence are profound. Jesus promised in John 14:26 that "the Holy Spirit . . . will teach you all things and remind you of everything I have told you." This teaching ministry ensures that the revelation of Christ remains fresh and transformative in the believer's life, aligning us with His mission and equipping us to embody His presence in the world. Through the Spirit believers experience the continuous unveiling of Christ's teachings, character, and mission, becoming living testimonies of His essence.

PARTICIPATION IN THE ONGOING *PAROUSIA* THROUGH THE SPIRIT

The Holy Spirit not only reveals Christ's essence but also empowers believers to actively participate in His ongoing presence. This empowerment is the essence of the *Parousia*, equipping believers to embody Christ's life and extend His mission in the world. In Acts 1:8 Jesus declares, "You will receive power when the Holy Spirit has come on you, and you will be my witnesses." The Spirit's empowerment enables believers to testify to Christ's essence, bearing witness to His transformative presence in their words and actions. Romans 8:9–11 further emphasizes the Spirit's work in uniting believers with the ascended Christ, ensuring that His life and power are actively at work within us.

The indwelling of the Holy Spirit allows believers to experience the *Parousia* as a present reality, transforming us into living temples through whom Christ's essence is revealed. Paul affirms this in 1 Corinthians 3:16, stating, "Don't you yourselves know that you are God's temple and that the Spirit of God lives in you?" Through the Spirit's presence believers are transformed from within, becoming vessels of Christ's unveiled glory. This transformation is evidenced by the fruit of the Spirit, as described in Galatians 5:22–23, which manifests Christ's reign within the believer's life. Love, joy, peace, and self-control, among the other qualities, serve as visible expressions of the *Parousia*, demonstrating that Christ's presence is actively shaping and renewing the believer.

The Spirit's work in uniting believers extends beyond individual transformation to the corporate experience of the Church. Ephesians 4:4–6 highlights the unity fostered by the Spirit, declaring, "There is one body and one Spirit . . . one God and Father of all, who is above all and through all and in all." Through the Spirit the Church collectively participates in the *Parousia*, embodying Christ's essence and advancing His kingdom in the world. This unity is a powerful testimony to the reality of Christ's presence, as believers join together in worship, service, and mission.

Worship, in particular, is transformed through the Spirit's work in the *Parousia*. Jesus states in John 4:23–24 that "true worshipers will worship the Father in Spirit and in truth." Spirit-led worship becomes an encounter with Christ's unveiled presence, drawing believers into deeper communion with Him and aligning our hearts with His redemptive purposes. Through worship believers experience the fullness of the *Parousia*, responding to Christ's presence with adoration, submission, and renewed commitment to His mission.

The Holy Spirit's transformative work ensures that the *Parousia* is not merely an eschatological hope but a present reality that shapes both the individual believer and the collective Church. The Spirit empowers believers to embody Christ's essence, equips them for their mission, and fosters unity within the body of Christ. Through the ongoing revelation of Christ's presence, believers are invited to live as active participants in the unfolding *Parousia*, reflecting His glory and advancing His kingdom in a world longing for renewal.

THE TRANSFORMATIVE POWER OF THE SPIRIT IN BELIEVERS' LIVES

The Holy Spirit stands as the divine catalyst of transformation in the lives of believers, ushering us into the unfolding reality of the *Parousia*. Through the Spirit's work, regeneration, sanctification, and empowerment become tangible experiences that unveil the essence of Christ within those who belong to Him. The *Parousia*, therefore, is not a distant hope but a present and ongoing reality, made accessible through the Spirit's indwelling presence.

The transformative journey begins with the Spirit's work of regeneration and renewal, ushering believers into the reality of new life in Christ. Paul, in his letter to Titus, affirms that God "saved us . . . through the washing of regeneration and renewal by the Holy Spirit" (Titus 3:5–6). This regeneration is not merely an external change or moral improvement but signifies a profound rebirth in which believers are made new creations, infused with the life and essence of Christ. The Spirit's renewal is the foundation upon which the believer's participation in the *Parousia* is built, ensuring that our identity is firmly rooted in Christ's ongoing revelation.

Jesus emphasizes this necessity of spiritual rebirth in John 3:5–6, declaring that "unless someone is born of water and the Spirit, he cannot enter the kingdom of God." This rebirth, initiated by the Spirit, transcends human effort and connects believers to the unfolding reality of Christ's reign, enabling us to live as citizens of the kingdom. Through the Spirit's work of regeneration, believers are not only transformed individually but are also drawn into the communal experience of the *Parousia*, where Christ's presence is unveiled among His people.

SANCTIFICATION: THE PROGRESSIVE UNVEILING OF CHRIST'S ESSENCE

The Holy Spirit's role extends beyond regeneration to the continuous work of sanctification, wherein believers are progressively conformed to Christ's image. The apostle Peter affirms this work, stating that believers are chosen "according to the foreknowledge of God the Father, through the sanctifying work of the Spirit" (1 Peter 1:2). Sanctification is not an isolated event but an ongoing process in which believers, through the Spirit's power, are increasingly aligned with the essence of Christ. This ongoing transformation is the heart of the *Parousia*, as the unveiled presence of Christ reshapes every aspect of the believer's life.

Paul further elaborates on this dynamic in Romans 8:13–14, emphasizing that if "by the Spirit you put to death the deeds of the body, you will live. For all those led by God's Spirit are God's sons." The Spirit empowers believers to overcome sin, guiding us into a deeper alignment with God's will. This sanctifying work is evidence of the *Parousia's* present reality, wherein Christ's essence is progressively revealed in the daily lives of those who walk by the Spirit.

EMPOWERMENT FOR RIGHTEOUSNESS

The Holy Spirit not only regenerates and sanctifies but also empowers believers to live righteously, reflecting the character of Christ in their thoughts, actions, and relationships. Paul exhorts believers in Galatians 5:16–18 to "walk by the Spirit" so that they "will certainly not carry out the desire of the flesh." Walking in the Spirit is not a passive endeavor; it requires an active reliance on His power to manifest Christ's essence in daily life.

Furthermore, Paul reassures believers in Philippians 2:13 that "it is God who is working in you both to will and to work according to his good purpose." The Spirit works within the believer to shape our desires and actions, ensuring that we align with God's will and reflect the righteousness of Christ. This empowerment serves as a critical aspect of the *Parousia*, in which the unveiled presence of Christ transforms believers into vessels of His divine nature.

RESURRECTION AS PRESENT REALITY

The Holy Spirit bridges the perceived gap between traditional eschatological expectations and their fulfillment "in Christ," reframing concepts such as resurrection, judgment, and the kingdom of God as present spiritual realities. In Romans 8:11 Paul declares that "if the Spirit of him who raised Jesus from the dead lives in you, then he who raised Christ from the dead will also bring your mortal bodies to life through his Spirit." Resurrection, therefore, is not a distant hope but a present experience, unveiled through the Spirit's indwelling life and made visible in the way we live now.

An example of this is found in Colossians 3:1–4, where Paul declares that believers "have been raised with Christ" and are now called to "seek the things above." This passage reveals that resurrection is not something we await passively but a factor that actively reshapes how we engage with the world. Through the Spirit we are empowered to live with new priorities, eternal focus, and Christ-centered identity.

Resurrection life, then, touches every part of our daily experience. It reshapes how we love, how we labor, how we suffer, and how we think. In our relationships the Spirit teaches us to release pride and position, making room instead for forgiveness and reconciliation. We no longer relate to others from a posture of self-preservation but as those who have been raised with Christ, those who live from the abundance of His grace.

In our work we are no longer driven by personal success or ambition. Rather, we begin to serve with the quiet intention of reflecting God's excellence and love, knowing that even the ordinary can become sacred when done in the Spirit. In our suffering and struggle we do not respond as the world responds. We endure with hope because resurrection has already begun within us. We know that Christ has triumphed over death, and we share in that victory now.

Even in our thoughts, in the private, unseen places of our hearts, the Spirit leads us to lay down anxiety, greed, and comparison. We are no longer defined by what we lack or by how we measure up. Our life is already secure, hidden with Christ in God. This is the power of resurrection: not only that we will be raised one day but that we have already been raised into a new way of seeing, living, and loving.

Imagine someone who once pursued status, consumed by material gain and self-glorification. Before encountering Christ their identity was tethered to what they could achieve or accumulate. But through the Spirit's regenerating work their values shift. They begin to seek the things above, fixing their hearts and minds on Christ. This inward resurrection transforms their priorities, not only changing their behavior but reshaping their desires. Now, decisions about time, money, and ambition are filtered through a kingdom lens: "Will this reflect the life of Christ in me?"

This aligns with Paul's assertion in Colossians 3:3, which reminds believers that "your life is hidden with Christ in God." That hidden life is not a secret life; it is a spiritual reality unveiled through the *Parousia*. The Spirit reveals Christ in us and through us, even when the world cannot see it. The *Parousia*, then, is not only the final unveiling of Christ in glory but also the daily unveiling of His life through those who live in resurrection power now.

To live as resurrected people is to live Spirit-led lives that make the unseen visible. Through the Spirit's work we embody resurrection, not in grand gestures but in everyday faithfulness, in how we forgive, how we speak, how we spend, how we rest, and how we love. The Spirit reveals Christ in the very fabric of our ordinary lives, turning mundane moments into sacred ones. This is resurrection now. This is the *Parousia* unfolding.

JUDGMENT AS PURIFICATION

Likewise, the Spirit transforms the notion of judgment from condemnation to purification. In John 16:8–11 Jesus describes the Spirit's role in convicting the world concerning sin, righteousness, and judgment. This conviction is not punitive but redemptive, aligning believers with Christ's essence and guiding us more deeply into the transformative reality of the *Parousia*. The unveiling of Christ's presence does not crush the believer; it refines and reorients us.

One of the most vivid illustrations of this can be seen in Paul's conversion in Acts 9. Before encountering the risen Christ, Saul—later known as Paul—was a zealous Pharisee who believed he was serving God by condemning and persecuting Christians. His sense of judgment was rooted in self-righteousness, driven by law and tradition. But when Christ appeared to him on the road to Damascus everything changed. Saul's world was shaken, not by divine condemnation but by divine confrontation.

In that moment judgment became a means of purification. The Spirit did not leave him in shame but invited him into repentance, humility, and transformation. Saul, blinded by light, was given new eyes, not just to see Jesus but to see himself in the truth of Christ's mercy. He was realigned with Christ's mission, and the man who had once embodied condemnation became the apostle of grace.

Paul would later call himself the worst of sinners (1 Timothy 1:15), not to wallow in guilt but to glorify the grace that had reshaped him. His life testified to the kind of judgment the Spirit brings, not a verdict of despair but a refining fire that separates the false from the true, the proud from the surrendered.

This same Spirit-led purification continues in the lives of believers today. When the *Parousia* of Christ presses in, it reveals not only the beauty of His essence but the places in us that resist it. The Spirit convicts us, not to shame us but to free us. This conviction may come through a moment of tension in a conversation, a quiet rebuke in prayer, or a dawning awareness of motives that are out of step with Christ. We begin to perceive our pride, our unforgiveness, our need for control. But instead of defending or excusing, the Spirit invites us to surrender. And in the surrender something beautiful happens: we are purified. We become more like Christ, not only in belief but in temperament, in relationships, in the quiet contours of our inner life.

A believer who once judged harshly may find himself softened by compassion. One who held grudges may begin to forgive without being asked. One who relied on moral performance may learn to live in grace. Judgment, when it comes through the Spirit, doesn't drive us away from God but draws us nearer. It reminds us that purification is not punishment. It is love in motion, reshaping us from the inside out, aligning us with Christ's heart and inviting us into His mission of reconciliation.

CONCLUSION

The kingdom of God, too, is no longer a distant expectation but a present reality within believers through the Spirit's indwelling. Paul reminds the Church in Philippians 3:20 that "our citizenship is in heaven," emphasizing that through the Spirit believers are already active participants in the reign of Christ. The Spirit enables us to embody kingdom values, living in righteousness, peace, and joy as evidence of Christ's present rule.

The Holy Spirit is the indispensable agent of the *Parousia*, ensuring that Christ's essence is progressively unveiled in the lives of believers. Through regeneration, sanctification, and empowerment the Spirit facilitates the transformative experience of Christ's ongoing presence. This chapter affirms that the *Parousia* is not a distant event but a dynamic and present reality, made tangible through the Spirit's work within believers and the Church.

Through the Spirit's regenerative work believers are born anew, entering into the unfolding reality of Christ's presence. In sanctification the Spirit continually aligns our lives with Christ's essence, revealing His glory through our daily transformation. Empowered by the Spirit believers are equipped to walk in righteousness, living as visible expressions of the *Parousia* in the world.

Yet the work of the *Parousia* is not confined to individual transformation; it extends to the corporate identity and mission of the Church. The next chapter will explore how the Church, as the body of Christ, is both the recipient and the vessel of the Spirit's presence. United by the Spirit, the Church is called to embody Christ's essence, reflecting His glory, advancing His kingdom, and living as a tangible expression of the *Parousia* in a world longing for redemption.

CHAPTER 17

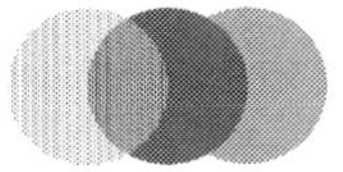

THE CHURCH'S PLACE WITHIN THE *PAROUSIA*

The Church stands at the heart of the ongoing unveiling of the *Parousia*, serving as the living vessel through which Christ's essence is revealed to the world. As the collective body of Christ, the Church is both the recipient and the instrument of His transformative presence, carrying forward His mission and embodying His character. Through worship, mission, and communal witness the Church manifests the reality of Christ's reign, providing the world with a foretaste of the New Jerusalem—the ultimate fulfillment of God's redemptive work.

The Church's place in the ongoing *Parousia* is not as a passive witness but as an active participant in the unfolding revelation of Christ's essence. At the heart of this participation is the reality of Imagoformity—the process by which believers, both individually and corporately, are shaped into the image of Christ through the Spirit's work. This transformation is not abstract or symbolic; it is lived and experienced as the Church progressively reflects the unveiled presence of Christ in the world.

Paul's description of the Church as Christ's body (Ephesians 1:22–23) affirms that the Church does not merely represent Christ but actively participates in His essence. This means that the unfolding of Imagoformity is not only an individual journey but also a communal reality. The Church, in its unity and diversity, is a living testament to the transformative power of Christ's presence, manifesting His glory in ways that draw others into His redemptive work.

This corporate transformation finds deep resonance in 2 Corinthians 3:18, where Paul declares, "We all, with unveiled faces, are looking as in a mirror at the glory of the Lord and are being transformed into the same image from glory to glory; this is from the Lord who is the Spirit." Here Paul emphasizes that the transformation into Christ's image is not instantaneous but progressive, unfolding through the ongoing work of the Holy Spirit. This passage affirms that Imagoformity is not simply about doctrinal knowledge or moral refinement but about a real and continuous unveiling of Christ's life within the believer and within the collective body of the Church. Just as the *Parousia* is an ongoing revelation rather than a singular future event, so too is Imagoformity an ever-deepening reality wherein believers, through worship, mission, and communion, are shaped into reflections of Christ's unveiled presence.

However, this process is not without struggle. The reality of Imagoformity acknowledges that sanctification is not effortless, nor does it occur without resistance. Just as the Church is called to reflect Christ's essence, it must also contend with the remnants of the old creation, wherein human frailty, division, and sin still threaten to obscure the clarity of Christ's image. The refining work of the Spirit ensures that the Church does not remain stagnant but is continuously drawn deeper into the unveiling of Christ's transformative presence.

This truth is exemplified in Paul's exhortation in Ephesians 4:22–24: "Take off your former way of life, the old self that is corrupted by deceitful desires, to be renewed in the spirit of your minds, and . . . put on the new self, the one created according to God's likeness in righteousness and purity of the truth." The Church, as the collective body of Christ, embodies this transitional journey, a calling to put off the remnants of the old creation and walk in the reality of the new. Imagoformity is the process by which this transition occurs, whereby the Church, through worship, mission, and communal accountability, is shaped not into its own image but into the image of Christ Himself.

In this way the Church is more than an institution or a gathering of believers—it is the sacred space in which Imagoformity is lived out, where Christ's unveiled presence is actively at work. Through worship the Church encounters the reality of Christ's essence, through mission it carries His presence into the world, and through communal life it serves as a visible testimony of the ongoing *Parousia* shaping and forming His people.

This reality calls believers to a deeper awareness of how we reflect Christ's essence, both as individuals and as a collective body. The Church is not simply a sign pointing toward Christ's return but a vessel through which His presence is actively unveiled. Every act of faith, every moment of worship, and every step taken in mission is a participation in Imagoformity—a sacred engagement with the ongoing unveiling of Christ's transformative presence.

Empowered by the Holy Spirit, the Church exists as a dynamic testimony of Christ's presence, demonstrating that the *Parousia* is not a distant event but an unfolding reality that touches every aspect of life. In unity and diversity, in service and in sacrifice, the Church reveals Christ's essence, drawing individuals and communities into the fullness of redemption.

THE CHURCH, AS CHRIST'S BODY, REVEALS HIS ESSENCE TO THE WORLD

The identity and purpose of the Church are rooted in its union with Christ, who is the head. As Paul declares in Ephesians 1:22–23, "He subjected everything under His feet and appointed him as head over everything for the church, which is his body, the fullness of the one who fills all things in every way." This profound union establishes the Church as the visible expression of Christ's spiritual reality, entrusted with unveiling His love, holiness, and authority to the world. Through its collective witness the Church becomes the means by which Christ's essence is made known, transforming lives and communities alike.

This unveiling takes place within the unity and diversity of the Church. Paul's metaphor of the body in 1 Corinthians 12:12–27 illustrates the interconnectedness of believers, each uniquely gifted and essential to the manifestation of Christ's presence. Just as the human body consists of different parts working together, so the Church in its diversity reflects the multifaceted nature of Christ. Every believer, endowed with spiritual gifts, contributes to the greater mission—whether through teaching, service, encouragement, or leadership. This diversity, when united in love, fully displays Christ's essence, showing the world a tangible expression of His grace and truth.

Reflecting on the Church's place within the *Parousia*, the apostle Paul's declaration in 2 Corinthians 3:1–3 offers a profound metaphor that vividly captures the believer's role as a living testimony of Christ's unveiled presence. Paul describes believers as "letters of Christ," written not with ink but with the Spirit of the living God, not on stone tablets but on human hearts. This powerful imagery underscores the reality that the Church, both individually and collectively, serves as a living epistle—an open letter that communicates the transformative essence of Christ to the world.

Through the *Parousia* Christ's presence is not merely a distant theological concept but a tangible, experiential reality that is meant to be read and understood by those around us. Just as a letter reveals the thoughts and intentions of its author, the lives of believers should reflect the heart and character of Christ, making His presence known in the world. The Spirit, as the divine author, inscribes the truth of Christ onto the hearts of those who believe, shaping us into visible expressions of His love, righteousness, and grace. This transformation calls believers to embrace our identity as "living letters," intentionally reflecting Christ's essence in our daily interactions, relationships, and communities.

Furthermore, Paul's contrast between the Old Covenant, inscribed on stone tablets, and the New Covenant, written on hearts, highlights the profound shift brought about by the Spirit's work in the *Parousia*. The Church is defined not by external adherence to laws, traditions, doctrines, and rituals but by an internal transformation that unveils the essence of Christ in everyday life. This distinction challenges believers to consider the depth of our witness—whether our lives authentically reflect the grace, love, and truth of Christ or if our message is obscured by inconsistency and complacency.

As the body of Christ, the Church collectively embodies this role, demonstrating to the world what it means to live in union with the unveiled presence of Christ. Each believer, as a unique letter, contributes to the larger narrative of redemption, showcasing the power of Christ's ongoing work through the *Parousia*. This reality calls the Church to greater accountability and purpose, ensuring that its mission, worship, and communal life align with the essence of Christ and the unfolding revelation of His kingdom.

Incorporating this metaphor into the believer's understanding of the *Parousia* serves as both an encouragement and a challenge. It invites personal reflection: How well does my life reflect Christ's character? Do my actions, attitudes, and relationships serve as a faithful testimony of His presence? Likewise, it challenges the Church to corporately examine whether it is living in alignment with Christ's unveiled essence, serving as a beacon of hope and transformation in the world.

Ultimately, the *Parousia* calls believers and the Church to embrace their sacred role as letters of Christ, written by the Spirit and sent into the world to reveal the fullness of His glory. This invitation is not passive but demands an active participation in Christ's mission, ensuring that every interaction, decision, and act of service reflects the ongoing unveiling of His transformative presence.

EXPERIENCING THE *PAROUSIA*: THE CHURCH AS THE LIVING ENCOUNTER OF CHRIST'S PRESENCE

As the Church participates in the unfolding *Parousia*, it does not merely represent Christ's presence—it becomes the very context in which His essence is encountered, known, and revealed. This unveiling of Christ is not reserved for an extraordinary or future age; rather, it is accessible now, through the sacred rhythms of faithful life together in the Spirit. Yet these channels of encounter are often counterintuitive, even to spiritually minded believers, as they are not apprehended through worldly logic or personal ambition but received by grace through surrender and attentiveness.

The Church first encounters the *Parousia* through the indwelling Holy Spirit, who unveils Christ's essence to believers, guiding, sanctifying, and empowering them (John 16:13–14). The Spirit does not simply impart knowledge; He manifests presence. John's declaration in Revelation 1:10—"I was in the Spirit on the Lord's day"—anchors the entire vision of the unveiled Christ that follows. Through the Spirit the Church is drawn into the already-but-not-yet reality of union with Christ, wherein His image is progressively formed in His people.

A second channel of encounter is the Word of God, which reveals the glory of Christ to those who believe (2 Corinthians 4:3–4). Scripture is not a static record but a living testimony, breathing forth the presence of the One who *is* the Word made flesh (John 1:14). Christ is unveiled through the Word, not as concept but as reality, calling the Church into alignment with His truth, authority, and grace. As Revelation 19:13 declares, "His name is called the Word of God." In meditating upon the Word, believers encounter the *Parousia*—the unveiled presence of the living Christ who transforms the heart and renews the mind.

The sacraments, too, are sacred encounters with the *Parousia*. In baptism believers are united with Christ in His death and resurrection (Romans 6:3–4), participating in the mystery of His unveiled life. In the Lord's Supper the bread and wine become not mere symbols but windows into communion with the crucified and risen Christ (Matthew 26:26–28; 1 Corinthians 10:16–17). These moments of sacramental participation unveil Christ's essence as both the Lamb of God and the risen Lord, and they reorient the Church to its shared identity as His body in the world.

In prayer the Church enters the very presence of Christ. Whether in personal devotion or communal intercession, prayer draws believers into the mystery of communion, wherein the Spirit unveils the heart of Christ. On the Mount of Transfiguration (Luke 9:28–36), during Pentecost (Acts 1:14–2:4), and in Paul's intercessions for the Church (Ephesians 1:17–23) we see how prayer functions as a threshold through which the unveiled glory of Christ is perceived and received. In prayer believers experience the *Parousia*—not as abstraction but as intimacy.

In both corporate and personal worship the Church is lifted into the heavenly chorus that proclaims the worthiness of the Lamb (Revelation 5:11–14). True worship is not performance; it is encounter. In Spirit and in truth (John 4:23–24) worship unveils the majesty, mercy, and authority of Christ, binding the worshiper to the reigning King whose presence sanctifies, heals, and commissions.

The Church also encounters the *Parousia* in acts of loving service. When believers serve the vulnerable, care for the poor, and extend compassion, they do not merely reflect Christ's values—they encounter His essence (Matthew 25:40). As 1 John 4:12 affirms, "If we love one another, God remains in us and his love is made complete in us." The perfection of God's love is the unveiling of Christ's presence within the servant-hearted believer.

In genuine fellowship and unity the Church becomes the living temple in which Christ dwells (Matthew 18:20; Acts 2:42–47). Unity in the Spirit is not simply agreement—it is a manifestation of divine communion, wherein the presence of Christ is made tangible through shared life, mutual love, and corporate witness. In this fellowship believers experience the *Parousia* in the midst of their togetherness, bearing witness to the relational nature of Christ's unveiled reign.

The Church likewise encounters the essence of Christ through creation, as the beauty and order of the natural world reflect the attributes of the Creator (Psalm 19:1–2; Romans 1:20). In reverent attentiveness to the created world, believers can perceive the sustaining presence of Christ and respond with awe and stewardship, recognizing that the One who made all things now dwells among us and within us.

Perhaps most paradoxically, the *Parousia* is revealed in suffering. In the fellowship of Christ's sufferings believers often perceive His presence with greater clarity and dependence (2 Corinthians 12:9; Philippians 3:10). In weakness grace is unveiled. In affliction His strength is made perfect. The cruciform path of the Church becomes the context in which Christ is most vividly encountered and His essence most deeply engraved.

Through meditation-focused reflection on Christ's Word, presence, and kingdom, the veil is thinned. Psalm 1:2–3 celebrates the one whose delight is in the Lord's instruction, meditating day and night. In stillness the Church is reminded that revelation does not always thunder from above; it often whispers in the depths of still hearts prepared to receive Him.

The Church also encounters the *Parousia* through prophecy, as the Spirit reveals the mind and will of Christ to His people (Acts 10; 1 Corinthians 14:1). Prophetic vision—whether through words, dreams, or discernment—unveils the glory, mercy, and mission of Christ in real time, affirming that He is not distant but present, not silent but speaking.

And finally, the *Parousia* is encountered through selfless humility—the kind exemplified by Zacchaeus (Luke 19:1–10), who in childlike surrender climbed a tree to see Jesus and found himself transformed by His gaze. As Christ taught, the "first will be last, and the last first" (Matthew 19:30). Humility creates the inner space wherein Christ is unveiled. In yielding, we receive. In surrendering self, we behold glory.

These channels of encounter are not manufactured by human striving; they are received through grace. They represent the unforced rhythms of life in the Spirit, wherein the essence of Christ is progressively unveiled to those who walk in faith. Just as the sheep in Matthew 25:31–46 were unaware that they had served Christ, so too the Church often encounters the *Parousia* in unanticipated and counterintuitive ways—not through control but through communion.

In this way *nuncmillennialism* offers a vision of the Church that is not merely awaiting the return of Christ but abiding in His presence now. These encounters are not isolated experiences; they are the lifeblood of a Church indwelt by Christ, shaped into His image, and sent into the world as His living presence.

WORSHIP AND MISSION, PREACHING AND TEACHING

The Church's engagement with the *Parousia* finds its expression in two key avenues: worship and mission. Worship serves as an encounter with the unveiled Christ, while mission extends His presence into the world. The two are intertwined, as worship fuels mission and mission leads back to deeper worship.

In His conversation with the Samaritan woman, Jesus declares in John 4:23–24, "True worshipers will worship the Father in Spirit and in truth." This statement underscores the reality that worship is more than ritual; it is an intimate experience of Christ's essence. As the Church gathers to worship it enters into communion with Christ, aligning its heart with His and experiencing the transformative power of His presence. Worship draws believers into deeper fellowship with Christ, renewing our minds, strengthening our faith, and empowering us to live out His mission in the world.

The Church's mission, rooted in the Great Commission of Matthew 28:18–20, flows from this place of worship. Christ's command to "go . . . and make disciples of all nations" is accompanied by the promise, "I am with you always." This assurance highlights that the mission of the Church is not merely about spreading information but about embodying the essence of Christ in a way that invites others into relationship with Him. Through acts of love, proclamation of the gospel, and works of justice and mercy, the Church reveals the present reality of the *Parousia* to a world longing for light and liberty.

The interplay between worship and mission is exemplified in the early Church's communal life, as described in Acts 2:42–47. The believers devoted themselves to the apostles' teaching, fellowship, the breaking of bread, and prayer—experiencing the reality of Christ's presence in their midst. Their worship overflowed into mission, drawing others to faith and fostering a community marked by generosity, unity, love, and joy. This model demonstrates how the *Parousia* is both experienced within the Church and extended to the world, making the invisible kingdom of God visible through the lives of His people.

In every aspect of its existence—whether in the unity of believers, the fervency of worship, or the pursuit of its mission—the Church stands as the visible sign of Christ's ongoing *Parousia*. It carries forward His essence, inviting the world to encounter the transformative reality of His presence and pointing toward the ultimate fulfillment of God's redemptive plan.

The Church's mission in proclaiming Christ's spiritual reign is foundational to its identity and purpose. As the collective body of Christ, the Church is called to unveil His essence to the world through its witness, teaching, and active participation in the ongoing *Parousia*. This sacred calling is not simply about proclamation but is about embodying the reality of Christ's reign within the life of believers. In Luke 17:21 Jesus declares, "The kingdom of God is in your midst," affirming that His reign is not a distant hope but a present reality experienced within those who belong to Him. The Church, therefore, exists to manifest this kingdom to the world, reflecting the transformative power of the *Parousia* as Christ's essence is progressively unveiled in the lives of believers.

This proclamation takes shape through faithful preaching and teaching, which serve as vital tools for revealing the dynamic nature of Christ's kingdom. The early Church, as described in Acts 2:42, devoted themselves to teaching, fellowship, and prayer—practices that facilitated their experience of Christ's ongoing presence and empowered their witness. Through Spirit-led proclamation believers are invited to transition from passive anticipation to active participation in the *Parousia*. The message of Christ's reign is not merely information to be conveyed but a reality to be lived out, calling believers into deeper communion with Him and aligning our lives with His kingdom purposes.

The unveiling of Christ's presence continues through the guiding work of the Holy Spirit, who leads the Church into all truth. In John 16:13 Jesus promises that the Spirit will "guide you into all truth," ensuring that the Church remains a living witness to the ongoing *Parousia*. The Spirit's role is crucial in unveiling the depths of Christ's essence, transforming believers into His likeness and empowering them to embody His mission in the world. As the Spirit reveals Christ's presence the Church is continually renewed, becoming an active participant in God's redemptive plan and a conduit for the transformative power of Christ's reign.

EMBODYING AND PROCLAIMING CHRIST'S REIGN

The Church plays an indispensable role in the ongoing *Parousia*, serving as the body of Christ through which His essence is revealed and His kingdom advanced. As both the recipient and the vessel of His presence, the Church is tasked with embodying Christ's reign in unity, diversity, worship, love, and mission. Through faithful proclamation and Spirit-led living, the Church transitions believers from passive waiting to active engagement with Christ's unveiled essence.

Throughout this exploration of the Church's role within the *Parousia*, a central theme emerges: the Church's embodiment of Christ's reign. As the visible representation of His presence in the world, the Church serves as a living testimony of His transformative power. This embodiment goes beyond mere representation; it is an active participation in Christ's ongoing work wherein believers, individually and collectively, reflect His love, grace, and truth. In doing so the Church becomes an agent of transformation, offering a glimpse into the kingdom's reality through its unity, service, and faithfulness.

Closely tied to this embodiment is the Church's responsibility to proclaim Christ's spiritual kingdom. Through faithful teaching and witness the Church calls believers into a deeper awareness of and participation in the present reality of the *Parousia*. The proclamation of Christ's reign is not limited to words but is demonstrated through lives marked by the Spirit's transformative work. As the Church teaches and exemplifies Christ's essence, it invites others to experience the ongoing unveiling of His presence, drawing them into the fullness of life "in Christ." This mission underscores the Church's role as a conduit of God's redemptive purposes in the world.

Integral to both embodiment and proclamation is the Church's call to stewardship and accountability. The Church is entrusted with aligning its mission, worship, and communal life with Christ's essence, ensuring that His kingdom is faithfully represented. This stewardship demands intentionality and faithfulness, as the Church is accountable for how it reflects the *Parousia* in its collective witness. Each act of service, teaching, and worship contributes to the unveiling of Christ's essence, and the Church must remain vigilant in its commitment to faithfully represent His kingdom. By embracing this responsibility the Church fulfills its sacred calling to reflect Christ's transformative presence to the world.

CONCLUSION

Through its worship, mission, and communal witness the Church reveals Christ's ongoing presence to the world, drawing others into the transformative reality of His reign. This sacred calling demands a renewed commitment to living as faithful stewards, ensuring that every aspect of the Church's life contributes to the ongoing revelation of God's redemptive plan.

As the focus shifts to the next chapter, we delve more deeply into the concept of accountability within the *Parousia* by examining the Judgment Seat of Christ. This exploration will illuminate how the Church and individual believers are evaluated in light of Christ's unveiled presence, shaping our understanding of sanctification and our participation in His kingdom. The Judgment Seat serves as a pivotal aspect of the *Parousia*, reinforcing the call to live in faithful anticipation and active stewardship of the divine reality unfolding within and through the Church.

CHAPTER 18

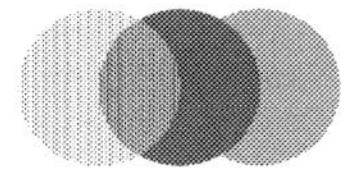

THE JUDGMENT SEAT OF CHRIST: ACCOUNTABILITY IN THE *PAROUSIA*

The Judgment Seat of Christ occupies a central, yet often misunderstood, role in Christian theology. Traditionally, it has been framed within eschatological contexts as a future moment of ultimate accountability, frequently associated with fear, reward, or condemnation. However, when understood through the lens of the *Parousia*, the Judgment Seat emerges as a profound mechanism of grace and transformation. Rather than being a singular, distant event, it represents an ongoing divine process—an ever-present spiritual assessment and realignment with Christ's essence that unfolds continuously in the life of every believer and the collective mission of the Church.

Through the *Parousia* the Judgment Seat of Christ transcends the binary notions of condemnation or reward. Instead it serves as an invitation to deeper participation in the redemptive and transformative work of Christ. It becomes an opportunity for believers to enter into greater conformity with His essence, revealing the truth of our spiritual walk and refining us for more effective service in God's kingdom. This chapter explores the theological and scriptural foundations of the Judgment Seat, highlighting its dynamic role in aligning believers with Christ's unveiled presence, fostering spiritual growth, and advancing God's redemptive purposes in the world.

SCRIPTURAL FOUNDATIONS FOR THE JUDGMENT SEAT OF CHRIST

The Judgment Seat of Christ is firmly rooted in Scripture, offering a perspective that shifts its focus from punitive judgment to a transformative assessment of faithfulness. Paul's words in 2 Corinthians 5:10 provide a pivotal understanding: "For we must all appear before the judgment seat of Christ, so that each may be repaid for what he has done in the body, whether good or evil." Paul uses the Greek term bema, which is translated "judgment seat." It refers to a seat of public accountability that historically was used for legal declarations, recognition, and reward. In the context of the *Parousia*, this appearance is not merely a legal evaluation but a profound unveiling of the believer's life in relation to Christ's transformative mission. It is through this unveiling that believers come to understand how their lives align with the essence and mission of Christ.

Paul further reinforces the personal nature of this divine assessment in Romans 14:10–12, where he states, "We will all stand before the judgment seat of God. . . . So then, each of us will give an account of himself to God." This underscores that the believer's relationship with Christ takes precedence over external evaluations, emphasizing personal alignment with His character and mission. The Judgment Seat is meant not to evoke fear but to call believers to embrace an ongoing journey of transformation and participation in God's redemptive work.

Paul's metaphor in 1 Corinthians 3:10–15, where he compares believers' works to materials tested by fire, provides additional insight into the Judgment Seat's purpose. Works that are built upon eternal values (symbolized by gold and precious stones) endure, whereas works rooted in self-serving or temporal pursuits, like wood, hay, and straw, are consumed. This metaphor highlights the refining aspect of the Judgment Seat, encouraging believers to build their lives on the foundation of Christ's essence, ensuring that their work reflects His eternal purposes.

When viewed through the framework of the *Parousia*, the Judgment Seat of Christ is not an event of condemnation but rather a continuous process of refining and alignment with Christ's essence. As believers encounter His unveiled presence they are invited into a process of ongoing purification that draws them more deeply into communion with Him.

Jesus's words in John 3:17, "For God did not send His Son into the world to condemn the world, but to save the world through him," affirm that the Judgment Seat functions not to punish but to refine believers, shaping them ever more fully into the likeness of Christ. For instance, worship serves as a crucible of purification, where motives and priorities are tested. As believers engage with the presence of Christ they are confronted with the areas in their lives that require transformation, producing a deeper conformity to His character.

This transformative assessment unfolds in both present and future dimensions. In the present, the convicting work of the Holy Spirit acts as an ongoing form of divine discipline, aligning believers with Christ's mission. The writer of Hebrews explains this dynamic in Hebrews 12:5–11, where God's correction is portrayed as an act of love designed to produce the fruit of righteousness. In the future the Judgment Seat will unveil the fullness of Christ's essence within believers, culminating in their ultimate sanctification. As John affirms in 1 John 3:2, "When he appears, we will be like him because we will see him as he is." This final unveiling is the culmination of a lifetime of transformation, where believers are brought into full alignment with Christ's glory.

SPIRITUAL FRUITFULNESS AS EVIDENCE OF THE JUDGMENT SEAT

The Judgment Seat not only assesses outward actions but also examines the motivations and spiritual alignment behind them. The fruit of the Spirit, as outlined in Galatians 5:22–23, serve as a measure of Christ's life and essence actively at work within the believer. Love, joy, peace, patience, kindness, goodness, faithfulness, gentleness, and self-control are not just qualities but tangible evidence of transformation. Acts of service and ministry that stem from self-interest or ambition may be consumed in the refining fire, while those motivated by Christlike love and humility will endure, testifying to the transformative power of the *Parousia* in the believer's life.

Through the lens of the *Parousia*, the Judgment Seat challenges believers to examine their lives with honesty and humility, recognizing that spiritual growth is not a static event but an ongoing journey of renewal and conformity to Christ. By embracing the continual unveiling of His presence, believers are invited into a deeper experience of grace, transformation, and purpose, ensuring that our lives reflect the fullness of His essence.

The Church, as the body of Christ, holds a profound responsibility in stewarding the unveiled presence of Christ within the *Parousia*. Beyond individual accountability, the Judgment Seat of Christ underscores the collective responsibility of the Church to align its worship, mission, and communal life with His essence. The Church's role in revealing Christ to the world is not a passive one; it is an active participation in the ongoing unveiling of His transformative presence.

The letters to the seven churches in Revelation 2 and 3 serve as a compelling illustration of Christ's collective assessment of His people. In these letters Christ evaluates entire communities, commending their strengths while addressing their shortcomings and calling them to realignment with His essence. For instance, the Church in Ephesus is praised for its perseverance but admonished for abandoning its first love, revealing the delicate balance between encouragement and correction inherent in the process of collective accountability. This biblical model emphasizes that the Church is not judged solely on numerical growth, the size of its buildings, or outward success but on its faithfulness to embodying the love, truth, and mission of Christ.

The early Church provides a powerful example of collective alignment with Christ's essence. In Acts 2:42–47 the believers devoted themselves to teaching, fellowship, and prayer, creating a vibrant community that reflected the presence of Christ and drew others into His kingdom. This model highlights how the *Parousia* shapes communal life, demonstrating that the Church's witness extends beyond individual efforts to a corporate reflection of Christ's transforming presence.

PROCLAIMING CHRIST'S SPIRITUAL REIGN AND ONGOING REVELATION

The Church's proclamation of Christ's reign is central to its identity and mission within the *Parousia*. Jesus declared in Luke 17:21, "The kingdom of God is in your midst," emphasizing the present reality of His rule within believers. The Church is called to embody this reign, living as a tangible manifestation of Christ's kingdom in the world. The *Parousia* is not a distant hope but an unfolding reality, inviting believers to demonstrate Christ's presence in our daily lives and communities.

Faithful preaching and teaching serve as vital tools for unveiling the truths of Christ's spiritual reign, transitioning believers from passive anticipation to active engagement. The early Church's devotion to the apostles' teaching in Acts 2:42 reveals how instruction fosters a deeper participation in the *Parousia*, equipping believers to align their lives with Christ's mission. Biblical preaching emphasizes the "already-but-not-yet" nature of Christ's kingdom, affirming its present reality while pointing toward its ultimate fulfillment. Through Spirit-led teaching believers are continually drawn into a fuller understanding of their calling to embody Christ's essence in every aspect of life.

The Holy Spirit plays a crucial role in the ongoing revelation of Christ's presence, guiding the Church into deeper truth and empowering its mission. Jesus promised in John 16:13, "When the

Spirit of truth comes, he will guide you into all truth." This ongoing revelation ensures that the Church remains a living witness to the *Parousia*, continually transformed by Christ's essence and equipped to reflect His love and holiness to the world.

THE CHURCH'S ACCOUNTABILITY BEFORE CHRIST

The Church's participation in the *Parousia* comes not only with revelation but also with responsibility. As recipients of Christ's unveiled presence we are called to respond with faithfulness, not only in mission but in character, integrity, and love. As Paul writes, "We will all stand before the judgment seat of God. . . . Each of us will give an account of himself to God" (Romans 14:10–12). This judgment is not about condemnation but about alignment—an unveiling not only of Christ but of how we have received and responded to Him.

This accountability is not punitive but purifying. The Judgment Seat is the place where motives, not just actions, are weighed, where hidden things are brought to light, not to shame us but to refine what will last. As Paul says elsewhere, "Each one's work will become obvious. . . . The fire will test the quality of each one's work" (1 Corinthians 3:13). This is not condemnation; it is calibration. The Church, as the bearer of Christ's presence, will be measured by how faithfully it has carried what was revealed.

The parable of the talents (Matthew 25:14–30) illustrates this kind of evaluation. The servants are not judged by how much they earned but by how faithfully they responded to what they were given. In the same way the Church is not accountable for outcomes beyond its control but for its response to the truth it has received. The Spirit does not only reveal Christ so we can admire Him. He reveals Christ so we can reflect Him. And the Judgment Seat of Christ is the place where that reflection is brought into full view.

This is why Paul urges the Church to "pay careful attention to how you walk . . . making the most of the time, because the days are evil" (Ephesians 5:15–16). To live in the *Parousia* is to live in the light. It means that our time, our gifts, our relationships, our teaching, all are lived under the gaze of the One who has already been unveiled. This does not induce fear but invites faithfulness. The Spirit is not only preparing us to meet Christ someday but is forming in us the Christ who is already present. And when we stand before Him fully it will not be a surprise. It will be the culmination of a life already being lived in His light.

IMPLICATIONS FOR WORSHIP, MISSION, AND TRANSFORMATION

The Judgment Seat offers a transformative perspective on worship, mission, and personal growth within the *Parousia*. Worship becomes more than a ritual; it becomes an act of preparation, aligning believers with Christ's unveiled presence. Jesus declared in John 4:23–24, "True worshipers will worship the Father in Spirit and in truth." True worship is a spiritual encounter that draws believers more deeply into communion with Christ, refining them for greater participation in His mission.

The mission of the Church is another key aspect of accountability, extending Christ's presence to the world through acts of love, service, and proclamation. The Great Commission in Matthew 28:18–20 entrusts the Church with the responsibility of making disciples, equipping this work with the assurance of Christ's abiding presence. The Judgment Seat evaluates the Church's faithfulness in fulfilling this mission, highlighting the importance of engaging the world with the transformative power of Christ's unveiled essence.

Personal transformation is an integral component of the *Parousia*. Paul, in Romans 8:26–30, provides a comprehensive illustration of how the Judgment Seat of Christ operates within the transformative work of the *Parousia*. As previously mentioned, verse 26 highlights the Holy Spirit's intercession on behalf of believers, addressing our weaknesses and unfaithfulness. In verse 27 Paul explains that the Spirit searches our hearts and provides the necessary remedies to align us with God's will. Verse 28, often misinterpreted, emphasizes that the Spirit's refining work is ultimately for our good and flows from God's loving purpose. In verse 29 Paul clarifies that believers are predestined—not, as is often assumed in popular Calvinist interpretations, in a deterministic sense of who will be saved or lost but in order for them to be conformed to the image of Christ.

This is not about exclusion or fixed eternal destinies but about God's loving purpose to shape those in Christ into the likeness of His Son. Predestination here refers to the goal of transformation, not the mechanism of salvation. This conformity is God's ultimate goal for believers, and in verse 30 Paul affirms that our glorification at the Judgment Seat of Christ is the fulfillment of this transformative process.

This transformation is not passive but an ongoing journey in which believers continually grow into deeper likeness to Christ, reflecting more and more His love, grace, and holiness in our daily lives. The Judgment Seat serves as a measure of this transformation, evaluating how believers have allowed Christ's presence to shape our character and actions.

THE JUDGMENT SEAT AND ESCHATOLOGICAL FULFILLMENT

Ultimately, the Judgment Seat culminates in the full realization of the *Parousia*, whereby Christ's essence is unveiled in its fullness within the Church. In Revelation 21:3 the voice from the throne proclaims, "Look, God's dwelling is with humanity." This consummation marks the fulfillment of God's redemptive purposes, as the Church is fully conformed to Christ's image and enters into eternal union with Him.

Eternal rewards, as described in 1 Corinthians 9:24–25, are not material but relational and transformative, representing the joy of a deeper and fuller union with Christ. Paul speaks of the "crown of righteousness" in 2 Timothy 4:8, which signifies the believer's ultimate alignment with Christ's glory and reign. These rewards are not earned but are the natural outcome of a life lived in faithful response to the unveiled presence of Christ.

The Judgment Seat of Christ, when viewed through the lens of the *Parousia*, is not an occasion for fear but a profound expression of grace and transformation. It serves as an ongoing invitation for believers to embody Christ's essence in worship, mission, and daily life. The Church, as the collective body of Christ, bears the responsibility of stewarding His unveiled presence and advancing His kingdom in the world.

As we move forward, the next chapter will explore the practical applications of the *Parousia* for believers. This discussion will provide tangible ways for believers to actively participate in the ongoing unveiling of Christ's presence, ensuring that our lives reflect His transformative work in every sphere of influence we have in the world.

CHAPTER 19

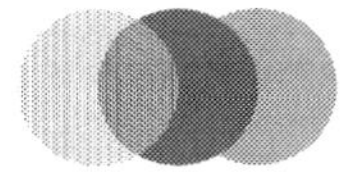

APPLICATIONS OF THE *PAROUSIA* FOR BELIEVERS

The *Parousia*, understood as the spiritual unveiling of Christ's essence, fundamentally reshapes how believers engage with everyday life. No longer waiting for a distant moment, we live in the present reality of His reign, empowered to embody His truth, love, and righteousness. This chapter offers a practical framework for integrating that unveiled reality into daily living. It explores how believers can align their hearts and minds with Christ's indwelling presence, participate in His kingdom's ongoing work, and serve as visible witnesses to His transforming power. As we walk in the light of His revealed glory, our lives are renewed in purpose, directed by the Spirit, and marked by a deeper participation in the redemptive work of God in a world still aching for restoration.

EMBRACING CHRIST'S UNVEILED ESSENCE

The continuous revelation of Christ's essence invites believers into an ongoing process of spiritual transformation that reshapes our identity, character, and purpose in profound ways. As Paul writes in 2 Corinthians 3:18, "We all, with unveiled faces, are looking as in a mirror at the glory of the Lord and are being transformed into the same image from glory to glory." This passage highlights that transformation is not a singular event but a progressive unveiling, drawing believers deeper into communion with Christ and equipping us to reflect His character in the world. The unveiling of Christ's glory cultivates humility, love, and service, aligning believers with His divine mission.

The transformation described by Paul is not achieved through human effort alone but through moments of *epiphaneia*, where Christ's essence is unveiled to the believer in greater measure. These moments act as spiritual breakthroughs, bringing deeper awareness, renewal, and clarity to the believer's walk.

Peter's confession in Matthew 16:16–17 serves as a clear example of *epiphaneia* leading to transformation. When Peter declared, "You are the Messiah, the Son of the living God," Jesus affirmed, "Flesh and blood did not reveal this to you, but my Father in heaven." This revelation was not the product of Peter's reasoning but a divine unveiling—an *epiphaneia* of Christ's essence that redefined Peter's understanding.

Likewise, every believer experiences progressive *epiphaneia* moments as we walk in faith. Each unveiling deepens our transformation, moving us from mere knowledge of Christ to an intimate awareness of His presence actively shaping our lives: "The path of the righteous is like the light of dawn, shining brighter and brighter until midday" (Proverbs 4:18). This verse encapsulates the journey of the believer in the *Parousia*—where each *epiphaneia* of Christ's essence illuminates a new dimension of our identity and calling.

The *Parousia* is not a theological construct but a lived reality, continually shaping the believer's daily walk. The transformative unveiling of Christ's essence is not something believers await passively but a reality they actively participate in, just as the first disciples did at Pentecost. What happened in Jerusalem was not only the fulfillment of Joel's prophecy but the beginning of an ongoing spiritual process whereby Christ's presence is continually revealed through the Spirit's work in His people.

At Pentecost the disciples were not merely given power; they were given perception. The Spirit opened their eyes to see Christ enthroned, just as He had promised: "I will not leave you as orphans; I am coming to you. In a little while the world will no longer see me, but you will see me. Because I live, you will live too" (John 14:18–19). The world could not see Him, but His followers could perceive Him—not with their physical sight but through the unveiled reality of the Spirit. This same unveiling continues for every believer who walks in the Spirit today.

Pentecost is not only a moment in history; it is the enduring pattern of Christ's unveiling through the Spirit. What began in that upper room continues in every believer who surrenders to the Spirit's presence. The transformation of the disciples—fear replaced by boldness, doubt replaced by faith—reveals what happens when Christ is truly seen. As Paul affirms, "We all, with unveiled faces, are looking . . . at the glory of the Lord and are being transformed into the same image from glory to glory" (2 Corinthians 3:18). This unveiling is not a one-time event but a way of life. Each moment of deeper surrender brings a fresh revelation of Christ's essence and a fuller participation in His kingdom. To live by the Spirit is to live in the ongoing reality of Pentecost, a reality that still reshapes the world through those who behold His glory.

The disciples were not only transformed internally; they stepped into authority. Christ's final words to them were not merely a command but an unveiling of the reality they now lived in: "All authority has been given to me in heaven and on earth. Go, therefore, and make disciples of all nations" (Matthew 28:18–19). What changed between fearful disciples hiding behind locked doors and bold apostles turning the world upside down? At Pentecost they received an *epiphaneia* of Christ's reign—not just as a doctrinal truth but as a spiritual reality unveiled through the Spirit.

Paul later expresses this transformation when he declares, "Christ in you, the hope of glory" (Colossians 1:27). The *Parousia* is not just about seeing Christ's authority; it is about walking in it. The Spirit's presence is the active unveiling of Christ's kingship in the believer, empowering them to stand in spiritual confidence against condemnation, exercise boldness in the mission of the kingdom, and overcome spiritual forces through discernment and divine power. Believers today experience the *Parousia's* power as they embrace their divine authority in Christ. The more they yield to the Spirit, the more they walk in boldness and victory.

Jesus declared, "The kingdom of God is not coming with something observable; no one will say, 'See here!' or 'There!' For you see, the kingdom of God is in your midst" (Luke 17:20–21). Pentecost confirmed this truth: the kingdom is not merely a future event but a present reality, breaking into the lives of those who live in the Spirit. When the disciples received the Spirit they immediately began living out the kingdom. They worshiped in unity; shared all things as an expression of kingdom life; and saw miracles, signs, and wonders that testified to Christ's reign. Believers today participate in the *Parousia* by recognizing that the kingdom is already here. Walking in the Spirit means living as active citizens of Christ's reign, manifesting His presence in relationships, service, and mission.

Pentecost was the beginning of the great unveiling—the moment when Christ's presence became a tangible, experienced reality for His people. That same unveiling continues today in the life of every believer who walks in the Spirit. Just as the disciples' eyes were opened to see Christ's reign at Pentecost, so too must every believer seek continual *epiphaneia*—the ongoing revelation of Christ's unveiled presence. This is not a singular event but a lifelong journey wherein each new unveiling deepens transformation, empowers authority, and strengthens kingdom participation. The question is not whether the *Parousia* has begun—it has. The question is: Are believers actively engaging with it?

Pentecost calls every believer to embrace the Spirit's work in ongoing transformation, to walk in the unveiled authority of Christ's reign, and to live daily as participants in His kingdom reality. The unveiling of Christ's essence is not something ahead—it is now. The *Parousia* is unfolding. Christ is here. Those who walk in the Spirit will see it.

This transformation is further illustrated in Ephesians 4:22–24, where Paul urges believers to "take off your former way of life . . . and . . . put on the new self, the one created in God's likeness in righteousness and purity of the truth." The renewal of the inner self requires a conscious effort to discard condemning tendencies and embrace the new identity found in Christ. As believers yield to the Holy Spirit's work we become living testimonies of the ongoing *Parousia*, reflecting Christ's essence in our daily actions and interactions. Through this spiritual renewal believers gain clarity of purpose, enabling us to walk in holiness, righteousness, and truth.

WALKING IN AUTHORITY (*EXOUSIA*)

The practical expressions of this authority manifest in various aspects of the believer's life. First, believers are empowered to overcome condemnation and guilt. Paul declares in Romans 6:14, "Sin will not rule over you, because you are not under the law but under grace." This empowerment frees believers from the bondage of guilt, enabling us to walk in the victory Christ has provided. Through the *Parousia* believers are continually strengthened to resist the temptations of condemnation that once held us captive, reflecting Christ's righteousness in our daily lives.

Second, believers are called to live as ambassadors of Christ's kingdom. In 2 Corinthians 5:20 Paul writes, "We are ambassadors for Christ, since God is making his appeal through us." As representatives of Christ, believers are entrusted with the mission to embody His love, peace, and righteousness in our communities and relationships. Our transformed lives serve as a powerful witness, drawing others into the ongoing revelation of Christ's presence.

Furthermore, believers are equipped to engage in spiritual warfare with confidence and victory. Ephesians 6:10–12 exhorts believers to "put on the full armor of God so that you can stand against the schemes of the devil." The *Parousia* empowers believers to stand firm against spiritual opposition, equipped with Christ's authority to confront the forces that seek to hinder our spiritual growth and our mission to spread the kingdom of God. Through reliance on Christ's presence and power, we walk in boldness, knowing we are more than conquerors through Him.

The empowerment granted through *exousia* is made possible by the Holy Spirit, who serves as the conduit of Christ's authority. Acts 1:8 declares, "You will receive power when the Holy Spirit has come on you, and you will be my witnesses." This divine empowerment enables believers to fulfill our calling, walking in alignment with Christ's will and purpose. As we yield to the Spirit's guidance we experience the fullness of Christ's unveiled presence, living lives marked by purpose, power, and victory.

Walking in spiritual authority requires a deep reliance on the Holy Spirit and a continual engagement with Christ's presence. It is through this reliance that believers are equipped to overcome life's challenges, embody Christ's character, and actively participate in the unfolding reality of the *Parousia*. As ambassadors of Christ's kingdom, we carry His transformative presence into every aspect of our lives, advancing His mission and reflecting His glory to the world.

PARTICIPATING IN THE KINGDOM NOW

The *Parousia*, understood as the spiritual unveiling of Christ's essence, calls believers to live as active participants in His kingdom. This participation transforms both personal devotion and communal engagement, empowering believers to reflect Christ's presence in worship, mission, and daily life. The reality of Christ's reign is not confined to a distant future event but is experienced in the present, shaping the image-bearing of believers in how we live, share God's love, and serve others for His glory.

Participation in Christ's kingdom begins with recognizing and embracing the spiritual realities of His reign. These realities encompass peace, joy, and purposeful living, all rooted in the believer's union with Christ. Jesus proclaimed in Luke 17:21, "The kingdom of God is in your midst," highlighting that His reign is already established within the hearts of believers. This truth invites believers to align our daily lives with His kingdom values, transforming mundane activities into acts of worship and submission to His lordship. As we surrender to Christ's reign our lives become living testimonies of His transformative power.

The kingdom of God is marked not by visible signs or worldly spectacle but by the progressive unveiling of Christ's presence. As Jesus taught, it is already in our midst. This reality affirms that the *Parousia* is not about awaiting a distant event but about living within the ongoing *epiphaneia* of Christ's reign here and now.

The Transfiguration (Matthew 17:1–8) serves as a paradigm for this reality. Peter, James, and John were not witnessing a future event but were given a moment of *epiphaneia* wherein Christ's glory was unveiled in the present. The voice from heaven commanded them not to wait for His return but to listen to Him now.

Likewise, believers today do not merely anticipate the future kingdom but are called to perceive and embody Christ's unveiled presence in the present. Each *epiphaneia* strengthens our participation in His kingdom, aligning our thoughts, actions, and mission with His unfolding reign. As Paul told the Colossian believers, "Set your minds on things above, not on earthly things" (Colossians 3:2). The ability to see Christ's kingdom reality is directly connected to our willingness to engage with ongoing *epiphaneia*, making His presence the foundation of our daily life and mission.

The kingdom of God manifests through tangible spiritual realities that shape the believer's identity and relationships. The apostle Paul affirms in Romans 5:1, "Since we have been justified by faith, we have peace with God through our Lord Jesus Christ." This peace is not merely an absence of conflict but a deep-seated reconciliation that fosters inner harmony and unity with others.

Similarly, Paul declares in Romans 14:17, "The kingdom of God is not eating and drinking, but righteousness, peace, and joy in the Holy Spirit." Joy becomes a defining characteristic of life in the kingdom, grounded in the assurance of Christ's presence and promises. Moreover, believers are called to set their minds on eternal realities, as Paul urges in Colossians 3:1–2: "Set your minds on things above, not on earthly things." This heavenly perspective shapes our priorities and fuels a life of purpose aligned with Christ's mission.

Believers demonstrate the kingdom through our actions, reflecting Christ's character in the world. The prophet Micah encapsulates this calling in Micah 6:8: "to act justly, to love faithfulness, and to walk humbly with your God." As we embody these values believers make Christ's presence visible to the world, revealing His love, justice, and humility in their interactions with others.

The *Parousia* compels believers to share Christ's unveiled essence through our words, deeds, and transformed lives. Our participation in His kingdom extends beyond personal growth to our becoming ambassadors of His reign, reflecting His love and truth in every context. Jesus encourages His followers in Matthew 5:16, "Let your light shine before others, so that they may see your good works and give glory to your Father in heaven." Every act of kindness and service becomes a reflection of Christ's essence, drawing others into the reality of His presence. Paul reinforces this mission in 2 Corinthians 5:20: "We are ambassadors for Christ, since God is making his appeal through us." As representatives of Christ's kingdom, believers invite others to experience the transformative power of His reign.

Sharing Christ's essence takes various forms, from proclaiming the gospel to discipling others and demonstrating the fruit of the Spirit. Jesus commands in Mark 16:15, "Go into all the world and preach the gospel to all creation." This commission challenges believers to share the good news boldly, making Christ known through our words and actions. Additionally, the Great Commission in Matthew 28:19–20 emphasizes the importance of making disciples, guiding others into deeper conformity with Christ's image. The ongoing work of the Holy Spirit produces the fruit of the Spirit in believers' lives, as outlined in Galatians 5:22–23: "love, joy, peace, patience, kindness, goodness, faithfulness, gentleness, and self-control." These qualities serve as practical evidence of Christ's presence at work within us.

Living in the *Parousia* involves an ongoing transformation, whereby believers are progressively conformed to the image of Christ and reflect His glory and love. Paul asserts in Romans 8:29, "Those he foreknew he also predestined to be conformed to the image of his Son." This transformative process is not instantaneous but unfolds as believers surrender to the work of the Spirit in our lives. The hope of ultimate transformation fuels our present journey, as Paul writes in Philippians 3:20–21: "Our citizenship is in heaven, and we eagerly wait for a Savior . . . who will transform the body of our humble condition into the likeness of his glorious body." This transformation begins now, as believers mirror Christ's nature in our daily lives, anticipating its full realization in eternity.

As believers participate in the kingdom now, we become living expressions of Christ's unveiled presence, embodying His love, righteousness, and mission. The *Parousia* calls us to a life of active engagement wherein we continually experience and share the transformative reality of Christ's reign, bringing hope and redemption to a world in need.

As believers embrace the unveiled essence of Christ, we are called to live in the transformative reality of the *Parousia*. This transformation is not a passive process but an active participation in Christ's presence, shaping every aspect of our lives. Through the renewing power of the Holy Spirit, believers are invited to walk in divine authority, fully aware of our identity as children of God. John 1:12 affirms this truth, declaring that those who receive Christ are given the authority to become children of God. This divine empowerment enables believers to reflect Christ's character as His image-bearers in the world, demonstrating His love, righteousness, and grace in our daily interactions.

The ongoing unveiling of Christ's glory calls believers to a deeper journey of spiritual transformation. Paul's words in 2 Corinthians 3:18 capture this reality, describing how believers, with unveiled faces, are continually being transformed into the image of Christ from glory to glory. This transformation is a lifelong journey that shapes the believers' character, refining us to reflect the holiness and purity of Christ. As believers yield to the Spirit's work we increasingly embody the essence of Christ in our thoughts, attitudes, and actions, becoming living testimonies of His presence in the world.

The kingdom of God, as Jesus proclaimed in Luke 17:21, is not merely a distant future hope but a present, internal reality within believers. Christ's reign is established in the hearts of His followers, guiding us to live in alignment with His values and purposes. This internal reality empowers believers to live righteously and to extend the influence of Christ's kingdom into our families, workplaces, and communities. Every act of faith, love, and obedience becomes a tangible expression of the kingdom, as we walk in the power and authority given to us through Christ.

Living out the *Parousia* also involves a commitment to mission and witness. In Matthew 5:16 Jesus exhorts His followers to let their light shine before others so that they may see their good works and glorify God. The life of a believer, shaped by the ongoing *Parousia*, becomes a beacon of hope and transformation in a world longing for redemption. Whether through acts of service, sharing the gospel, or simply embodying Christ's character in daily interactions, believers participate in revealing the unveiled presence of Christ to those around them. This witness is not limited to words but is demonstrated through the integrity of a life lived in alignment with Christ's mission.

Paul's exhortation in Ephesians 4:22–24 further emphasizes the practical outworking of the *Parousia* in daily life. He urges believers to put off their old selves, which are corrupted by deceitful desires, and to put on the new self, created in the likeness of God in true righteousness and holiness. This transformation is not achieved through human effort alone but through a continual dependence on the Spirit's power, enabling believers to walk in righteousness, reflect God's holiness, and fulfill His purposes.

Ultimately, the goal of the *Parousia* is conformity to the image of Christ. Romans 8:29 reveals that believers are predestined to be conformed to the likeness of Christ, an ongoing process that reaches its fulfillment in the believer's complete transformation. This divine purpose calls for a life of surrender, growth, and reflection of Christ's love and truth in every aspect. As believers embrace this transformative journey we are equipped to live with purpose and confidence, secure in the knowledge that we are being shaped into the likeness of our Savior.

The *Parousia* calls believers to pursue continuous spiritual growth, aligning their character with Christ's essence. It challenges them to walk in the authority granted by Christ, overcoming condemnation, guilt, fear, and spiritual opposition. The *Parousia* also invites believers to live as active citizens of God's kingdom, advancing His authority within their lives and communities. Through worship believers cultivate a deeper connection with Christ's unveiled presence, experiencing renewal and transformation.

The reality of the *Parousia* inspires believers to share Christ's essence with the world as ambassadors and witnesses of His glory. Additionally, the *Parousia* calls believers to live as the body of Christ, fostering unity, love, understanding, and compassion within the community of faith. As believers embrace the *Parousia* they reflect the hope and assurance of the ultimate fulfillment of God's redemptive plan.

SURRENDER: THE KEY TO UNVEILED GLORY

However, before the applications of the *Parousia* can take root and flourish in a believer's life, they must first surrender. Jesus emphasized this in Luke 9:23, saying, "If anyone wants to follow after me, let him deny himself, take up his cross daily, and follow me." Surrender requires laying down personal ambitions and embracing God's purposes for the world to come. The depth of one's surrender directly influences the degree to which the *Parousia* shapes their spiritual journey "in Christ."

Epiphaneia does not come to the passive observer but to the one who surrenders completely. Christ's essence is unveiled to those who desire Him above all else, making surrender the gateway to deeper revelation.

The rich young ruler (Mark 10:17–22) provides a stark contrast to Paul's surrender in Acts 9. The young man desired life in the kingdom, yet he refused to release his earthly attachments. In contrast, Paul surrendered everything—his identity, ambitions, and security—leading to a life of profound *epiphaneia*. The degree of *epiphaneia* in the believer's life is directly tied to the depth of surrender. Jesus declared, "Anyone who loses his life because of me will find it" (Matthew 10:39).

Each act of surrender invites a greater unveiling of Christ's essence, leading to increased transformation, deeper authority, and greater kingdom participation. Surrender is not a one-time event but a daily posture—one that continually positions the believer to receive fresh *epiphaneia*, unlocking new dimensions of the *Parousia's* reality.

Peter's spiritual journey exemplifies this principle of proportional surrender. Initially, Peter followed Jesus with enthusiasm, yet he struggled with personal ambitions and fears, as seen in Matthew 16:22–23. However, after his denial of Christ and subsequent restoration (John 21:15–19) Peter's surrender deepened, and he was transformed into a bold apostle, fully committed to God's purposes. His life demonstrates that full surrender leads to greater conformity to Christ's image and a more profound experience of His unveiled presence.

Each believer must prayerfully commune with the Spirit of Christ and examine their willingness to surrender fully to His will. Surrender is not a one-time decision but a daily commitment, as Jesus taught in Luke 9:23. When believers hold back areas of their lives from Christ's authority, their spiritual growth and transformation are hindered. However, full surrender unlocks the divine power of the *Parousia*, allowing the Holy Spirit to work mightily within them.

Paul affirms this truth in Galatians 2:20, declaring, "I have been crucified with Christ, and I no longer live, but Christ lives in me." His life, along with the lives of many disciples, illustrates the profound impact of complete surrender in unleashing the transformative power of the *Parousia*. This surrender aligns believers with Paul's exhortation in Romans 12:1–2: "Therefore, brothers and sisters, in view of the mercies of God, I urge you to present your bodies as a living sacrifice, holy and pleasing to God; this is your true worship. Do not be conformed to this age, but be transformed by the renewing of your mind, so that you may discern what is the good, pleasing, and perfect will of God."

CONCLUSION

Despite the transformative nature of the *Parousia*, its understanding as a present spiritual reality has not been without challenges. Throughout Christian history various interpretations and misunderstandings have led to differing perspectives regarding its significance, eschatological implications, and practical applications. Some have viewed the *Parousia* solely as a future physical event, while others have struggled to comprehend its present transformative impact. Addressing these misconceptions is essential to maintaining a biblically sound and theologically coherent understanding of Christ's ongoing unveiling.

In the next chapter we will explore key objections and counterarguments to the interpretation of the *Parousia* as the spiritual unveiling of Christ's essence. Through careful scriptural engagement and theological reflection we will address these challenges, reinforcing the transformative reality of the *Parousia* and its profound implications for the believer's daily life. By doing so believers can gain greater confidence in their understanding of the *Parousia* and be equipped to articulate its significance with clarity and conviction.

CHAPTER 20

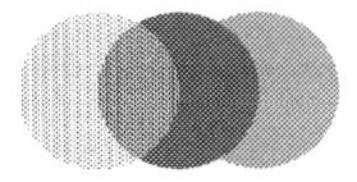

DEFENDING THE TRANSFORMATIVE RELATIONAL *PAROUSIA*

As believers embrace the transformative reality of the *Parousia* as the spiritual unveiling of Christ's essence, questions and objections naturally arise. These concerns often stem from long-standing eschatological traditions that anticipate Christ's return as a literal, visible, and future event that will be accompanied by a "rapture" of varying chronologies. Addressing these objections with theological clarity and scriptural insight is essential for affirming the *Parousia* as an ongoing spiritual reality rather than a distant physical occurrence.

Many of the objections to this interpretation focus on key scriptural passages traditionally understood to indicate a visible, bodily return of Christ. However, by carefully examining these texts within their historical, literary, and theological contexts, we can uncover their true meaning and deeper spiritual significance. This chapter aims to demonstrate how these passages align with the broader biblical narrative of divine presence and spiritual transformation, central themes of the *Parousia*.

MISUNDERSTANDINGS ABOUT THE TIMING OF THE *EPIPHANEIA*

One of the fundamental misunderstandings surrounding the *Parousia* stems from overlooking the significance of *epiphaneia* in Scripture. The *epiphaneia* of Christ—the manifestation or unveiling of His presence—occurs throughout redemptive history. It is often misunderstood as a delayed event when, in reality, it is an immediate and ongoing revelation for those who have spiritual eyes to see.

The destruction of Jerusalem in AD 70 stands as one of the most profound *epiphaneia* moments in redemptive history, a divine unveiling that reshaped the course of faith and worship forever. For those entrenched in the old system, the fall of the city and the fiery ruin of the temple signified devastation, loss, and divine abandonment. But for those who had embraced Christ it was a confirmation of His sovereign rule and the decisive fulfillment of His words. Jesus had spoken of this moment with unmistakable clarity when He warned His disciples that not one stone of the temple would remain upon another. The judgment on Jerusalem was not simply a political tragedy but a theological watershed, marking the visible end of the Old Covenant and the full inauguration of the New Covenant.

Josephus, the Jewish historian, recorded the unimaginable suffering within the city's walls: famine reducing people to desperation; factions turning on one another; and finally, the merciless assault of the Roman army. Even hardened Roman soldiers were taken aback by the carnage, and when the temple, once thought indestructible, was set ablaze, all recognized that God's hand had brought about its destruction. What unfolded with the destruction of Jerusalem was not merely a military conquest but a divine *epiphaneia*, an unveiling of Christ's authority as the true temple.

With the temple's destruction the last vestiges of the old sacrificial system were swept away. No longer would priests stand before the altar, and no longer would the courts be filled with worshipers offering sacrifices. The reality that Jesus had declared years before, that true worshipers would no longer be bound to a place but would worship in spirit and truth, was now fully revealed. The *Parousia* was not a distant event to be anxiously awaited but a present reality, one that had already begun shaping the world in ways that could not be reversed. The removal of the earthly temple only served to unveil the true dwelling place of God: Christ Himself, enthroned in the heavenly Jerusalem, and His presence abiding in His people.

Paul repeatedly links *epiphaneia* with the *Parousia*, emphasizing that Christ's appearing is not an end-time event but an ongoing unveiling of His glory. He writes in 2 Timothy 1:10, "This has now been made evident through the appearing (*epiphaneia*) of our Savior Christ Jesus, who has abolished death and has brought life and immortality to light through the gospel."

Here *epiphaneia* does not refer to a postponed second coming but to the revelation of Christ's essence already realized through the gospel. Likewise, Titus 2:11–13 describes both a present and a future *epiphaneia*, where Christ's grace is unveiled now while awaiting its full consummation. This pattern of progressive unveiling is foundational to the transformative relational *Parousia* (TRP). The *Parousia* is not a singular future event but an unfolding revelation of Christ's presence, accessible to those who live by faith rather than sight (2 Corinthians 5:7). In this light hear what Jesus was saying in Matthew 5:8: "Blessed are the pure in heart, for they will see God."

MISUNDERSTANDINGS ROOTED IN LITERALISM

Beyond addressing objections, this discussion seeks to equip believers with a robust framework for defending and articulating the *Parousia* as an ongoing reality. By deepening their understanding believers can confidently embrace Christ's unveiled presence in their lives, participating fully in the transformative work of His kingdom.

One of the strongest affirmations of the transformative relational *Parousia* is found in the progressive unveiling of Christ's presence within believers—a process that is not static but continually forming them into His image. This concept, which can be best described as Imagoformity, offers a direct counterpoint to the argument that the *Parousia* must be a single, climactic future event. Rather than viewing Christ's coming as an external spectacle that has yet to occur, Imagoformity reveals that His presence is already actively transforming His people, progressively conforming them to His essence.

Paul speaks directly to this ongoing unveiling in 2 Corinthians 3:18: "We all, with unveiled faces, are looking as in a mirror at the glory of the Lord and are being transformed into the same image from glory to glory; this is from the Lord who is the Spirit." Here Paul describes transformation not as an instantaneous occurrence but as a process of increasing conformity to Christ's image. This is not an eschatological event that believers merely anticipate; it is the very essence of the *Parousia* actively unfolding in their lives. If the *Parousia* is the unveiling of Christ's presence, then Imagoformity is the natural outcome—believers are being reshaped by this presence, becoming living testimonies of His reality.

This challenges the literalist objection that claims Christ's coming must be a global, physical event to be meaningful. If that were the case, then the process of Imagoformity—this progressive conforming into Christ's image—would be meaningless in the present. But Scripture consistently testifies that believers are already participating in Christ's coming, for His presence is actively shaping them into His likeness.

EVALUATING CLAIMS OF A LITERAL SECOND COMING

Many traditional eschatological perspectives assert that the *Parousia* refers to a single, climactic future event in which Christ will return physically to establish His kingdom on earth. These interpretations often arise from a literal reading of apocalyptic and prophetic texts, which can obscure the deeper symbolic and spiritual meanings woven throughout Scripture. While the hope of Christ's return remains central to the Christian faith, it is important to recognize that the *Parousia* is not limited to a distant event but is an ongoing, transformative reality in the lives of believers.

The New Testament consistently presents the kingdom of God as a present reality accessible to those who have been spiritually awakened. Jesus's declaration in Luke 17:21, "The kingdom of God is in your midst," underscores the idea that His reign is already established within the hearts of those who believe. When viewed through this lens the *Parousia* is not an event to be awaited passively but a reality to be embraced actively.

In defending the transformative relational *Parousia*, it becomes evident that the focus should shift from anticipation of a physical return to the ongoing unveiling of Christ's essence in the lives of believers. Through worship, mission, and spiritual growth the presence of Christ is continually revealed, shaping the Church and advancing His redemptive work in the world.

In Romans 8:29 Paul emphasizes this transformative purpose: "Those he foreknew he also predestined to be conformed to the image of his Son, so that he would be the firstborn among many brothers and sisters." This means that the *Parousia* is not something to be awaited passively—it is a present spiritual reality that is reshaping the believer's identity. To argue that Christ's presence is significant only when physically manifested ignores the greater theological truth that He is already present in His people, changing them from within.

Thus, Imagoformity directly addresses the eschatological misinterpretation that the *Parousia* must be a delayed or yet-unfulfilled event. If Christ's presence were truly absent, then there would be no transformation—no progressive unveiling of His glory in the Church. Yet the testimony of Scripture and the lived experience of believers confirm that His presence is indeed at work, forming them into His image.

Furthermore, this spiritual transformation aligns with Paul's teaching in Colossians 3:10, where he speaks of believers who have "put on the new self. You are being renewed in knowledge according to the image of your Creator." The renewal into Christ's image is not a future event. It is an ongoing work of the Spirit that testifies to the reality of the *Parousia* in the present.

If the *Parousia* were merely a delayed physical event, then this transformation would lack its immediate significance. But because Imagoformity is happening now we see that Christ's presence is already revealed in His people and that His unveiling is continuing to reshape them into His essence.

For this reason the biblical doctrine of Imagoformity offers one of the strongest theological witnesses to the reality that the *Parousia* is not a postponed event but an ongoing spiritual unveiling of Christ's presence. It refutes the notion that Christ must physically return for transformation to occur, demonstrating instead that His unveiled presence is already actively conforming believers to His image.

MISINTERPRETED BIBLICAL TEXTS: ACTS 1:11, REVELATION 19:11–16, AND MATTHEW 24:30

One of the most frequent challenges to the concept of the *Parousia* as a present spiritual reality is the interpretation of key biblical texts that appear to suggest a physical and visible return of Christ. Among these, Acts 1:11, Revelation 19:11–16, and Matthew 24:30 are often cited to support the belief in a future bodily return of Christ to establish His kingdom on earth.

In Acts 1:11 the angels declare to the disciples, "This same Jesus, who was taken from you into heaven, will come in the same way that you have seen him going into heaven." This statement is commonly interpreted to mean that Christ will return in a literal and physical form, just as He visibly ascended into the clouds. However, a closer examination of the phrase "in the same way" within its broader theological context suggests a deeper spiritual reality. Just as Christ's ascension was not merely a physical departure but a transition to a higher realm of divine authority, His "return" can be understood as His ongoing unveiling to those who have the faith to perceive His presence. This perspective aligns with Jesus's promise in John 14:19, "In a little while the world will no longer see me, but you will see me," emphasizing the selective perception of His presence by believers.

The misunderstanding of Acts 1:11 arises from assuming a purely physical interpretation of Christ's departure and return rather than recognizing *epiphaneia* as the disciples' actual experience. The angels' words—"This Jesus . . . will come in the same way that you have seen him going"—do not necessitate a future bodily descent but rather point to a recurring pattern of divine unveiling.

Throughout Scripture, as we have seen, clouds symbolize divine presence rather than a literal transportation method. The cloud at Christ's ascension mirrors the cloud on Sinai (Exodus 19:9), the glory cloud in the tabernacle (Exodus 40:34–38), and the cloud at the Transfiguration (Matthew 17:5)—each representing an *epiphaneia* of divine glory rather than an observable departure.

Christ's "return" is thus an ongoing unveiling of His presence rather than a long-delayed second coming. This aligns with Jesus's own words in John 14:18–19, "I will not leave you as orphans; I am coming to you. In a little while the world will no longer see me, but you will see me." The contrast between the world's blindness and the disciples' perception affirms that the *Parousia* is a revealed reality rather than a postponed event—one that believers experience through ongoing *epiphaneia*.

Similarly, Revelation 19:11–16 presents a powerful vision of Christ descending on a white horse, bearing the title "Faithful and True" and judging in righteousness. The vivid apocalyptic imagery is often interpreted to support a dramatic future event in which Christ returns in glory to establish His kingdom physically. However, within the symbolic language of Revelation, this vision serves to illustrate the ongoing and active reign of Christ over spiritual forces and the continual victory of His essence in the lives of believers. The white horse represents purity and divine authority, and the imagery reflects Christ's triumphant presence, which is progressively revealed in the hearts and lives of those who are "in Him."

The apocalyptic imagery of Revelation 19 aligns perfectly with the *epiphaneia* of Christ's unveiled reign rather than a physical future invasion. John sees heaven opened, revealing Christ as the victorious King of kings. However, His sword is not in His hand but in His mouth—a clear indication that His victory is spiritual, not militaristic (Revelation 19:15).

This symbolism echoes Paul's description of Christ's *epiphaneia* in 2 Thessalonians 2:8: "The Lord Jesus will destroy [the lawless one] with the breath of his mouth and will bring him to nothing at the appearance (*epiphaneia*) of his coming (*Parousia*)." Here Christ's victory is accomplished not through physical conquest but through His revealed presence, just as in Revelation 19. The *Parousia*, then, is not an event that remains future but an active reality manifesting Christ's reign in the lives of believers now.

Matthew 24:30, which states, "They will see the Son of Man coming on the clouds of heaven with power and great glory," further reinforces the expectation of a visible future *Parousia*. The reference to Christ coming "on the clouds" evokes Old Testament imagery of divine presence and authority rather than a literal physical descent. Throughout Scripture clouds symbolize God's glory and guidance, as seen in Exodus 13:21 and Daniel 7:13. Thus, Christ's coming in the clouds signifies His ongoing presence and authority revealed in the spiritual realm to those who have eyes to see Him.

The image of "coming on the clouds" (Matthew 24:30) must be understood through the lens of *epiphaneia*, aligning with Old

Testament divine enthronement imagery rather than a physical return event. This is evident in Daniel 7:13, where the Son of Man is depicted as "coming with the clouds of heaven"—not descending to earth but being enthroned in glory. When Jesus applies this passage to Himself, He is not predicting a future spectacle but declaring that His reign will be unveiled through *epiphaneia*. Those who "see" the Son of Man coming are those whose eyes have been opened to His kingdom—a fulfillment already experienced by the early Church (Acts 7:55–56).

Paul confirms this reality in 1 Timothy 6:14–16, referring to Christ's *epiphaneia* "in [God's] own time," which already illuminates believers while awaiting its full realization. This is consistent with Jesus's promise that the pure in heart will "see God" (Matthew 5:8), highlighting that the *Parousia* is not an external event to be observed but a spiritual reality to be perceived.

REBUTTAL: CONTEXTUALIZING THE PASSAGES

A thoughtful examination of the scriptural passages often cited in support of a future physical *Parousia* reveals a deeper spiritual reality that aligns with the transformative and relational unveiling of Christ's essence. Understanding these passages within their biblical and theological contexts provides clarity and reinforces the ongoing nature of Christ's presence rather than confining it to a singular future event.

REINTERPRETING KEY "SECOND COMING" PASSAGES

Acts 1:11—A Clouded Assumption

The angelic message in Acts 1:11—"This Jesus . . . will come in the same way that you have seen him going into heaven"—is commonly taken as a prediction of Christ's literal, physical return. However, this interpretation overlooks the symbolic language embedded in the passage. The phrase "in the same way" (*houtōs*) does not necessarily imply a visible, bodily reenactment but rather a continuity in spiritual revelation.

Christ's ascension was not primarily spatial—it was theological. It marked His exaltation to divine authority and the beginning of His universal reign made accessible through the Spirit. The cloud that received Him (Acts 1:9) is not a vehicle but a biblical symbol of divine presence and glory (cf. Exodus 40:34–35; Matthew 17:5). Thus the promise of His "return" is fulfilled not by a sky-splitting descent but by the ongoing unveiling of His presence in and through the Spirit-filled community. The *Parousia* here is relational and unfolding, not postponed or distant.

Revelation 19:11–16—Victory, Not Violence

This dramatic vision of Christ riding a white horse is often cited as evidence of a future physical return marked by violence and warfare. But Revelation's apocalyptic style demands a symbolic reading—one rooted in the spiritual reality of Christ's present reign rather than literal military conquest. The white horse signifies purity, triumph, and righteous authority, not an actual warhorse descending from the sky. This vision unveils not an impending battle of bloodshed but the ongoing victory of Christ's Word, Spirit, and truth over the forces of darkness.

The heavenly armies, clothed in fine white linen (v. 14), symbolize the redeemed—those made righteous not by their own merit but through Christ's righteousness (cf. Revelation 19:8). The sharp sword proceeding from Christ's mouth (v. 15) is not a weapon of physical violence but a powerful image of the Word of God, echoing Hebrews 4:12, which describes the word as "living and effective . . . sharper than any double-edged sword." Through this imagery Revelation proclaims that Christ conquers not with violence but with truth—piercing hearts, disarming lies, and setting captives free.

This scene also echoes Ephesians 6:12, where Paul reminds believers that their struggle is not "against flesh and blood" but against spiritual forces of evil. Christ's victory is not geopolitical but spiritual—

rooted in His redemptive mission, not in military power. Revelation 19 thus portrays the ongoing reality of Christ's *Parousia*: a transformative reign already disarming spiritual powers and forming His people into agents of reconciliation and righteousness (cf. Colossians 2:15).

Far from pointing to a distant future event, this apocalyptic vision reveals a present truth: Christ's kingdom is advancing now—not by force but by the Spirit, through the lives of those who bear His name and live in the light of His unveiled presence.

Matthew 24:30—The Son of Man on the Clouds

Jesus's words in Matthew 24:30—All peoples "will see the Son of Man coming on the clouds of heaven with power and great glory"—are frequently interpreted as a literal description of His return. Yet the imagery of "coming on the clouds" is a symbolic motif used throughout Scripture to signify divine authority and presence.

In Daniel 7:13, which Jesus directly echoes, the Son of Man is not descending to earth but being enthroned in heaven, receiving dominion and glory from the Ancient of Days. Likewise, in Exodus 16:10 and Hebrews 12:1 clouds represent the manifestation of God's presence and the gathered community of faithful witnesses. In this context "coming on the clouds" refers to Christ's heavenly exaltation and ongoing reign, not to a visible descent.

This vision is fulfilled in the spiritual unveiling of Christ's kingdom, manifested in the lives of believers and the spread of the gospel. The *Parousia* in Matthew 24 is not a single climactic spectacle but the revelation of Christ's authority breaking into the world through His Spirit-filled Church.

REINTERPRETING THE CONCEPT OF "COMING"

This book asks us to reinterpret the concept of "coming" not as a delayed event waiting to break into history but as a present, relational unveiling of Christ's glory through the Spirit. While many believers imagine the *Parousia* as a dramatic future return, Scripture invites us to see it as a continuous revelation of Christ's presence in the lives of His people. This reinterpretation shapes how we understand eschatology, spiritual transformation, and the kingdom of God.

A deeper exploration of the term often translated as "coming" (Greek: *parousia*) reveals a broader and more relational meaning. The word *parousia* conveys the idea of presence or arrival, not merely in a physical sense but as an ongoing and unfolding reality. This perspective aligns with Paul's usage in Philippians 1:26, where he expresses his desire to be present with the Philippians, highlighting an experiential and relational aspect of presence rather than a single physical event.

Understanding the *Parousia* in this relational light emphasizes the continuous unveiling of Christ's presence in the lives of believers. It is not an event restricted to the future but rather a transformative experience unfolding through faith, obedience, and surrender to the Holy Spirit.

CHRIST'S VICTORY OVER SPIRITUAL FORCES

The imagery in Revelation 19 emphasizes Christ's victory over spiritual forces, a theme that runs throughout the New Testament. Rather than predicting a future physical battle, this passage declares the all-encompassing nature of Christ's spiritual reign. His triumph is not limited to a single event but is an ongoing reality that is progressively unveiled in the lives of believers. This perspective aligns with the apostolic teaching that Christ has already disarmed the powers of darkness and reigns victoriously through His Word and Spirit (Colossians 2:15).

The portrayal of Christ as a conquering King serves as a powerful assurance that His presence is continually at work, dismantling the forces of sin and darkness within individuals and communities. This spiritual reign invites believers to participate in His mission, bearing witness to the reality of His kingdom through lives transformed by His unveiled essence.

A BROADER THEOLOGICAL FRAMEWORK

The tendency to emphasize a physical return of Christ can inadvertently limit the transformative impact of the *Parousia* in the present. By focusing solely on a future event, believers risk neglecting the immediate and profound reality of Christ's presence available to them now. Recognizing the *Parousia* as a spiritual unveiling allows believers to fully engage in the work of Christ, aligning their lives with His kingdom and living in the power of His presence today.

The *Parousia* encapsulates the "already-but-not-yet" tension of the kingdom of God—where Christ's reign is actively at work in the world—while also pointing to its ultimate fulfillment. This understanding encourages believers to embrace their role in advancing Christ's mission, living as reflections of His unveiled glory while awaiting the consummation of His redemptive work.

ALIGNMENT WITH CHRIST'S KINGDOM TEACHINGS

The spiritual nature of Christ's kingdom is a recurring theme in His teachings. In John 18:36 Jesus clearly states, "My kingdom is not of this world," underscoring its spiritual and eternal nature rather than a political or earthly dominion. Likewise, in Luke 17:21 He declares, "The kingdom of God is in your midst," affirming the present and internal reality of His reign among those who believe. These statements shift the focus from external manifestations of Christ's coming to the inward transformation brought about by His presence through the *Parousia*.

Rather than anticipating a dramatic physical return, believers are called to recognize and experience Christ's presence now. The ongoing unveiling of His essence through the *Parousia* invites them to live as active participants in His kingdom, embodying His values of righteousness, peace, and joy (Romans 14:17). The imagery of Christ coming on the clouds serves as a powerful reminder of His continuous presence, reigning through His Spirit and working through the lives of those who surrender to Him.

CLOUDS IN DANIEL 7:13: THE OLD COVENANT REDEEMED

The imagery of clouds within Scripture is one of the most profound symbols of God's interaction with humanity, particularly within the context of His covenantal relationship with His people. Far from being mere atmospheric phenomena, clouds consistently signify God's presence and glory and the gathered community of the redeemed. By examining Daniel 7:13 through the lens of the New Testament, we uncover a rich theological framework in which clouds symbolize the redeemed people of God across both the Old and New Covenants. This interpretation provides significant support for the transformative relational *Parousia*, highlighting the unveiling of Christ's presence among His covenant people.

In Daniel's vision the "Son of Man" is described as coming "with the clouds of heaven" to the "Ancient of Days" (Daniel 7:13). This throne room imagery underscores divine authority and glory, yet the role of the clouds requires careful theological consideration.

The Son of Man's appearance takes place in the presence of the Ancient of Days, where God's ultimate authority is already manifest. The clouds, therefore, cannot simply represent God's presence or divine authority, as these elements are already intrinsic to the throne room scene. Instead, the clouds must signify a distinct and integral aspect of God's redemptive work—namely, His covenantal relationship with the redeemed with the Son of Man as their Redeemer.

THE REDEEMED AS THE CLOUDS

A consistent interpretation is that the clouds represent the Old Covenant saints, those justified by faith, who accompany the Son of Man into the presence of God. These are the faithful witnesses of the Old Covenant described in Hebrews 11, whose righteousness through faith enabled them to participate in the establishment of Christ's everlasting kingdom. This view aligns with the symbolic use of clouds throughout Scripture to represent God's covenant people.

BIBLICAL PRECEDENT FOR CLOUDS AS THE REDEEMED

The use of clouds to symbolize the redeemed covenantal community finds further support in key biblical passages. Hebrews 12:1 refers to a "large cloud of witnesses" surrounding believers, representing the faithful saints of the Old Covenant who testify to God's redemptive work. Similarly, Revelation 1:7 declares, "Look, he is coming with the clouds, and every eye will see him," where the clouds signify the gathered saints who share in Christ's glory and reign (cf. Revelation 5:9–10). In both instances clouds serve as a metaphor for the covenant community of the redeemed.

CLOUDS AS A COVENANT MARKER

Throughout the Old Testament clouds are frequently associated with God's presence as He interacts with His covenant people. In Exodus 13:21 a cloud leads the Israelites during the Exodus, symbolizing God's guiding presence. At Mount Sinai a dense cloud signifies God's covenantal engagement with Israel (Exodus 19:9). Likewise, in 1 Kings 8:10–11 the cloud that fills the temple reflects God's glory dwelling among His people. In Daniel 7:13 this symbolism extends to the faithful saints of the Old Covenant who accompany the enthronement of the Son of Man in God's presence.

CLOUDS IN THE NEW TESTAMENT: THE REDEEMED IN THE *PAROUSIA*

The New Testament continues the symbolic use of clouds, connecting them to the redeemed community of the New Covenant and their participation in Christ's glory. This continuity underscores the relational and transformative nature of the *Parousia*. Several key passages illustrate this connection:

In 1 Thessalonians 4:16–17 Paul describes the Lord's descent: "For the Lord himself will descend from heaven with a shout, with the archangel's voice, and with the trumpet of God, and the dead in Christ will rise first. Then we who are still alive, who are left, will be caught up together with them in the clouds to meet the Lord in the air, and so we will always be with the Lord." The clouds here symbolize the unification of believers with Christ in His spiritual presence. Rather than a physical ascent the clouds represent the gathered community of the redeemed brought into relational unity with Christ.

Matthew 24:30 reads, "Then the sign of the Son of Man will appear in the sky, and then all the peoples of the earth will mourn; and they will see the Son of Man coming on the clouds of heaven with power and great glory." In this passage the clouds signify the manifestation of Christ's authority, accompanied by the presence of His redeemed people who share in His victory and glory.

Revelation 14:14–16 states, "Then I looked, and there was a white cloud, and one like the Son of Man was seated on the cloud, with a golden crown on his head and a sharp sickle in his hand." The Son of Man seated on a cloud underscores the connection between clouds and the redeemed, highlighting their participation in Christ's reign and judgment.

In Ephesians 2:6 Paul writes, "He also raised us up with him and seated us with him in the heavens in Christ Jesus." Although this verse does not explicitly mention clouds, it emphasizes the spiritual reality of believers already united with Christ in His heavenly presence, consistent with the metaphor of clouds as the gathered redeemed.

The promise of "new heavens and a new earth, where righteousness dwells" (2 Peter 3:13) and the vision of the "new heaven and a new earth" (Revelation 21:1) both emphasize the ultimate fulfillment of God's promises. These passages highlight the transformed reality of God dwelling with His people, a theme that culminates in the relational and communal fulfillment of the *Parousia*. The clouds, as symbols of the redeemed, align with this eschatological vision, representing the unified community of believers in God's renewed creation.

In Colossians 1:27 Paul declares, "Christ in you, the hope of glory," encapsulating the relational and transformative nature of the *Parousia*. The indwelling presence of Christ in His people represents the unveiling of His glory within the redeemed community, a reality symbolized by the clouds throughout Scripture.

THE UNITY OF THE REDEEMED ACROSS COVENANTS

This interpretation of clouds emphasizes the continuity of God's covenantal people throughout redemptive history. In Daniel 7:13 the clouds represent the faithful saints of the Old Covenant who, through their faith, bear witness to God's redemptive plan. In the New Testament the clouds expand to include the redeemed of the New Covenant, united with Christ through faith in His fulfillment of God's promises. Together these clouds symbolize the unified redeemed community—the Church—testifying to the relational and transformative nature of the *Parousia*.

THEOLOGICAL IMPLICATIONS FOR THE TRANSFORMATIVE RELATIONAL *PAROUSIA*

By interpreting clouds as the gathered community of the redeemed across both the Old and New Covenants, this framework reinforces the transformative relational *Parousia* as the unveiling of Christ's presence:

The *Parousia* is not a delayed physical event but a spiritual reality in which Christ's presence is unveiled through the gathering of His people (cf. Colossians 1:27). The clouds represent the relational and communal aspect of Christ's presence, where His glory is revealed in and through His people. The unified testimony of the clouds across Scripture reflects the fulfillment of God's covenantal promises, culminating in the relational dwelling of God with His people (cf. 2 Peter 3:13; Revelation 21:1).

The metaphor of clouds provides a cohesive and consistent theological framework for understanding the *Parousia*. In Daniel 7:13 the clouds symbolize the Old Covenant saints who witness the enthronement of the Son of Man. In the New Testament the clouds represent the New Covenant redeemed, gathered into Christ's relational presence. Together they form a unified redeemed community across redemptive history. This interpretation reinforces the transformative relational *Parousia* as the unveiling of Christ's essence and presence among His people, fulfilling God's promise to dwell with His covenantal community for eternity.

SPIRITUAL REALITIES OVER PHYSICAL MANIFESTATIONS

The *Parousia* is best understood as an ongoing spiritual revelation of Christ's glory and presence, aligning with the New Covenant's emphasis on internal transformation. Rather than anticipating a singular physical manifestation, Scripture consistently points to the *Parousia* as a dynamic process in which believers are progressively conformed to the image of Christ. As Paul declares in 2 Corinthians 3:18, "We all, with unveiled faces, are looking as in a mirror at the glory of the Lord and are being transformed into the same image from glory to glory." This transformation reflects the believer's journey of spiritual renewal, where Christ's unveiled presence brings about deeper communion, greater maturity, and increasing alignment with His essence.

BROADER SCRIPTURAL HARMONY

The overarching narrative of Scripture prioritizes spiritual fulfillment over physical spectacle, demonstrating that God's redemptive work is centered on internal renewal and transformation. Christ's resurrection body, for example, transcended material limitations, pointing to the spiritual realities of His glorified essence (John 20:19–29). His post-resurrection appearances, marked by His ability to move beyond physical constraints, reveal that His glorified presence is not bound by earthly limitations but is instead an ongoing spiritual reality available to those who believe.

Furthermore, the Holy Spirit continues Christ's mission by unveiling His presence in the lives of believers, reinforcing the reality of the *Parousia* as a present and active experience. Jesus assured His disciples in John 14:16–17 that the Holy Spirit would dwell within them, bringing the reality of Christ's presence into their everyday lives. This promise was fulfilled at Pentecost, as recorded in Acts 2:1–4, when the Spirit-empowered believers to experience the ongoing unveiling of Christ's essence. The Spirit's indwelling presence serves as the primary means by which believers participate in the transformative work of the *Parousia*, aligning their hearts and minds with the realities of Christ's kingdom.

FROM PHYSICAL AND PREDICTED TO SPIRITUAL AND PRESENT: REINTERPRETING THE *PAROUSIA* IN LIGHT OF REVELATION

The book of Revelation consistently portrays Christ's essence as divine light and authority, emphasizing the spiritual nature of His ongoing presence. In Revelation 21:23 the vision of the New Jerusalem illustrates this reality: "The city does not need the sun or the moon to shine on it, because the glory of God illuminates it, and its lamp is the Lamb." This passage affirms that the *Parousia* is not defined by physical manifestations but by the transformative illumination of Christ's essence in the lives of His people. His glory, shining forth in and through believers, testifies to the ongoing nature of the *Parousia* as an ever-present spiritual reality.

The ongoing unveiling of Christ's glory is facilitated by the Holy Spirit, aligning believers with His essence and preparing them for the fullness of His kingdom. As Paul writes in Galatians 5:5, "We eagerly await through the Spirit, by faith, the hope of righteousness." This anticipation is not passive; rather, it is an active participation in the transformative work of Christ's presence, allowing believers to embody His righteousness and reflect His character in their daily lives. The *Parousia*, therefore, is something not to be awaited with idle expectation but embraced through faith as a present reality that progressively shapes and renews those who surrender to Christ.

The spiritual interpretation of the *Parousia* finds its foundation in the broader scriptural narrative, emphasizing Christ's ongoing unveiling rather than a single future event. Scripture consistently affirms that the *Parousia* is an ongoing spiritual revelation, consistent with the New Covenant's focus on internal transformation and divine presence. The destruction of Jerusalem and the temple in AD 70 stands as a pivotal moment in redemptive history that reinforces this interpretation. Jesus's prophecy in Matthew 24:1–2 foretold the fall of the temple as a sign of the end of the Old Covenant age, marking the transition from a localized, temple-based worship system to the universal and spiritual reign of Christ. This catastrophic event served as both a divine judgment and a prophetic fulfillment, demonstrating that Christ's kingdom was not of this world (John 18:36) but was being established through His unveiled presence in the lives of believers.

The symbolic texts often interpreted as references to a future physical return—such as Acts 1:11, Revelation 19:11–16, and Matthew 24:30—align more accurately with the spiritual realities of Christ's reign, highlighting the transformative work of His presence rather than predicting physical events. The fall of Jerusalem affirmed that the *Parousia* was not to be understood in merely external terms but as the progressive and relational unveiling of Christ's authority, visible through the spiritual transformation of His people and the establishment of the New Covenant reality.

The spiritual focus of the *Parousia* reflects the teachings of Christ regarding His kingdom, which prioritize inner renewal over external spectacle. Jesus stated clearly in John 18:36 that "My kingdom is not of this world," reinforcing the idea that His reign is spiritual in nature. Similarly, Galatians 5:5 demonstrates that Paul and the early believers eagerly awaited the fulfillment of Christ's righteousness through the unveiling of His essence rather than through a physical event.

Key scriptural references affirm the perspective that the *Parousia* is an ongoing spiritual reality rather than a singular future event. Acts 1:11 highlights Christ's return as a continuation of His spiritual glory, pointing believers to the ongoing revelation of His presence rather than to a physical reappearance. Similarly, Revelation 19:11–16 employs apocalyptic imagery to emphasize Christ's spiritual victory, portraying His triumph through righteousness and truth rather than through a literal battle. In Matthew 24:30 the imagery of Christ coming on the clouds serves as a powerful symbol of divine presence and authority, reinforcing the notion that His reign is manifest through spiritual transformation rather than a physical descent.

Paul's words in 2 Corinthians 3:18 further underscore this transformation, describing how believers are progressively conformed to Christ's image as His unveiled glory is revealed in their lives. Likewise, Jesus affirms the spiritual nature of His kingdom in John 18:36, declaring that it is not of this world but exists within the hearts and lives of those who believe. Galatians 5:5 emphasizes the believer's anticipation of righteousness through the ongoing unveiling of Christ's essence, highlighting the transformative power of the *Parousia* in shaping their journey of faith. Together these passages present a cohesive biblical framework that aligns with the transformative relational *Parousia*, encouraging believers to embrace Christ's presence as a present and active reality in their daily lives.

By addressing common objections and clarifying the spiritual significance of the *Parousia*, this chapter reaffirms its theological coherence and alignment with the broader scriptural narrative. It invites believers to embrace the ongoing transformative realities of Christ's unveiled presence, participating fully in His kingdom and serving as active agents of His mission in the world. This perspective not only offers a deeper understanding of the *Parousia* but also equips believers to live with confidence, purpose, and a renewed sense of identity in Christ.

Understanding the *Parousia* as a transformative, relational unveiling invites believers to reframe their spiritual journey as an ongoing process of becoming more like Christ. In the next chapter we will explore how this relational dynamic deepens the believers' connection with Christ, transforming their identity and empowering them to live in greater alignment with His presence. This exploration will provide practical insights for believers seeking to experience the fullness of the *Parousia* in their daily walk with Christ.

CHAPTER 21

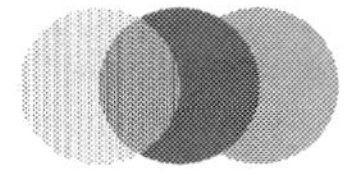

THE MYSTERY OF THE *PAROUSIA* MADE ALIVE

The *Parousia* is the ongoing spiritual unveiling of Christ's essence, an eternal reality that transcends eschatological speculation and becomes a lived experience in the believer's daily walk. Far from being a distant theological concept, the *Parousia* invites believers to actively embody Christ's presence in their lives, transforming passive anticipation into dynamic participation. Paul captures the transformative nature of this mystery in Colossians 2:12–15, where he anchors the believer's identity and renewal in their union with Christ's death and resurrection. Through this union the essence of Christ becomes a tangible and transformative reality, shaping every aspect of life and illuminating the paths of faith, hope, and love.

At the heart of the *Parousia* made alive is the radiant unfolding of *epiphaneia*—not as a distant spectacle but as the present-tense appearing of Christ's essence in the believer's life. Paul speaks of this unveiling in 2 Timothy 1:10, where Christ's appearing abolishes death and brings immortality to light through the gospel. This ongoing *epiphaneia* is not confined to doctrinal affirmation but becomes the light by which the believer walks daily, drawing them into communion with Christ and shaping their inner world by the power of His resurrected life. Through this light the *Parousia* becomes not a theological destination but a spiritual reality that permeates heart, mind, and action.

This present-tense unveiling is also captured in Titus 2:11–12, where Paul states, "For the grace of God has appeared (*epiphaneia*), bringing salvation for all people, instructing us to deny godlessness and worldly lusts and to live in a sensible, righteous, and godly way in the present age."

Through *epiphaneia* believers are continually instructed, transformed, and empowered to reflect Christ's unveiled presence to the world. The mystery of the *Parousia* becomes alive when believers recognize that the appearing of Christ is not simply a future hope but a present, unfolding reality.

This ongoing unveiling challenges believers to see the *Parousia* not as a distant promise but as a present invitation to divine communion. Even the most mundane moments of life become sacred opportunities to reflect the glory of Christ. In this way the believer's journey is transformed into active participation in the kingdom of God, where each step reveals the power of Christ's resurrection and the beauty of His essence made alive. Through worship, service, and daily surrender the believer reflects the mystery of the *Parousia*, unveiling Christ's presence to the world.

At the heart of the *Parousia* made alive is the reality of Imagoformity—the divine process by which believers are progressively conformed into the image of Christ. This transformation is not merely theoretical but is tangible, experiential, and eternal, marking the ongoing unveiling of Christ's presence within His people. To understand the mystery of the *Parousia*, one must grasp the profound reality that Christ's coming is not just an event to anticipate but an experience to embody.

Paul affirms this relational transformation in Romans 8:29, stating, "For those he foreknew he also predestined to be conformed to the image of his Son, so that he would be the firstborn among many brothers and sisters." This passage unveils the true nature of the *Parousia*—not simply as Christ's return but as His unfolding essence within the redeemed, shaping them into His divine image. This process of being conformed to Christ is what Imagoformity encapsulates. It is the *Parousia* in motion, the progressive revelation of His presence that transfigures believers from glory to glory (2 Corinthians 3:18).

Just as Jesus is the visible image of the invisible God (Colossians 1:15), believers are being formed into His image, reflecting His unveiled presence in the world. This transformation is the very mystery that Paul labored to proclaim—the *Parousia* is not external; it is Christ in you, the hope of glory (Colossians 1:27).

The mystery of the *Parousia* made alive is fulfilled in Imagoformity. As believers yield to the Holy Spirit's work, their very existence becomes an *epiphaneia*—a radiant unveiling of Christ's essence. Every moment of faithfulness, every act of love, every surrender to divine truth manifests the reality of Christ's coming within them.

Paul emphasizes this in Galatians 4:19, declaring, "My children, I am again suffering labor pains for you until Christ is formed in you!" Here Paul does not speak of a future, distant return but of a present, living transformation—Christ being formed within His people. The *Parousia* is the formation of Christ's image in those who walk by the Spirit, and Imagoformity is the tangible reality of this formation.

This spiritual unveiling of Christ's essence also fulfills the promise Jesus made in John 14:23: "If anyone loves me, he will keep my word. My Father will love him, and we will come to him and make our home with him." The coming of Christ is not restricted to an external, apocalyptic event but is manifested as the indwelling presence of the Father and the Son. This divine inhabitation is the culmination of Imagoformity—the realization of the believer's destiny in Christ, wherein God's presence permeates their being, shaping them into living testaments of His *Parousia*.

Thus, to experience the *Parousia* is to undergo Imagoformity—to become the unveiling of Christ's presence in the world. This reality transcends eschatology and reframes the Christian life, not as waiting for an external event but as walking in the unveiled presence of Christ, where His divine image is revealed in us and through us.

The resurrection of Christ serves as the hinge between the temporal and the eternal, the physical and the spiritual, death and life. It is the definitive act by which believers are transitioned from the realm of sin and death into the reality of the new creation. In this transformative process believers are empowered to live as citizens of His kingdom, embracing both the "already" of His reign and the "not yet" of its consummation. This chapter delves into how the mystery of the *Parousia* becomes alive in the believer's life, inspiring a transformative walk in faith, worship, and mission.

THE RESURRECTION OF CHRIST: THE BRIDGE BETWEEN TWO WORLDS

The resurrection of Christ is the turning point between two realms—the temporal and the eternal, the earthly and the heavenly, death and life. It is not only the foundation of the believer's hope but also the catalyst for a radically transformed way of living. In the power of His resurrection, believers are called into the reality of the new creation, where the *Parousia* becomes a present, spiritual unveiling of Christ's reign. This chapter explores how the resurrection empowers a life of faith that trusts without striving, worship that flows from union with Christ, and mission that reflects His presence rather than ambition. It also examines how this resurrection life reshapes the believer's entire orientation toward the world, not as a place to escape but as the very ground on which the unveiled essence of Christ is made visible through them.

Christ's resurrection is not an isolated event fixed in time; it is the opening act of a grand narrative—the unveiling of a new humanity. The writer of Hebrews describes Christ as the "forerunner" who has entered the heavenly sanctuary on behalf of His people (Hebrews 6:20). In this role Christ demonstrates the journey from death to life, from the flesh to the Spirit, and from the transient to the eternal. His victory over death becomes a divine guarantee that those who are "in Him" will share in His triumph. As the forerunner Christ leads believers into a life that reflects His glory and power, a life marked by the transformative essence of His resurrection.

Paul identifies Christ as "the firstborn from the dead" (Colossians 1:18), signifying that His resurrection is the prototype for all who belong to Him. This truth moves believers from being mere spectators of Christ's work to active participants in the redemptive power of His resurrection. United with Christ, believers step into the reality of the new creation, wherein their identity is defined no longer by the limitations of the old but by the boundless potential of life "in Christ." This new creation transforms their perspective, empowering them to view every challenge and triumph as part of God's redemptive story.

The *epiphaneia* of Christ's resurrection life is not confined to the past or delayed to the future—it is made alive in the believer now. Paul proclaims in 2 Timothy 1:10 "Christ Jesus, who has abolished death and has brought life and immortality to light through the gospel."

This statement affirms that resurrection is not merely a future expectation but a present, revealed reality, made known through *epiphaneia*. Just as Christ is the firstborn from the dead, His resurrection unveils the transformation of all who are "in Him." This truth aligns with Colossians 3:1–4, where Paul exhorts, "So if you have been raised with Christ, seek the things above, where Christ is, seated at the right hand of God. . . . When Christ, who is your life, appears (*epiphaneia*), then you also will appear with him in glory." Here Paul connects *epiphaneia* to the believer's resurrection identity, emphasizing that to live in Christ is to experience resurrection life now, anticipating its fullness in glory. The *Parousia* is thus made alive in the present through the unveiled resurrection life of Christ in the believer.

The resurrection of Christ calls believers to embrace a vision of life that transcends the temporal. It challenges them to anchor their purpose, identity, and hope in the transformative power of Christ's victory. As both forerunner and firstborn, Christ invites all who follow Him to rise into the fullness of their calling. They are summoned to live as emissaries of His kingdom, reflecting His essence in their worship, their relationships, and their daily lives. Through the resurrection the bridge between two worlds is firmly established, allowing believers to walk confidently in the power and promise of Christ's eternal reign.

DYING IN JESUS: THE CALL TO LEAVE THE WORLD BEHIND

The mystery of the *Parousia* cannot be fully made alive without a willingness to embrace the cruciform life—a life shaped by the death and resurrection of Christ. This cruciform existence is the spiritual framework by which believers are conformed to the pattern of Christ's death and resurrection, not only through suffering and surrender but also through the redemptive victory that emerges from them. This paradox—life through death, glory through humility, and victory through submission—defines the Christian journey. Just as Christ embraced the cross to reveal the glory of resurrection, believers are called to take up their own cross daily (Luke 9:23), dying to themselves so that Christ may live in them (Galatians 2:20).

At the heart of the cruciform life is surrender—not a passive resignation but an active yielding of one's will, desires, and self-interest to the will of God. This surrender is the threshold to transformation: what is broken is made whole, what is temporary is exchanged for the eternal, and self-reliance gives way to the freedom found in Christ's lordship. It is through this cruciform existence that the believer's true identity as an image-bearer of God is revealed and restored. Paul illustrates this truth in Romans 6:5–6: "For if we have been united with him in the likeness of his death, we will certainly also be in the likeness of his resurrection. For we know that our old self was crucified with him so that the body ruled by sin might be rendered powerless so that we may no longer be enslaved to sin."

To live in the *Parousia* is to die to self and to the values of the world. Yet this death is not the end; it is the gateway to true freedom, identity, and purpose "in Christ." As Paul expresses in Romans 6:3–4, "Are you unaware that all of us who were baptized into Christ Jesus were baptized into his death? Therefore we were buried with him by baptism into death, in order that, just as Christ was raised from the dead by the glory of the Father, so we too may walk in newness of life."

The cruciform life is not a one-time event but a daily act of surrender—a deliberate choice to take up one's cross and follow Christ (Luke 9:23). In this spiritual crucifixion the believer is united with the redemptive power of the cross, breaking the chains of sin and self and replacing them with the liberating presence of Christ. As Paul proclaims, "I have been crucified with Christ, and I no longer live, but Christ lives in me. The life I now live in the body, I live by faith in the Son of God, who loved me and gave himself for me" (Galatians 2:20).

Through this union believers no longer rely on their own strength but are empowered by the same glory and power that raised Christ from the dead. The *Parousia*, the unveiled presence of Christ, elevates those who embrace this cruciform reality above sin, condemnation, and self-interest.

CRUCIFORMITY, IMAGOFORMITY, AND THE *PAROUSIA*: THE RESTORATION OF GOD'S IMAGE

Cruciformity and Imagoformity are inextricably linked within the transformative reality of the *Parousia*. While cruciformity speaks of the believer's participation in Christ's death and resurrection, Imagoformity unveils the ultimate purpose of this transformation: the restoration of humanity to its original design as image-bearers of God. "In Christ" the distorted image of God caused by sin is renewed and perfected, bringing believers into alignment with their true identity in Him. Paul emphasizes this restoration in 2 Corinthians 3:18: "We all, with unveiled faces, are looking as in a mirror at the glory of the Lord and are being transformed into the same image from glory to glory; this is from the Lord who is the Spirit."

Here the unveiling (*apokalypsis*) of Christ's presence through the *Parousia* is tied directly to the process of becoming like Him. As believers embrace the cruciform life, the veils of self, sin, condemnation, and worldly identity are removed, allowing them to reflect the true image of Christ. Just as the cross was the necessary path to the resurrection, cruciformity is the necessary path to Imagoformity—where the believer's participation in Christ's suffering leads to their full conformation to His image.

The *Parousia*, therefore, is not merely a future event but the ongoing revelation of Christ in the believer's life. This unveiling occurs as believers live in surrender, allowing their old nature to be put to death so that the "new self"—created in the image of Christ—can emerge. Paul describes this transformation in Colossians 3:9–10: "You have put off the old self with its practices and have put on the new self. You are being renewed in knowledge according to the image of your Creator."

Thus cruciformity leads to Imagoformity, and Imagoformity is realized through the *Parousia*—the spiritual unveiling of Christ's life within the surrendered believer. This is why the cruciform life is indispensable to experiencing the full mystery of the *Parousia*: without dying to self, there can be no resurrection into the restored image of God.

THE *EPIPHANEIA* OF THE CRUCIFORM LIFE: THE VISIBLE *PAROUSIA*

Dying in Jesus also means relinquishing the false identities imposed by the world—identities rooted in status, achievements, and fear. This surrender is not a loss but a divine exchange, trading the fleeting for the eternal, the fractured for the whole, and the temporal for the divine. In this act of dying, believers are freed to embrace their true identity as children of God and heirs of His Kingdom. As Paul affirms in Romans 8:16–17, "The Spirit himself testifies together with our spirit that we are God's children, and if children, also heirs—heirs of God and coheirs with Christ—if indeed we suffer with him so that we may also be glorified with him."

The epiphaneia of Christ's cruciform life is the paradoxical path to transformation. To live in the unveiled presence of Christ is to embrace the cross, for it is through death that resurrection is revealed. Paul affirms, "We always carry the death of Jesus in our body, so that the life of Jesus may also be displayed in our body" (2 Corinthians 4:10–11). This passage reveals that the *Parousia* is made alive through epiphaneia in suffering, where the dying of self makes way for the appearing of Christ's life. Just as epiphaneia unveils resurrection, so too does it reveal the crucified Christ within the believer's surrender.

Paul intensifies this reality in 2 Timothy 4:8, where he describes a *"crown of righteousness"* that will be given to those who *"have loved His appearing (epiphaneia)."* To love Christ's appearing is not merely to long for a future event but to embrace His unveiled presence in the daily walk of faith, where death to self makes way for the fullness of life.

Through this cruciform *epiphaneia* the *Parousia* becomes visible, not in the spectacle of clouds or cataclysms but in the quiet radiance of a life laid down. This is the paradox of the "Visible *Parousia*": that the glory of Christ's reign is made manifest, not by outward signs but by inward transformation. When believers surrender self-interest, bear the cross of love, and walk in faith-filled obedience, they unveil Christ's essence in real time. In this way the *Parousia* becomes not only spiritually discerned but publicly embodied, seen in lives shaped by humility, service, and joy—and even in suffering. It is a visibility not of optics but of essence, the visibility of glory refracted through human weakness.

This new identity reshapes every aspect of life, reordering priorities, values, and relationships in alignment with Christ's reign. No longer defined by the transient pursuits of the world, believers are called to live as vessels of Christ's essence, bearing witness to His love, grace, and truth. This surrender does not diminish individual *Parousia* but transforms ordinary moments into acts of worship and every interaction into an opportunity to reveal Christ's essence.

LIVING IN CHRIST: THE ESSENCE OF THE *PAROUSIA* REVEALED

To live "in Christ" is to live in the unveiled presence of the risen King. The *Parousia* is not a far-off future event but the present and personal transformation that occurs when Christ becomes the very atmosphere of one's life, not just its goal but its source. In this union the believer's life is no longer compartmentalized between sacred and secular but is entirely redefined by the indwelling glory of Christ.

Paul's call in Colossians 3:2 to "set your minds on things above" is not a withdrawal from the world but an invitation to see it rightly through the lens of resurrection. Believers, as citizens of the kingdom, are sent not to escape the world but to reveal the reign of Christ within it. Every act of grace, every decision marked by love, and every response shaped by faith becomes a visible echo of the *Parousia*.

In this way the Church becomes the *epiphaneia*, the radiant unveiling of Christ's essence to the world. The Holy Spirit empowers believers to reflect this glory, not only in moments of worship but in the patterns of ordinary life. As Paul writes, "Now you are light in the Lord. Walk as children of light" (Ephesians 5:8). This light is not self-generated; it is the refracted glory of Christ's own appearing through His people.

To declare, as Paul does, that "Christ . . . is your life" (Colossians 3:4) is to confess that the *Parousia* is not simply something we await but Someone we embody. It is Christ made visible in and through us, in weakness and in strength, in joy and in suffering. This is the mystery made alive: the believer no longer lives, but Christ lives in them. And in that life the world begins to see—however dimly—the shape of His eternal reign.

THE KINGDOM OF GOD: A PRESENT AND FUTURE REALITY

The *Parousia* unveils the kingdom of God, not as a distant hope but as a present, spiritual reign made visible through the lives of those who walk in Christ. It is a kingdom that has already come in power through the resurrection and ascension of Jesus and yet awaits its full unveiling in the renewal of all things. This tension is not meant to create confusion, but clarity: believers live between the triumph of Christ's appearing and the consummation of His reign.

To live in this kingdom now is to embody its values in a world shaped by opposing forces. Jesus's words "The kingdom of God is in your midst" (Luke 17:21) become not merely a declaration of proximity but a call to recognition that where Christ reigns the kingdom is present. Through the *Parousia* His essence is spiritually discerned and made visible in the faithful lives of His people. Every act of mercy, justice, and humility becomes a revelation of His rule.

But this kingdom is not advanced through dominance, strategy, or control. It is unveiled in cruciform love, the way of Christ reflected in those who bear His image. This is how the *Parousia* reshapes mission: not as conquest but as presence. Believers are not merely proclaimers of truth but vessels of it, a living *epiphaneia* of Christ's reign in real time.

This is what makes kingdom living a form of eschatological hope: not waiting idly for heaven but bearing heaven's reality into earth's brokenness. The kingdom that will one day be seen in fullness is already being revealed, person by person, act by act, moment by moment—through those in whom the *Parousia* has become alive.

THE MYSTERY MADE ALIVE: A LIFE OF UNION WITH CHRIST

The *Parousia* is the unveiling of Christ's essence within the believer, a mystery made alive through their union with Him. This union is not a distant theological concept but a lived reality, transforming every aspect of life and empowering believers to reflect His glory in all they do. Through this divine connection the presence of Christ reshapes identity, renews purpose, and anchors destiny in the reality of His kingdom.

Paul's declaration "Christ in you, the hope of glory" (Colossians 1:27) encapsulates the heart of the *Parousia*. This indwelling presence of Christ is both the source and the culmination of the believer's transformation. It is through this indwelling that believers are empowered to live as reflections of Christ's essence, bringing hope, renewal, and light into a broken world. The *Parousia* is not simply a future expectation; it is an active reality by which Christ's presence transforms every thought, action, and interaction, making His glory manifest in and through His people. This continual unveiling of Christ within gives rise to what might best be called a daily resurrection, a rhythm of dying and rising that defines life in the *Parousia*.

THE RESURRECTION OF THE DAY: LIVING IN THE RHYTHM OF THE *PAROUSIA*

To live in the *Parousia* is to experience a daily resurrection. As Paul writes in 2 Corinthians 4:16, "Even though our outer person is being destroyed, our inner person is being renewed day by day." This renewal is not only the result of spiritual effort but the ongoing effect of Christ's unveiled presence within the believer. The *Parousia*, rightly understood, is not a singular moment to await but a living rhythm of death and life—an unceasing transformation by which the old self is crucified and the new self is raised in the likeness of Christ.

In this sense *resurrection* is not only our future hope; it is our present participation. Each day brings with it the divine opportunity to enter this sacred rhythm. As the Spirit calls us to die to selfish ambition, fear, pride, and control, we are not diminished but resurrected. This is the mystery and the miracle: through surrender we rise. Through weakness we are filled with power. Through letting go we receive the very life of Christ. Paul's declaration in Galatians 2:20 frames this mystery plainly: "I have been crucified with Christ, and I no longer live, but Christ lives in me."

This daily resurrection is not a burden of moral effort but the fruit of relational participation in the *Parousia*. It is the evidence that the *Parousia* is active, that Christ is enthroned and His reign is transforming hearts. The believer who walks in faith is not merely imitating Christ but being conformed to Him, moment by moment. Colossians 3 speaks to this dynamic: "You died, and your life is hidden with Christ in God. When Christ, who is your life, appears, then you also will appear with him in glory" (vv. 3–4). The appearing of Christ—His *Parousia*—is already happening in the hidden places where lives are being daily surrendered and raised anew.

Thus, to walk in this world as a child of the kingdom is to live in continual resurrection. Every act of forgiveness, every moment of trust in suffering, every decision to bless instead of curse—these are not small things. They are death undone. They are resurrected alive. They are the unfolding of the kingdom.

In this way the mystery of the *Parousia* becomes a living testimony. Christ is not only returning in glory; He is appearing now in the glory of transformed lives. Heaven breaks into earth not by spectacle but by the slow and radiant unveiling of Christ in those who die and rise with Him—not once, but every day.

HOPE AND ASSURANCE IN THE *PAROUSIA*

The *Parousia* provides a profound source of hope that sustains believers through trials and suffering. Paul's vision in Romans 8:18–25 captures this dynamic, as he writes, "For I consider that the sufferings of this present time are not worth comparing with the glory that is going to be revealed to us." This passage highlights the groaning of creation and humanity in anticipation of redemption, framing the *Parousia* as the resolution to suffering and decay.

This hope is not passive but active, empowering believers to persevere and embody Christ's presence in a world longing for renewal. The promise of the *Parousia* infuses the believer's life with meaning and purpose, enabling them to navigate tribulation with resilience and faith. Through their participation in the *Parousia's* transformative power, believers become conduits of hope, reflecting the glory of Christ to a world in need.

The *Parousia* guarantees Christ's ultimate victory, grounding the believer's confidence in His eternal reign. Paul's declaration in 1 Corinthians 15:57 underscores this assurance: "Thanks be to God, who gives us the victory through our Lord Jesus Christ." This victory over sin, death, and darkness provides the Church with an unshakable foundation for its mission and life.

The certainty of Christ's triumph strengthens the Church to remain faithful, knowing that His redemptive purposes will be fulfilled. This assurance anchors the believers' faith and fuels their commitment to living as vessels of His transformative presence, embodying the kingdom's values and anticipating the ultimate renewal of all things.

The *Parousia*, as the spiritual unveiling of Christ's essence, reshapes eschatology by grounding it in the reality of Christ's transformative presence. It calls believers to actively participate in His ongoing kingdom work, embracing the tension between the "already" and the "not yet." Through the lens of the *Parousia*, eschatology shifts from distant anticipation to present engagement, inviting believers to live as vessels of Christ's unveiled glory.

This understanding of the *Parousia* equips the Church to reflect Christ's reign through worship, mission, and community life. It also provides hope amid tribulation and assurance of ultimate victory, anchoring faith in the certainty of Christ's presence and redemptive purposes. The *Parousia* is not only a theological framework but a lived reality that shapes the identity, purpose, and destiny of believers.

As this journey of theological reflection reaches its conclusion, we turn to the practical outworking of the *Parousia* in the believer's life. Chapter 22 will illuminate how the unveiled essence of Christ moves from concept to lived experience. It will explore how believers embody the transformative reality of the *Parousia*, allowing Christ's essence to animate their worship, relationships, and daily lives.

This transition from theological depth to practical application mirrors the essence of the *Parousia* itself: a movement from reflection to action, from unveiling to embodiment. Just as the *Parousia* invites believers into the ongoing reality of Christ's presence, so too does the next chapter invite us to make this mystery alive in our own lives, becoming conduits of His essence in a world longing for redemption.

CONCLUSION: THE *PAROUSIA* AS THE BELIEVER'S PRESENT AND ETERNAL REALITY

The *Parousia*, once shrouded in mystery, now stands unveiled as the believer's present and eternal reality. Through union with Christ in His death and resurrection, believers are invited to step into the fullness of His presence, experiencing the power of His essence in their lives. This is the great mystery made alive: Christ in us, the hope of glory. It is a reality that transforms our lives, calls us to reflect His kingdom to the world, and invites us to participate in His ongoing reign.

The *Parousia* challenges believers to live boldly and faithfully, allowing the unveiled presence of Christ to shape every thought, word, and action. It is an invitation to walk in the light of His glory, to embrace our cross in life, and to embody the values of His kingdom in a world longing for redemption. As Jesus said in Luke 9:23, "If anyone wants to follow after me, let him deny himself, take up his cross daily, and follow me. Now, in the light of the *Parousia*, his statement is clear. To live in the *Parousia* is to live in the reality of Christ's presence, allowing His essence to permeate every aspect of our existence.

Recall what Jesus told His disciples in Luke 11:34–36: "Your eye is the lamp of the body. When your eye is healthy [undivided], your whole body is also full of light. But when it is bad [divided], your body is full of darkness. Take care, then, that the light in you is not darkness. If, therefore, your whole body is full of light, with no part of it in darkness, it will be entirely illuminated, as when a lamp shines its light on you." In light of the *Parousia* being the present unveiling of the essence of Christ standing before us in heaven, how do we see? When our vision is fixed on His unveiled essence, the light of His *epiphaneia* (shining revelation) compels us into cruciformity (living in His self-giving way), which in turn brings about imagoformity (our transformation into His image). This moment-by-moment transformation is the heart of the *Parousia's* work in the believer.

The *Parousia* continually unveils what darkness seeks to obscure: that Christ has already triumphed over death and reigns with all authority in heaven and earth. To walk in the light of the *Parousia* is to live in the reality of His victory, allowing no shadow of doubt or deception to dim His revealed presence. The *Parousia* progressively brings light (Imagoformity) to those whose spiritual eyes are open (*epiphaneia*) and focused on it (cruciformity). Our transformation in the *Parousia* depends on the clarity of our spiritual vision—how fully we receive the radiance of Christ's ascended presence within us.

Let the mystery of the *Parousia* be made alive in your life. Let it guide your worship, fuel your mission, inspire your hope, and unbridle your love. "In Christ" we find the fullness of life, the power to overcome, and the vision to see His kingdom come on earth as it is in heaven. Let this divine unveiling of the essence of Christ shape not only your present but your eternity as you live in the transformative reality of His essence, now and forever.

In light of this profound reality, consider the charge given by the apostle Paul in Romans 12:1–2: "Therefore, brothers and sisters, in view of the mercies of God, I urge you to present your bodies as a living sacrifice, holy and pleasing to God; this is your true worship. Do not be conformed to this age, but be transformed by the renewing of your mind, so that you may discern what is the good, pleasing, and perfect will of God."

Paul's exhortation resonates deeply within the context of the *Parousia*. Consider the depth of God's mercy toward those who believe. Through faith He grants us access to the very essence of His Son (*epiphaneia*—the unveiling of Christ's presence), who reigns with all power in heaven and earth. Therefore, surrender fleeting ambitions and embrace your divine calling, offering yourselves as a living sacrifice (cruciformity—a life shaped by the cross) that reflects Christ to the world (Imagoformity—being transformed into His image). This is the worship that pleases God. Turn away from the fleeting images of this age and fix your gaze on the eternal image of Christ—the essence of the new creation.

CHAPTER 22

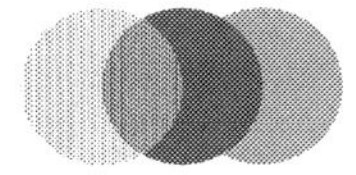

THE *PAROUSIA* AS A TRANSFORMATIVE RELATIONAL UNVEILING

Throughout this book we have reinterpreted the *Parousia* not as a distant, climactic event but as a present and unfolding spiritual reality, the continual unveiling of Christ's essence through the Spirit. This final chapter brings the journey to its fulfillment by drawing together the book's central insights: that Christ's reign is already active, His presence is already transforming, and His kingdom is already advancing through His people. At the same time this transformation is not yet complete. The tension between the *already* and the *not yet* of God's kingdom points us toward the ultimate fulfillment of the *Parousia*, when all things are renewed and Christ is fully revealed in glory.

Here we explore how the ongoing *Parousia* continues to shape individuals and communities today, even as it anticipates the final consummation of God's redemptive plan. Believers are invited to live faithfully in this tension, participating in Christ's reign now while longing for the day when His unveiled presence will fill all things in heaven and on earth.

THE ALREADY-BUT-NOT-YET NATURE OF THE KINGDOM

The kingdom of God, inaugurated through Christ's incarnation, death, resurrection, and ascension, is an active, spiritual reality accessible to believers now. Jesus declared, "The kingdom of God is in your midst" (Luke 17:20–21), pointing to its present and dynamic operation in the world. Paul echoes this reality, affirming that believers have been rescued "from the domain of darkness and transferred" into the kingdom of "the Son he loves" (Colossians 1:13–14).

Believers encounter the transformative power of the *Parousia* through the indwelling of the Holy Spirit, who reveals Christ's presence and empowers spiritual renewal. As Paul writes, "We all, with unveiled faces, are looking as in a mirror at the glory of the Lord and are being transformed into the same image from glory to glory" (2 Corinthians 3:18). This transformation reflects the ongoing unveiling of Christ's essence in the life of the believer. The Holy Spirit serves as both guide and guarantee of the ultimate fulfillment of God's redemptive plan. Through the Spirit's work believers are prepared to participate more fully in Christ's reign and to experience His glory being progressively unveiled in their lives.

While the kingdom is present now, its complete realization awaits the renewal of all things. John's apocalyptic vision captures this future hope: "Then I saw a new heaven and a new earth. . . . Then the one seated on the throne said, 'Look, I am making everything new'" (Revelation 21:1–5). This ultimate renewal signifies the culmination of God's redemptive plan, whereby the *Parousia* will bring Christ's essence fully into view for all creation. The cosmic scope of this revelation is echoed in Paul's declaration that "at the name of Jesus every knee will bow . . . and every tongue will confess that Jesus Christ is Lord" (Philippians 2:10–11). The *Parousia*, therefore, is not merely a moment of fulfillment but the unveiling of Christ's eternal reign, transforming the cosmos into a place where God's glory is fully revealed and His purposes are perfectly realized.

Believers are called to embrace the dual reality of the kingdom by living as its citizens in the present while anticipating its future fulfillment. Paul captures this tension in Romans 8:18–25, where he describes creation itself as eagerly awaiting liberation alongside believers. This cosmic anticipation emphasizes the interconnectedness of human and cosmic redemption within the *Parousia*. As Paul notes, "We know that the whole creation has been groaning together with labor pains until now. . . . We also groan within ourselves, eagerly waiting for adoption, the redemption of our bodies" (Romans 8:22–23).

This tension invites believers to lead lives marked by faith, hope, and love. Paul's reminder that "now these three remain: faith, hope, and love—but the greatest of these is love" (1 Corinthians 13:13) encourages believers to root their lives in the values of the kingdom while they wait. Living in this tension fosters active participation in God's transformative work, aligning the believer's life with the mission of the kingdom and the ongoing unveiling of Christ's essence.

THE PRESENT EXPERIENCE OF THE *PAROUSIA* AS A PRELUDE TO ITS FULFILLMENT

The ongoing unveiling of Christ's essence transforms believers, preparing them for the ultimate renewal promised in the *Parousia*. This transformative power lies at the heart of the believers' sanctification and mission, shaping their lives to reflect the character of Christ. As Paul writes in Romans 8:29, "Those he foreknew he also predestined to be conformed to the image of his Son." Through the work of the Holy Spirit, believers are continually molded into Christ's likeness, manifesting His essence in their actions, attitudes, and relationships.

The Holy Spirit's sanctifying work serves as both a guide and a foretaste of the glory to come. Paul describes the Spirit as a "down payment of our inheritance, until the redemption of the possession, to the praise of his glory" (Ephesians 1:13–14), highlighting the connection between present transformation and the future fulfillment of God's promises. The Spirit empowers believers to experience the transformative presence of Christ now, offering a glimpse of the eternal glory that awaits them in the *Parousia*.

The Church's mission to embody and proclaim Christ's essence serves as a living reflection of the *Parousia's* ultimate unveiling. Jesus's Great Commission in Matthew 28:18–20 calls believers to "Go, therefore, and make disciples. . . . And remember, I am with you always, to the end of the age." This mission underscores the Church's role as a visible witness to Christ's transformative presence in the world. Through worship, acts of love, and gospel proclamation the Church becomes a microcosm of the kingdom, reflecting the ultimate fulfillment of Christ's reign.

Believers participate in this mission by embodying Christ's essence in their daily lives. The prophetic call in Micah 6:8 to "act justly, to love faithfulness, and to walk humbly with your God" captures the essence of Christian living as a reflection of the *Parousia*. Worshiping in spirit and truth, engaging in acts of compassion, and proclaiming the gospel are practical ways believers align themselves with Christ's redemptive work, drawing others into the transformative power of the kingdom.

The present experience of the *Parousia* sustains believers through trials, anchoring them in the hope of future glory. Paul's words in Romans 5:3–5 encourage believers to rejoice in their sufferings, knowing that "affliction produces endurance, endurance produces proven character, and proven character produces hope. This hope will not disappoint us." This hope, grounded in the reality of Christ's presence, transforms suffering into a pathway for deeper reliance on His essence and greater spiritual growth.

In 2 Corinthians 4:16–18 Paul further emphasizes the eternal perspective believers are called to adopt: "Therefore we do not give up. . . . For our momentary light affliction is producing for us an absolutely incomparable eternal weight of glory." This assurance of ultimate renewal allows believers to endure trials with steadfast faith, confident that their lives are aligned with God's eternal purposes.

Living in this hope fosters resilience and purpose, enabling believers to actively participate in God's redemptive work while anticipating the *Parousia's* final consummation. It is in this tension between the present experience of Christ's reign and the future fulfillment of His promises that believers find the strength to persevere, the joy to worship, and the courage to reflect His glory in a world longing for redemption.

THE FINAL UNVEILING OF CHRIST'S ESSENCE IN THE RENEWAL OF ALL THINGS

The ultimate *Parousia* encompasses the renewal of all creation, described in Scripture as the advent of the "new heavens and new earth" wherein righteousness will dwell. This renewal is not merely a resetting of creation but a transformative restoration in which God's purposes are fully realized. Peter's declaration in 2 Peter 3:13, "We wait for new heavens and a new earth, where righteousness dwells," encapsulates the believer's hope for a reality imbued with God's justice and glory. John's apocalyptic vision in Revelation 21:1 reinforces this expectation, proclaiming, "Then I saw a new heaven and a new earth."

This cosmic restoration reflects the comprehensive alignment of all creation under Christ's authority and the harmony of God's redemptive plan. Paul writes in Ephesians 1:10 that God's purpose is "to bring everything together in Christ, both things in heaven and things on earth," demonstrating that Christ's reign encompasses every dimension of existence. This unification is not simply hierarchical but relational, bringing creation into perfect alignment with its Creator. The Alpha and the Omega—Christ's eternal identity as the beginning and end of all things—stands at the center of this transformation, as affirmed in Revelation 22:13: "I am the Alpha and the Omega, the first and the last, the beginning and the end."

The *Parousia* also represents the ultimate fulfillment of God's promise to dwell with His people. This theme of divine presence is woven throughout Scripture, reaching its zenith in the vision of

Revelation 21:3: "Look, God's dwelling is with humanity, and he will live with them. They will be his peoples." In this moment the relational essence of God's covenantal promises is fully realized, as humanity enters into unbroken fellowship with its Creator.

This fulfillment is embodied in Christ, who is Immanuel, "God with us" (cf. Matthew 1:23). His presence transforms all creation, illuminating it with divine glory. John's vision continues in Revelation 22:5, where he describes a world no longer dependent on external sources of light: "People will not need the light of a lamp or the light of the sun, because the Lord God will give them light." Here Christ's essence radiates throughout the cosmos, signifying the complete transformation of creation into a place where God's glory dwells eternally.

Central to the *Parousia* is Christ's definitive victory over sin, death, and all forces of darkness. Paul triumphantly declares in 1 Corinthians 15:54–57, "Death has been swallowed up in victory. . . . Thanks be to God, who gives us the victory through our Lord Jesus Christ." This victory is not merely symbolic but is enacted in the full eradication of sin and death, ensuring that nothing impedes the perfect communion between God and His creation.

This triumph is vividly portrayed in the worship of the multitude before the throne in Revelation 7:9–17. The text describes an innumerable crowd from every nation, tribe, and language standing before the Lamb. They proclaim, "Salvation belongs to our God, who is seated on the throne, and to the Lamb!" The Lamb, who stands at the center of the throne, leads His people to "springs of living water" and wipes away every tear from their eyes. This imagery conveys the relational and restorative aspects of the *Parousia*, as Christ's presence becomes the source of eternal comfort, life, and joy for the redeemed.

The unveiling of Christ's essence as the Lamb of God reveals the depth of God's redemptive love. His victory ensures eternal life and righteousness for those who belong to Him, highlighting the relational nature of the *Parousia* as the culmination of God's redemptive purposes.

ESCHATOLOGICAL IMPLICATIONS OF NUNCMILLENNIALISM

Nuncmillennialism offers a distinct perspective on the *Parousia*, contrasting with more conventional eschatological frameworks. Premillennialism envisions a future, literal millennium following Christ's return, emphasizing physical reign and cataclysmic events. Postmillennialism, in turn, anticipates a golden age of Christian influence ushering in peace before Christ's return. Nuncmillennialism diverges from both by affirming that Christ's reign is already active—spiritually present and transformative within the lives of believers—while acknowledging that its ultimate fulfillment is still to come.

Rather than expecting a future utopia or dramatic geopolitical intervention, Nuncmillennialism embraces the ongoing challenges of embodying the kingdom in a broken world. These trials are not detours but opportunities—places where the power of Christ's unveiled presence meets human frailty, reshaping individuals and communities from the inside out.

This theological framework—embraced throughout this book—emphasizes the "now" of Christ's reign while holding in tension the "not yet" of its final consummation. It views the *Parousia* as an ongoing spiritual reality, distinguishing it from interpretations that reduce it to a singular future event. This perspective anchors believers in the present experience of Christ's transforming presence, while sustaining hope for the complete renewal of all things.

Revelation 20:1–6 stands as a key text for Nuncmillennialism. The imagery of Satan's binding and the first resurrection is interpreted symbolically, not literally. Satan's binding represents the limitation of his ability to deceive the nations—an accomplished reality secured through Christ's crucifixion and resurrection. The first resurrection symbolizes the spiritual regeneration of believers who are now alive in Christ, having been raised with Him in newness of life.

This reading aligns with the New Testament's pervasive "already-but-not-yet" motif. Jesus's declaration in Luke 17:21, "The kingdom of God is in your midst," affirms the accessibility of His reign in the present. At the same time Revelation 21:1–4 gestures forward to the ultimate fulfillment of God's promises: the creation of a new heaven and new earth wherein God dwells fully with His people.

Nuncmillennialism thus provides a robust, Christ-centered eschatology. In 1 Corinthians 15:24–28 Paul describes the climax of redemptive history: "Then comes the end, when he hands over the kingdom to God the Father, when He abolishes all rule and all authority and power." This vision situates the *Parousia* within God's larger purpose—to bring all things under Christ's rule until God is "all in all." Christ's reign is not delayed; it is active and advancing, preparing all creation for this final unveiling.

Within this view the *Parousia* is understood as the gradual but transformative unveiling of Christ's essence in the world—an unveiling that reshapes the hearts of believers, conforms them to His image, and equips them to participate in God's redemptive mission.

Nuncmillennialism also reframes apocalyptic imagery and final judgment as symbolic of deeper spiritual realities. The great white throne in Revelation 20:11–15 represents the unveiled presence of Christ, before whom all humanity stands accountable—not merely in the future but even now. In John 5:24 Jesus says, "Anyone who hears my word and believes him who sent me has eternal life and will not come under judgment but has passed from death to life." This present-tense salvation reveals that final judgment is not only a future event but an ongoing unveiling of divine justice and mercy.

Rather than evoking fear, apocalyptic literature in this framework becomes a call to spiritual alignment. Its visions invite believers to active participation in the kingdom, not passive waiting. Through the *Parousia* God is not only revealing His justice but also restoring His creation.

Nuncmillennialism ultimately calls believers to live now in the transformative power of Christ's unveiled presence. It unites apocalyptic imagery and eschatological hope into a single vision of divine justice, mercy, and restoration. The *Parousia*, rightly understood, is not only something we await but something we inhabit as Christ reigns in and through His people.

THE *PAROUSIA* AS THE SPIRITUAL UNVEILING OF CHRIST'S ESSENCE

The *Parousia* transcends the traditional expectation of a physical return by centering on the ongoing spiritual unveiling of Christ's essence. John writes, "The Word became flesh and dwelt among us. We observed his glory, the glory as of the one and only Son from the Father, full of grace and truth" (John 1:14). This moment of incarnation is not confined to a historical event but represents the perpetual revelation of Christ's glory through the Holy Spirit in the life of the believer. The *Parousia*, in this sense, is a continuous unveiling of Christ's divine essence, inviting believers into a deeper relational knowledge of Him.

This interpretation aligns seamlessly with Christ's teachings, which consistently emphasize spiritual realities over worldly manifestations. When Jesus declared, "My kingdom is not of this world" (John 18:36), He invited His followers to embrace a kingdom that transcends material limitations. This spiritual nature of His reign calls believers to look beyond physical expectations and recognize the transformative power of His presence in their lives. Christ's kingdom is present, active, and transformative, revealing itself in the hearts and lives of those who walk in faith.

Believers are called to grow in their understanding of Christ's unveiled essence, which reveals His glory, authority, and divine nature. As Peter reminds us, "His divine power has given us everything required for life and godliness through the knowledge of him who called us by his own glory and goodness" (2 Peter 1:3). A deeper grasp of Christ's essence equips believers to reflect His character, embody His mission, and participate in the ongoing work of His kingdom.

The ongoing revelation of Christ's essence empowers believers to live transformed lives, walking in the authority granted to them as children of God. John writes, "To all who did receive him, he gave them the right to be children of God" (John 1:12). This spiritual authority enables believers to overcome the condemnation of sin, participate in His reign, and share His unveiled glory with the world.

The transformative power of the *Parousia* manifests in the lives of believers through faithful worship, missional engagement, and spiritual growth. Faithful worship involves encountering Christ's essence through worship in spirit and truth, as Jesus explained to the Samaritan woman at the well: "Those who worship [God] must worship in Spirit and in truth" (John 4:23–24). In worship believers align themselves with the presence of Christ, allowing His glory to shape their hearts and minds.

Missional engagement represents another vital expression of this transformative power. By living out the Great Commission believers share the gospel through both word and action. Jesus's command, "Go, therefore, and make disciples of all nations. . . . And remember, I am with you always, to the end of the age" (Matthew 28:19–20), reflects the Church's calling to embody the *Parousia's* reality. In doing so the Church draws others into Christ's redemptive work, serving as a visible testimony to His ongoing reign.

Spiritual growth, too, emerges as a critical aspect of the *Parousia's* transformative power. Believers are called to abide "in Christ," who is the source of life and fruitfulness. As Jesus declared, "Remain in me, and I in you. Just as a branch is unable to produce fruit by itself unless it remains on the vine, neither can you unless you remain in me" (John 15:4–5). Through this abiding relationship believers experience continual renewal, becoming vessels of Christ's essence and participants in His kingdom.

REAFFIRMING THE FRAMEWORK OF NUNCMILLENNIALISM

The Nuncmillennialist perspective bridges the tension between the "already" and the "not yet" dimensions of Christ's reign, offering a holistic understanding of His transformative presence. Jesus's proclamation, "The kingdom of God is in the midst of you" (Luke 17:21), underscores the immediacy of His reign, made accessible to believers now through the Holy Spirit. At the same time the vision in Revelation 21:1–4 points forward to the future fulfillment of the *Parousia*, when God's dwelling with humanity will be fully realized and creation will be renewed.

Nuncmillennialism offers a compelling framework that challenges traditional eschatological views by emphasizing the spiritual activity of Christ's reign in the present age while affirming its future consummation. The symbolic depiction of the binding of Satan and the first resurrection in Revelation 20:1–6 aligns with the spiritual realities of Christ's kingdom, showcasing the present limitation of Satan's power and the new life believers experience through spiritual regeneration.

Paul's description of Christ's ultimate victory in 1 Corinthians 15:24–28 further highlights the cosmic scope of the *Parousia*. He writes, "Then comes the end, when he hands over the kingdom to God the Father, when he abolishes all rule and all authority and power." This passage underscores the transformative and relational nature of the *Parousia*, through which all creation is brought into alignment with God's purposes and Christ's reign culminates in the renewal of all things.

THE *PAROUSIA'S* TRANSFORMATIVE IMPACT ON CHRISTIAN LIVING

The apocalyptic language of Scripture, including the vivid depictions of final judgment, is best understood as symbolic representations of spiritual realities rather than as literal predictions. These symbols help believers grasp the deeper truths of divine justice and mercy that permeate the kingdom of God. John's vision of the great white throne in Revelation 20:11–15 reflects this ultimate unveiling of divine purpose: "I . . . saw the dead, the great and the small, standing before the throne, and books were opened. Another book was opened, which is the book of life." This vision underscores both the accountability of humanity and the triumph of God's mercy before His unveiled presence.

Jesus affirms this spiritual lens in John 5:24: "Anyone who hears my word and believes him who sent me has eternal life and will not come under judgment but has passed from death to life." Here faith is revealed as the gateway into the transformative reality of the *Parousia*—not merely as future escape but as present participation in eternal life.

Believers are called not to passively await the culmination of the *Parousia* but to actively live within its unfolding reality. The Church, as the visible body of Christ, becomes a foretaste of the New Jerusalem—a living testimony of Christ's unveiled essence in worship, fellowship, and mission. As Paul writes in Colossians 1:27, "Christ in you, the hope of glory." This indwelling presence is not symbolic alone—it is the very power by which the kingdom is revealed through our lives.

The transformative power of the *Parousia* finds expression in three key aspects of Christian life:

- *Worship* is where believers encounter Christ's presence in spirit and truth, aligning their lives with His purposes and glorifying God as a gathered body. Here worship becomes both adoration and transformation.
- *Fellowship* reflects the relational reality of the kingdom, as believers build up one another in love, unity, and mutual service. The Church's shared life becomes a living picture of the community of the redeemed.
- *Mission* extends the reality of Christ's reign into the world. As believers bear witness through word and deed they embody the gospel of the kingdom, drawing others into the

redemptive presence of God. The Church becomes a radiant outpost of heaven in a world still longing for restoration.

This chapter has explored the *Parousia* as a transformative, relational unveiling—a reality both present and future, both personal and cosmic. The "already-but-not-yet" dynamic of the kingdom calls believers to live in the tension of Christ's current reign and the anticipation of the final renewal of all things. Nuncmillennialism provides the interpretive framework by which this unfolding reality is discerned, aligning the apocalyptic imagery of Scripture with the ongoing spiritual reign of Christ.

Believers are invited to embrace the *Parousia* as a living truth: to deepen their understanding of Christ's unveiled essence, to walk daily in the Spirit, and to reflect the reign of Christ through worship, community, and mission. This vision not only reorients eschatological thought; it offers a renewed way of life. The *Parousia* is not merely something to be awaited—it is something to be inhabited.

Through the Church's faithful witness the kingdom of God is proclaimed, not as a distant hope but as an active, radiant reality. As believers participate in the ongoing unveiling of Christ's glory they help bring His light into the shadowed corners of the world, bearing the image of the King they serve. This is the vision with which this book concludes: the *Parousia* as the presence of Christ transforming His people now, even as we await the day when His unveiled glory fills all creation.

EPILOGUE

HEBREWS 12: FROM ANCIENT TRUTHS TO A NEW HEAVEN

In this final chapter we reach the culmination of our unveiling of the transformative journey—a journey marked by both destruction and revelation. As the world around us burns the fleeting structures of earthly life are consumed, making way for the radiant revealing of a heavenly reality. Here we not only recapitulate the theme of the transformative relational *Parousia* but also explore how ancient truths continue to speak powerfully to our modern experience of faith.

The first-generation believers in Christ were deeply rooted in Jewish tradition, culture, laws, and rituals. Their entire worldview was filtered through the sacred lens of the Torah, as taught by priests, prophets, and scholars. It was within this context that the disciples first carried the transformative message of Jesus, proclaiming the fulfillment of the Old Testament prophecies about the Messiah-King—a truth verified by His death, resurrection, and ascension. While the gospel eventually reached the Gentiles, it was these Jewish roots that initially fueled the kingdom's expansive mission, spreading from Jerusalem throughout Judea and into the far-flung towns of the Roman and Greek worlds.

Every New Testament letter, from Paul's epistles to the pastoral letters, was written for communities steeped in this shared heritage of Jewish laws, rituals, and traditions. In Rome, for example, even as Paul addressed both Jewish and Gentile believers, it was the Jews who first received the Good News. This foundational context illuminates the character of the book of Hebrews—a work written for those who were deeply ingrained in the Jewish way of life.

Although the exact authorship of Hebrews remains uncertain, one compelling premise is that it was the product of a collective of disciples—possibly including figures such as Paul, Barnabas, and Silas. This "Circuit Sermon" model, whereby early Christian leaders traveled and shared a unified message tailored to diverse communities, explains how the teachings of Hebrews could have resonated widely among believers. Drawing on their Judaic tradition, Hebrews affirms Christ's fulfillment of the Torah and the prophets, unveiling His identity as the Savior-King and framing the trials of early believers within the context of an enduring hope in His promised kingdom.

Now, as I conclude this revelatory message of relational transformation, I must turn our focus to Hebrews 12—a pivotal text that bridges the lived experience of the early Church with our contemporary quest for a heavenly *Parousia*. Written to believers enduring trials, Hebrews 12 speaks of divine discipline, a process in which life's challenges are not merely sufferings but essential steps toward a refined and resilient faith. Its closing verses present a resounding summation: the eternal promise of God's unshakable kingdom far outweighs any temporal struggle. This call to let go of the temporary and embrace the transforming power of divine truth is as relevant today as it was for those first-century disciples.

Drawing upon the rich imagery and profound symbolism of Hebrews 12, we are invited to step into a teaching tradition that employs parables and metaphors to reveal deeper spiritual truths. Just as the early believers were encouraged to look beyond the immediacy of their broken world to the promise of God's eternal kingdom, we too are called to see with new eyes and listen with new ears—to perceive the eternal values hidden behind the transient veil of our everyday existence.

Building on this tradition, Jesus's teaching method was as revolutionary as it was subtle—a method that beckoned His listeners to engage with the divine mysteries beneath the surface of everyday life. Through the artful use of parables and metaphors, He communicated profound spiritual truths in a language that was both accessible and richly layered. Rather than proclaiming doctrinal absolutes in plain terms, Jesus wove stories that bridged the gap between the seen and the unseen, inviting His audience to discover the eternal within the temporal.

Indeed, this pedagogical approach was not accidental; it was designed to engage hearts and minds willing to search for deeper meaning. His words carried a dual purpose: for those with receptive ears and discerning eyes, they revealed the hidden architecture of God's kingdom—its promises of renewal and transformation—while for others the lessons remained obscured, a gentle reminder of the cost of spiritual indifference. As Jesus Himself explained to His disciples in Luke 8:10, "The secrets of the kingdom of God have been given to you to know, but to the rest it is in parables; so that looking, they may not see, and hearing they may not understand.'" This deliberate use of parables underscores His intention to illuminate profound truths for those who truly sought them, while leaving the unprepared in a state of spiritual blindness.

The disciples, having witnessed firsthand the power of these symbolic narratives, embraced this teaching method as a core aspect of their ministry. They learned that understanding the mysteries of faith often required an openness to interpret beyond literal words—to see the world through the lens of transformation and grace. Today this same method challenges us, calling us to approach Scripture not merely as a historical document but as a living parable, urging us to look beyond the superficial and into the depths in which the eternal meets our everyday reality.

In embracing Jesus's teaching method we are invited to become active participants in the unfolding mystery of God's kingdom—a kingdom revealed gradually through stories that speak to the soul, transforming our perceptions of the world and our place within it. Paul captures this transformative trek in 2 Corinthians 3:18, reminding us that "we all, with unveiled faces, are looking as in a mirror at the glory of the Lord and are being transformed into the same image from glory to glory." As we engage with the living parables of Scripture our very nature is refined and reshaped, drawing us ever closer to the divine likeness. This active, ongoing transformation calls us to not merely observe but to participate fully in the dynamic *Parousia* of God's eternal glory.

This call to transformation resonates throughout Scripture in the lives of those who chose eternal promises over fleeting pleasures. In Hebrews 11 the faithful are presented as enduring examples of this courageous choice. Consider Abraham, who, upon hearing the divine call, abandoned the comforts of his familiar world to embrace an uncertain future defined solely by God's promise. Reflect on Sarah, who embraced the possibility of a child despite the seeming obstacle of her advanced age. And think of Rahab, who trusted in God's grace even amid circumstances that appeared irredeemable. Each of these journeys of faith epitomizes the bold decision to pursue a destiny shaped by divine promise and heavenly glory rather than the temporary security of worldly gains.

Likewise, the prophets offer powerful testimony. In a culture deeply entrenched in the allure of immediate rewards, they dared to proclaim a vision of a kingdom not bound by the fleeting nature of this life—a kingdom anchored in justice, mercy, and everlasting truth. Their words, often delivered in the language of metaphor and parable (as seen in passages like Isaiah 61), invited their listeners to look beyond the superficial glitter of earthly existence toward a radiant, enduring reality of God's righteousness, power, and authority.

Continuing this pattern, the New Testament further illuminates the transformative journey through the lives of the early disciples.

Many left behind stable livelihoods and cherished relationships to follow a master who led them into a life of sacrificial love, faith, and hope in a transformative promise. Their radical commitment was not a denial of life but an embrace of a deeper, more meaningful existence that transcended the temporal—a transformation powerfully exemplified in the conversion and ministry of Peter, John, James, and Paul, among others.

These biblical exemplars remind us that, even as the world around us burns with the impermanence of the physical, the eternal beckons us with an unwavering light. Their stories challenge us to reexamine our own priorities and to invest our lives in the lasting treasures of God's kingdom. Their enduring faith invites us to not only reflect on our past but to actively pursue a future shaped by divine promise and transformative hope.

In our modern landscape the ancient wisdom of Scripture continues to resonate, inviting us to listen with new ears and see with new eyes. This call is not merely about adopting a fresh perspective; it is a transformative invitation to align our very senses with the eternal. As we sift through the cacophony of modern distractions, we are challenged to discern the subtle, yet profound, voice of the Spirit—a voice that calls us to prioritize lasting heavenly values over the ephemeral lures of the physical world.

To listen with new ears means to attune ourselves, as Elijah did, to the quiet whispers of divine guidance amid the noise of everyday life. It is an invitation to reject the superficial promises of immediate gratification and instead focus on the timeless truths that have sustained generations of faithful believers. As Jesus declared in John 10:27, "My sheep hear my voice," reminding us of the importance of tuning in to God's call. By embracing this deeper level of listening, we empower ourselves to recognize the divine in the ordinary and to appreciate the transformative power of God's presence through the *Parousia* in every moment unveiled to us.

Similarly, to see with new eyes is to perceive the world through a lens shaped by hope and eternal purpose. It transforms our understanding of what is truly valuable, shifting our focus from transient appearances to the underlying realities of grace and redemption. As Paul exhorts us in Romans 12:2, we are called to be transformed by the renewal of our minds. This renewed vision encourages us to look beyond the fleeting beauty of the material world and to embrace a perspective that values spiritual depth, growth, and the advancement of God's kingdom here and now.

In this contemporary application the teachings of our ancient faith are not relics of the past but living, dynamic guides for today. As we practice listening with new ears and seeing with new eyes, we find ourselves better equipped to navigate the complexities of modern life, empowered to pursue a path of genuine transformation that mirrors the eternal promise illuminated throughout this book.

Building on this transformative journey, we now arrive at the ultimate promise that has guided believers throughout the ages: the unveiling of heaven—not as a distant escape but as the fullness of God's presence revealed in Christ. As we draw this herald to a close, the unveiling of heaven stands as the culminating promise—a resplendent vision emerging from the ashes of a burning world. In these final reflections we are invited to embrace the transformative truth that the impermanence of our earthly existence is not an end but a doorway into eternal communion. The fading nature of the physical realm makes space for the reality that endures—the unveiled kingdom of God, radiant with glory, justice, and love.

Having contemplated the profound promise of heaven's unveiling—a reality emerging from the refining fire of our temporal existence—we now turn to one of the most striking passages in Scripture: Hebrews 12:14–29. In these verses the writers use vivid metaphor to unveil the transformation God's kingdom undergoes amid the trials of life, echoing the very teaching methods Jesus employed.

Just as He spoke in parables to engage hearts, challenge minds, and reveal deeper truths to those with ears to hear, so too does this passage call us to recognize the unfolding mystery of God's eternal kingdom.

As we turn to these verses we step into the world of the first-century disciples—men and women who read these words not merely as distant eschatological warnings but as a living invitation. To them the message of Hebrews 12 was not about a future event to be awaited with fear but about a present reality to be embraced through transformation. It was a call to step into the unfolding revelation of Christ's kingdom, to experience the transformative relational *Parousia* in real time. Through this lens we begin to see how these metaphors reveal God's refining work, drawing believers into a deeper participation in His unshakable kingdom.

The opening verse of this passage sets the stage for all that follows: "Pursue peace with everyone, and holiness—without it no one will see the Lord" (Hebrews 12:14). This is more than a command for ethical living; it is an invitation to transformation. The call to peace and holiness is not simply about external harmony or personal piety but about alignment with the nature of God Himself. Peace in this sense is not merely the absence of conflict but the presence of divine order—a state of being that flows from an intimate relationship with Christ.

Jesus frequently used parables to challenge old ways of thinking, revealing that peace and holiness are not only actions but conditions of the heart. In the same way this verse beckons us to see beyond superficial morality and into the deep relational transformation that takes place when we encounter the living God. To "see the Lord" in this context is not a distant hope for the afterlife but a call to experience His likeness, His rule, and His presence—now. It is the unveiling of divine reality, a truth that transcends external appearances and invites us into eternal communion with God.

Thus, peace and holiness are not mere ideals to be pursued in isolation; they are the very evidence of a life transformed by the presence of Christ. To seek them is to step more deeply into the relational unveiling of His kingdom, where the veils of the temporal world are drawn back, revealing the eternal. But the process of transformation is not without resistance. Just as peace and holiness are cultivated through alignment with Christ, so too can the forces of division and corruption take root if left unchecked.

Hebrews 12:15 warns of this danger: "Make sure that no one falls short of the grace of God and that no root of bitterness springs up, causing trouble and defiling many." Here the "root of bitterness" is not just a metaphor—it is a warning about the unseen forces that can undermine the transformative work of God. In the same way that a root remains hidden beneath the soil yet dictates the health of the entire plant, bitterness, when allowed to take hold, silently corrupts, spreads, and ultimately defiles the whole community. This is not just about personal resentment but about a spiritual condition—one that can hinder the work of grace and distort the relational reality of God's kingdom.

Jesus often used parables of growth, harvest, and soil to illustrate this very truth. He taught that, just as good seed must be cultivated to bear fruit, so the human heart must be guarded against the weeds of sin and hardness. Whether through the parable of the wheat and tares (Matthew 13:24–30) or that of the sower (Mark 4:3–9), His teachings emphasized that transformation requires both divine grace and human response.

Thus, this verse is not merely about avoiding bitterness—it is an urgent call to remain deeply rooted in grace. Just as unchecked bitterness can poison the soul, a heart yielded to God can flourish in peace and spiritual maturity. The presence of Christ in our lives is meant to be a continual process of refinement, whereby the old ways of the flesh are crucified and the new life of the Spirit takes shape.

The call to remain rooted in grace is not merely an individual pursuit—it is a safeguard for the entire community of faith. What we cultivate within our hearts does not remain hidden; it takes root, grows, and eventually bears fruit, affecting not only our own spiritual condition but also those around us. Whether we allow bitterness to spread or grace to flourish, the outcome is inevitable. The choice is before us: Will we cling to what is fleeting, or will we yield to God's refining work, allowing His grace to shape our lives into something eternal?

The writers of Hebrews now turn to a stark example of what happens when one chooses the temporary over the eternal—a lesson drawn from the life of Esau: "And make sure that there isn't any immoral or irreverent person like Esau, who sold his birthright in exchange for a single meal. For you know that later, when he wanted to inherit the blessing, he was rejected, even though he sought it with tears, because he didn't find any opportunity for repentance" (Hebrews 12:16–17).

Esau's decision to trade his birthright for a fleeting moment of satisfaction stands as a sober warning. His choice was not merely about food; it was a spiritual failure, a willingness to exchange an eternal inheritance for a temporary pleasure. In the heat of the moment, he valued what was immediate over what was lasting, and by the time he realized the weight of his decision the opportunity to reclaim his inheritance had passed.

This is more than just a historical account; it is a parable in itself, mirroring the teachings of Jesus. Again and again Jesus warned against the danger of prioritizing temporary gains over eternal realities. He spoke of the rich man who stored up treasure for himself but was not rich toward God (Luke 12:16–21); the foolish virgins who were unprepared for the bridegroom's arrival (Matthew 25:1–13); and the seed that fell among thorns, choked by the cares and pleasures of this world (Mark 4:18–19). In each of these lessons the pattern is the same: those who choose immediate gratification over spiritual endurance find themselves empty handed when the time of fulfillment arrives.

Esau's story presses the reader to reflect deeply: What are we willing to forfeit for temporary comfort? Are we exchanging the deep, transformative work of God for the fleeting indulgences of this world?

The warning is clear—if we reject the call to transformation, if we neglect the eternal for the sake of the temporary, we risk losing what truly matters.

The weight of Esau's decision serves as both a warning and an invitation. Unlike him, we still stand at the crossroads, with the opportunity to choose the eternal over the temporary, to hold fast to the inheritance set before us rather than surrendering it for fleeting satisfaction. The question remains: Will we recognize the surpassing worth of Christ's kingdom and embrace it, or will we, like Esau, be blinded by immediate desires and forfeit what is of infinite value?

To drive this contrast home, the writers of Hebrews shift their focus to an even greater reality—one that underscores the magnitude of the choice before us. The text takes us back to the moment when Israel stood before Mount Sinai, where the presence of God descended in fire, darkness, and trembling: "For you have not come to what could be touched, to a blazing fire, to darkness, gloom, and storm, to the blast of a trumpet, and the sound of words. Those who heard it begged that not another word be spoken to them, for they could not bear what was commanded: If even an animal touches the mountain, it must be stoned. The appearance was so terrifying that Moses said, 'I am trembling with fear'" (Hebrews 12:18–21).

This passage paints a scene of divine majesty and overwhelming fear. Even Moses—who had stood in the presence of God before—trembled at the display of His holiness. Though Sinai was a physical mountain that could be seen and touched, it remained untouchable, marked by fire and judgment, darkness and storm, and the deafening sound of divine command. The people, unable to withstand the voice of God, begged for silence, knowing that they could not bear the weight of His words.

Why do the writers remind us of this moment? Because what follows will redefine the nature of God's presence. The trembling at Sinai was not the final destination of God's revelation—it was a foreshadowing of something greater. Sinai represented a covenant of exposure, whereby God's majesty was undeniable but distant, real but unapproachable. It highlighted the separation between divine holiness and human frailty, making clear that, under the law, access to God was restricted and His presence was more of a warning than an invitation.

But now something has changed. A radical shift has taken place through Christ. The writer is about to unveil a new mountain—one that does not bring terror but invitation. Unlike Sinai, where the people trembled in fear, the next verses introduce Mount Zion—a place not of judgment but of joy, not of trembling but of belonging.

Before we can fully grasp the gift of Zion, we must first understand the weight of Sinai. This passage compels us to acknowledge the magnitude of God's holiness, the limitations of the old covenant, and the urgent need for something greater. The fear and trembling at Sinai pointed to the need for a mediator, for a better covenant—one that we now find in Christ.

A dramatic shift occurs as we arrive at Hebrews 12:22–24. The contrast between Sinai and Zion is not merely a change in location—it is a complete transformation of spiritual reality. It is the movement from distance to intimacy, from fear to joy, from law to grace: "Instead, you have come to Mount Zion, to the city of the living God (the heavenly Jerusalem), to myriads of angels, a festive gathering, to the assembly of the firstborn whose names have been written in heaven, to a Judge, who is God of all, to the spirits of righteous people made perfect, and to Jesus, the mediator of a new covenant, and to the sprinkled blood, which says better things than the blood of Abel."

Here the unshakable kingdom of God is revealed, and the presence of Christ is no longer distant, but near. The question now is clear: Will we cling to the fear of Sinai, or will we step forward into the unveiled reality of Christ's kingdom?

The words "you have come" (προσεληλύθατε) reveal a profound truth: this is not a future hope but a present reality. The author is not speaking of something yet to be attained but of something already entered into. This passage does not merely point to a kingdom to come; it announces a kingdom that is already here—a reality made accessible through Christ's presence and mediation. The transformative relational *Parousia* is fully realized in this moment: the hidden has been unveiled, and those in Christ now stand in the presence of the living God.

Mount Zion represents the fulfillment of all that Mount Sinai foreshadowed. Where Sinai was unapproachable, Zion is accessible. Where Sinai condemned, Zion welcomes. Where Sinai brought terror and trembling, Zion offers celebration and joy. Sinai was a mountain of separation, but Zion is a mountain of union—a dwelling place where heaven and earth intersect, where the redeemed already stand among the great assembly of angels and the righteous made perfect.

This unveiled reality is not merely a theological abstraction but a present invitation. Just as Jesus often used parables to shift the minds of His listeners from earthly to heavenly realities, so too does this passage invite believers to see beyond the visible and into the already-present kingdom of God. No longer is God's dwelling distant and veiled behind law and ritual; it is open, vibrant, and accessible through Christ's mediation.

Perhaps nowhere is this truth more vividly demonstrated than in the final moments of Stephen's life. As he stood before his accusers, about to be stoned, Scripture tells us that he "gazed into heaven. He saw the glory of God, and Jesus standing at the right hand of God" (Acts 7:55). In this moment Stephen did not see a future hope but a present reality. The veil between heaven and earth was drawn back, and the heavenly Zion was revealed in full glory.

Stephen's vision was not an isolated experience but a revelation of what Hebrews 12:22–24 declares: the kingdom of God is unveiled, and believers already participate in it. His death was not an end but a transition into the full realization of what he had already seen—the transformative relational *Parousia* in its completion.

Mount Sinai and Mount Zion serve as covenantal signposts, each representing an era of God's relationship with His people. Sinai speaks of distance, law, and the impossibility of approaching God through human effort. The trembling Israelites could not endure the presence of God, and even Moses feared the sight of divine majesty. It was a covenant of exposure—one that revealed sin but could not remove it.

Zion, by contrast, is a place not of fear but of belonging. It is "the city of the living God," a place where the spirits of the righteous are made perfect, where angels rejoice in celebration, and where Jesus Himself mediates a new covenant of grace. This is the heart of the transformative relational *Parousia*: what was once hidden in mystery is now revealed in relationship.

Jesus has not merely prepared a way to Zion; He has brought Zion to His people. The firstborn assembly, the great cloud of witnesses, the joyous celebration of heaven—all of it is already accessible "in Christ." This is not just the eschatological hope of a future Zion but the current reality in which believers now stand.

The authors of Hebrews are urging their readers to see what has already been unveiled. The transformation that once seemed distant and untouchable at Sinai is now the present experience of every believer in Zion. No longer must we stand trembling in fear; instead we enter with confidence, through the blood of Christ, into the fullness of God's presence.

This is why the sprinkled blood of Jesus speaks a better word than the blood of Abel. Abel's blood cried out for justice and retribution (Genesis 4:10), while Christ's blood declares forgiveness, reconciliation, and redemption. His blood does not demand vengeance—it proclaims victory.

Hebrews 12:22–24 is not merely a description of what will happen someday; it is a call to see what is already true today. Through the unveiling of Christ, through His mediation, through the transformative work of His presence we now dwell in Mount Zion—the city of the living God. This is the reality of the transformative relational *Parousia*: The separation between heaven and earth has been removed, and in Christ we now stand in the unveiled kingdom.

As the writers of Hebrews continue unfolding the contrast between the old and new covenants, we reach a moment of profound warning and revelation. Hebrews 12:25–27 states, "See to it that you do not reject the one who speaks. For if they did not escape when they rejected him who warned them on earth, even less will we if we turn away from him who warns us from heaven. His voice shook the earth at that time, but now he has promised, 'Yet once more I will shake not only the earth but also the heavens.' This expression, 'Yet once more,' indicates the removal of what can be shaken—that is, created things—so that what is not shaken might remain."

This passage calls us to attention—to listen carefully, for the voice that once thundered from Sinai now speaks from the heavenly realm. The contrast is striking. When God first spoke to His people from Mount Sinai, His voice shook the earth. The Israelites, overcome with fear, pleaded for the voice to cease, unable to bear the weight of divine revelation. Yet even in their trembling they could not escape the demands of the covenant given to them.

Now, the writers warn, if the people could not escape God's voice when He spoke on earth, how much more serious is it to reject His voice from heaven? This is not merely a message given through a prophet or through an earthly law—it is the very voice of Christ, enthroned in heaven, speaking the final and ultimate word of divine authority. To reject Him is to turn away from the only unshakable reality that will remain when all else is removed.

The reference to God's shaking of the earth and heavens is drawn directly from the prophet Haggai (Haggai 2:6–7), through whom God declares: "Once more, in a little while, I am going to shake the heavens and the earth, the sea and the dry land. I will shake all the nations so that the treasures of all the nations will come, and I will fill this house with glory." This shaking is not merely a sign of destruction—it is a divine removal of all that is temporary, making way for what is eternal. The heavens and the earth—the entire created order—are being tested, shaken, and refined so that only what is of God's kingdom will remain.

Throughout the biblical narrative shaking signifies divine intervention and the dismantling of earthly powers. Isaiah 13:13 describes the day of the Lord as a time when God "will make the heavens tremble, and the earth will shake from its foundations." Revelation 6:12–14 portrays the heavens shaking, stars falling, and mountains moving as signs of the old world passing away in light of God's sovereign reign. The shaking the writers of Hebrews speak of is not merely an eschatological event—it is the very process through which God is unveiling His kingdom. The old order is passing away, and through the transformative relational *Parousia* believers are being called into a new and unshakable reality.

Jesus Himself often spoke of this transition—using parables to reveal that God's kingdom would not be built upon what is unstable but upon what is eternal. In Matthew 7:24–27 He describes two builders—one who built on rock and the other on sand. When the storm came only one house remained. In John 15:1–6 He speaks of the vine and the branches, saying that what does not remain in Him will be cut off and burned. In Luke 3:17 John the Baptist declares that Jesus's "winnowing shovel is in his hand to clear his threshing floor and gather the wheat into his barn, but the chaff he will burn with fire that never goes out."

Each of these teachings mirrors the shaking in Hebrews 12:25–27. The storms, the shaking, and the fire all signify the same reality—God is refining the world, stripping away all that is temporary so that only what is of His kingdom remains.

This shaking, then, is not just about judgment—it is about transformation. It is through this shaking that believers are lifted into a new way of seeing, freed from the attachments of the temporal world. Just as Christ, in His resurrection and ascension, entered into the unshakable reality of the heavenly throne, so too are we being drawn into His eternal presence.

The writers of Hebrews are not simply describing a future apocalyptic event—they are revealing a present reality. Even now God is unraveling the old order, shaking the world free from its illusions, so that the eternal kingdom is made manifest. This is the very essence of the transformative relational *Parousia*. It is not just about Christ's future return—it is about His revealed presence, lifting us into His kingdom now. It is not merely a cosmic event—it is an inward transformation that dislodges the temporary attachments of our lives. It is not about earthly security—it is about finding unshakable foundation in Christ's eternal reign.

The passage ends with an invitation and a warning. If we remain attached to what can be shaken, we will fall with it. If we listen to Christ's voice and yield to His reign, we will stand in the unshakable kingdom. This passage is both a challenge and a comfort. It reminds us that everything we hold onto in this world will one day fall away, but it also declares the glorious reality that "in Christ" we have already entered into something eternal.

The shaking has been happening since the incarnation of Christ. The old world order is continuing to crumble and burn away, and it will keep crumbling and burning until God consummates His eternal plan. The systems built on human strength, temporary pleasures, and religious legalism are fading away. But for those who are "in Christ," what remains is unshakable. Therefore, the question posed to every believer is this: Will we cling to what is temporary, only to have it shaken from our grasp? Or will we embrace the reign of Christ and his *Parousia* and remain in what is unshakable? For what is shaken will pass away, but what is unshakable will endure forever. And when what is shaken is burned away, what remains, left unshaken, is the heavenly vision of the authority of the kingdom of the Son over all things.

The world has been shaken, the temporal has crumbled, and all that remains is what is unshakable—the kingdom of God. This is the moment of realization, the unveiling of what has been true all along: the reign of Christ is not just a future expectation but a present reality. The writers of Hebrews now lead us to the conclusion of this chapter, summing up everything that has been revealed through metaphor, warning, and invitation: "Therefore, since we are receiving a kingdom that cannot be shaken, let us be thankful. By it, we may serve God acceptably, with reverence and awe, for our God is a consuming fire" (Hebrews 12:28–29).

These verses do not merely conclude the passage—they summon us into participation. We are not waiting for this kingdom to arrive; we are receiving it even now. The contrast between what has been shaken and what remains points us to the essence of the transformative relational *Parousia*—the process through which the fleeting realities of this world dissolve, allowing the eternal to emerge.

What remains is not something fragile or temporary but something unshakable—a kingdom established not on human effort, not on religious systems, not on political power but on the presence of Christ Himself. This is the kingdom that will never collapse, a kingdom not built with human hands but one that has always been and always will be.

And how should we respond? With gratitude. This gratitude is not passive; it is active. It manifests in worship, reverence, and awe. The writers of Hebrews are calling us to a posture of deep awareness—a recognition that we stand in the presence of something immeasurably greater than ourselves.

Then comes the final declaration, the last word on transformation and revelation: "For our God is a consuming fire." This fire is not mere destruction; it is purification, refinement, and unveiling. Throughout Scripture fire is used not only as a symbol of judgment but as an agent of transformation. Just as gold is refined in the furnace, so too is everything subjected to the fire of God's presence. In Deuteronomy 4:24 God is called a consuming fire, a jealous God, meaning that He does not allow divided loyalties—only what is fully His will endure. In Malachi 3:2–3 the Messiah is described as a refiner's fire, purging away all impurity from His people. In 1 Corinthians 3:12–15 Paul describes the final judgment in which every person's work will be tested by fire—only that which is eternal will remain.

This is the fire of transformation, the fire that burns away what is perishable and leaves behind only that which is holy, enduring, and truly alive. The presence of God does not consume to destroy—it consumes to reveal.

This passage is not just a conclusion—it is an invitation. An invitation to live as citizens of the unshakable kingdom, to see through the veil of the temporary and to step fully into the reality of the eternal. The world may continue to burn with the impermanence of time, but those whose lives are aligned with Christ's presence will not be consumed.

We are called to worship God with reverence and awe, not out of fear but out of the overwhelming realization that we stand in the presence of something eternal, something weighty, something real. This is the very essence of the transformative relational *Parousia*—to not simply observe Christ's reign from a distance but to be swept up in it, changed by it, and made alive in it.

Let us not shrink back from this fire or turn away from this transformation. For what is being revealed is not just a future hope but a present reality—a kingdom that is already breaking through, a kingdom that is already in us, through us, and before us.

As we embrace the final words of this passage we step into the larger story—the story of a kingdom unveiled, of Christ's reign made known, and of lives set ablaze, not by destruction but by the consuming fire of divine love. May we live with eyes set on the heavenly, hearts kindled by the unshakable truth, and spirits transformed by the all-consuming presence of God.

In this unveiled kingdom we do not simply wait—we are called to embody. The *Parousia* is not an event to observe but a life to inhabit. And so this journey ends with a vision—and a call.

A VISION OF HOPE: A NEW HUMANITY, RESTORED IN GLORY

The end of this journey is not individual enlightenment but the restoration of all things in Christ. The *Parousia* is not just personal transformation—it is cosmic renewal. The unveiling of Christ's presence in the believer is a foretaste of the full unveiling of His kingdom, when all things will be restored and creation itself will be set free from corruption (Romans 8:19–21).

John's vision of the final unveiling, as he shares in 1 John 3:2, is breathtaking: "Dear friends, we are God's children now, and what we will be has not yet been revealed. We know that when he appears, we will be like him because we will see him as he is." This is the completion of Imagoformity—the moment when the process of transformation reaches its fulfillment, when the veil is completely lifted and believers behold Christ fully, as they become fully like Him.

But this unveiling is not only for the future. The mystery of the *Parousia* is already alive in those who yield to His presence now. The world longs for a glimpse of divine restoration, and the Church—formed into the image of Christ—is called to be that vision, a people unveiled in glory, radiating the essence of Christ to all creation.

FINAL CALL: LIVE AS THE UNVEILED REFLECTION OF CHRIST

This unimaginable invitation stands before each believer: live as the unveiled presence of Christ. Embrace Imagoformity as your calling. See your spiritual life not as a checklist of religious duties but as the unfolding revelation of Christ's essence in you. This is the reality of the *Parousia* made alive. This is the hope of glory. This is Imagoformity—the formation of a new humanity, restored in Christ, unveiled in glory, and forever transformed by His presence.

Let this unveiling shape your worship, fuel your mission, and transform your life. The Spirit of Christ is already at work in you—step into the fullness of His divine formation: "Christ in you, the hope of glory" (Colossians 1:27).

The *Parousia* is not waiting. The journey is happening. The unveiling is now.

APPENDIX 1

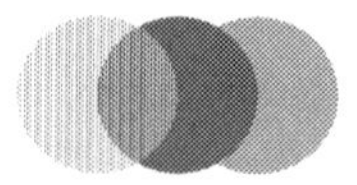

COMPARING THE MILLENNIAL VIEWS

Theology	Christ's Return	Millennium	Church's Role	Eschatological Outlook
Premillennialism	Before Millennium	Literal Future	Passive Waiting	Pessimistic
Postmillennialism	After Millennium	Figurative	Transforming World	Optimistic
Amillennialism	After Church Age	Symbolic/ Now	Proclaiming Gospel	Realistic
Nuncmillennialism	Ongoing/ Now	Present Reality	Living the Kingdom	Balanced Realism

APPENDIX 2

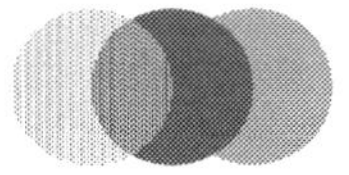

EARLY *PAROUSIA* THEOLOGY COMPARED

Church Father	Parousia as Ongoing Presence	Parousia as Future Event	Key Theme
Ignatius (35 AD–108 AD)	Strongly Emphasized	No Explicit Teaching	Christ Presence in Suffering and Unity
Polycarp (69 AD–155 AD)	Likely Emphasized	No Teaching on Bodily Return	Christ Presence in Martyrdom
Justin Martyr (100 AD–165 AD)	Partially Emphasized	Taught a Final Conclusion	Present Transformation and Future Fulfillment
Irenaeus (130 AD–202 AD)	Somewhat Emphasized	Affirmed a Final Conclusion	Transformation Now and Future Kingdom
Tertullian (155 AD–220 AD)	Decreased Emphasis	Emphasized a Conclusion	Physical Return and Apocalyptic Judgment
Origen (185 AD–253 AD)	Mystical Emphasis	Emphasized Future Final Fulfillment	Spiritualized Parousia Now and Future Culmination

APPENDIX 3

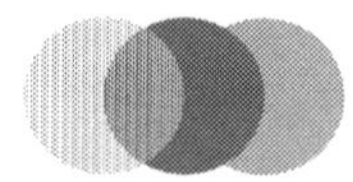

DEFINITION OF *IMAGOFORMITY* (NOUN):

The continual, Spirit-led process by which believers are transformed into the image of Christ, progressing from glory to glory through sanctification, faith, and divine participation until the final culmination in glorification at the *Parousia*. It reflects the believer's journey of being reshaped from the corruption of the old creation into the incorruptible likeness of the Son, preparing them for full union with God.

KEY THEOLOGICAL ELEMENTS IN THIS DEFINITION

1. *Ongoing Transformation*: Unlike the static concept of Imago Dei, Imagoformity emphasizes an active, dynamic process (Rom. 12:2; 2 Cor. 3:18).
2. *Spirit-Led*: Transformation occurs *through* the Holy Spirit's work (John 16:13; Gal 5:16–25).
3. *From Corruptible to Incorruptible*: The transition from the old Adamic nature to the perfected image of Christ (Rom. 5:12–21; 1 Cor. 15:49).
4. *Progressive Glorification*: Movement from one stage of divine reflection to another, culminating in final glorification at the *Parousia* (Phil. 3:21; 1 John 3:2).
5. *Theosis and Union with God*: Participating in the divine nature without losing individual identity (John 17:22–23; 2 Pet. 1:4).

APPENDIX 4

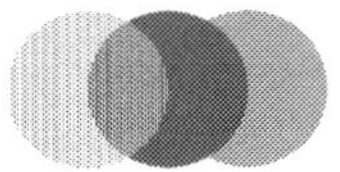

IMAGOFORMITY AS A THEOLOGICAL LIFE MODEL

The journey of the *Parousia* is not a distant event to be awaited but a lived reality to be unveiled. From the Garden to the cross, from Pentecost to the present, Christ's essence has been forming within those who walk by faith. The unveiling of His presence is not a passive occurrence but a transformative process—a calling, an invitation, a divine formation of His image within us. This is the heart of Imagoformity: the lifelong, Spirit-driven, eschatologically fulfilled transformation that defines the believer's existence in Christ.

Imagoformity (noun): *Imago Dei* (Latin for "Image of God") with formity (denoting formation or shaping). The continual, Spirit-led process by which believers are transformed into the image of Christ, progressing from glory to glory through sanctification, faith, and divine participation, until the final culmination in glorification at the *Parousia*. It reflects the believer's journey of being reshaped from the corruption of the old creation into the incorruptible likeness of the Son, preparing them for full union with God.

THE LIFELONG JOURNEY OF IMAGOFORMITY

To walk in Imagoformity is to see the Christian life not as an effort to be "good" but as a journey into divine formation. It is the process by which we are progressively conformed to the image of Christ—not by mere moral striving but by the Spirit's active work in unveiling His presence within us. Paul describes this reality in 2 Corinthians 3:18:

> We all, with unveiled faces, are looking as in a mirror at the glory of the Lord and are being transformed into the same image from glory to glory; this is from the Lord who is the Spirit.

This transformation is not self-generated; it is Spirit-driven. It is God's work in us, unfolding through every act of faith, every surrender to His presence, every moment wherein His essence is revealed in our thoughts, actions, and relationships. Imagoformity is not about behavioral modification—it is about identity formation, about becoming who we were created to be in Christ.

The end of the Christian life is not mere improvement but complete transformation. As Paul states in Philippians 3:20–21, "Our citizenship is in heaven, and we eagerly wait for a Savior from there, the Lord Jesus Christ. He will transform the body of our humble condition into the likeness of his glorious body, by the power that enables him to subject everything to himself."

This is the eschatological fulfillment of Imagoformity—the moment when the unveiling is complete, when what was sown in perishable form is raised in imperishable glory (1 Corinthians 15:42–44). But even now, before that day, this transformation is already unfolding. The believer is not waiting for a future moment to become like Christ; the process has already begun, and the Spirit is actively shaping those who yield to His work.

A PARADIGM SHIFT: FROM RELIGION TO TRANSFORMATION

For centuries Christian discipleship has often been framed as a moral endeavor, a call to "be good" and follow ethical teachings. While righteousness is essential, Imagoformity shifts the focus from morality to transformation, from human effort to divine formation. The question is no longer "Am I good enough?" but rather "Am I yielding to the Spirit's unveiling of Christ's essence in me?"

Jesus did not come merely to reform human behavior; He came to recreate humanity. The fall introduced fragmentation—sin severed humanity from its divine identity. But through Christ the image of God is restored, renewed, and revealed. The *Parousia* is not just Christ's presence coming upon us—it is His presence coming through us. This means that spiritual maturity is not about mastering religious disciplines but about experiencing the fullness of divine transformation.

Paul frames this shift in Colossians 3:9–10: "You . . . have put off the old self with its practices and have put on the new self. You are being renewed in knowledge according to the image of your Creator." This is the essence of the Christian journey—not merely following Christ's teachings but becoming His reflection, as the new creation He has made us to be.

THE CALL TO A TRANSFORMATIVE MINDSET

If the end goal of the Christian life is not merely salvation but transformation, then the journey requires intentional participation. Believers are not passive recipients but active participants in their sanctification. God does the work, but we partner with Him by yielding to the Spirit, embracing the disciplines of faith, and allowing Christ's image to be formed within us.

This means adopting a transformative mindset, which recognizes that:

- *Faith is not just belief—it is formation.* To have faith in Christ is to be shaped by His presence, conformed to His image through surrender and trust.

- *Sanctification is not self-improvement—it is self-abandonment.* Sanctification is not about trying harder to be holy but yielding more fully to the Spirit's transformative work.
- *Hope is not wishful thinking—it is expectation.* The believer does not hope for transformation as a distant possibility but expects it as an unfolding reality.

Paul captures this active participation in transformation in Romans 12:2: "Do not be conformed to this age, but be transformed by the renewing of your mind, so that you may discern what is the good, pleasing, and perfect will of God."

To embrace Imagoformity is to embrace the *Parousia* as an ongoing, lived experience—the reality of Christ's unveiled presence shaping the believer into His likeness.

ACKNOWLEDGMENTS

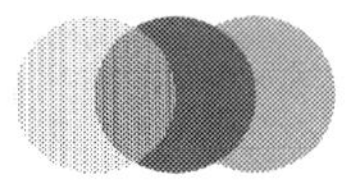

I wish to acknowledge Swiss Catholic theologian Hans Urs von Balthasar (1905–1988), Scottish Presbyterian theologian Thomas F. Torrance (1913–2007), and American Lutheran theologian Robert W. Jenson (1930–2017)—each of whom, in their own way, took a step forward in unveiling the mystery of the *Parousia* and the present glory of Christ's Kingdom. Though each of us stands singular in the inspiration we have received, I believe we have all carried the same torch—the epiphany of Christ's glory—for the sake of the body of Christ. It is a torch not lit by intellect or ambition, but by the Spirit of God, that others might see Christ lifted up and be transformed through relational faith, grace, and the unveiling of His glory.

Each of these theologians made a significant and unique contribution to the recovery of *Parousia* as a present reality—moving the Church away from a purely futuristic, cataclysmic expectation and toward the living reality of Christ's reign now. My own work is offered humbly, as one further step in this unfolding revelation. It has come not by study of their writings but by the Spirit's guidance and encouragement—through surrender, Scripture, and the breath of God. This, I believe, is further witness to the Spirit of Christ at work in His Body, for His glory.

I trust in Christ that there will be steps beyond mine—taken by others, in their own time, for their own generation—as the glory of the Lord continues to fill the earth. For the Kingdom is not postponed. It is present. And the unveiling is not finished.

Made in the USA
Las Vegas, NV
12 September 2025

e3c2f218-6129-42f6-8ee4-b2043454f62dR01